Recommended

COUNTRY INNS
The South

"Sara Pitzer's guide answers every conceivable question . . . and the personal touches are the crowning glory. Reading her book makes one realize that staying in an inn is not just renting a room from strangers. Instead, it's meeting new friends whom you feel you've known all your life."
—*The St. Augustine* (FL) *Record*

"We liked her choices, we liked her profiles, and we certainly liked her engaging style. . . . Sara Pitzer does it professionally and well."
—Norman Strasma, *Inn Review*

"Reading Sara Pitzer's vivid descriptions of unique and cozy inns conjures up images of some of the finest traditions of the old South. Take it from a native, Pitzer tells it like it is."
—Lenore Barkley, executive director,
  Vicksburg–Warren County (MS) Tourist Commission

"I read about all the inns I have visited, and Sara has them down to the letter. Her light, breezy style makes you want to go, even when you don't have a trip in mind."
—*The Charlotte* (NC) *Observer*

"An excellent introduction to the region."
—*Uncommon Lodgings*

"In the age of chain motels and fast-food dining, a good old inn is to be treasured more than ever. Sara Pitzer has sought out [129] of the South's finest, and written about them with grace, charm, and descriptive prose that makes you want to jump in the car and head for the nearest inn."
—John Egerton, author of *Southern Inn*

"Profiles [129] of the best and most interesting inns in ten southern states."
—*Chattanooga News–Free Press*

"The best guide I've seen to country inns . . . that little personal touch that gives the reader confidence . . . the information is exhaustive . . . Sara Pitzer has the place for you."
—*The Island Packet* (Hilton Head, SC)

"Recommended Country Inns" Series

"The guidebooks in this new series of recommended country inns are sure winners. Personal visits have ensured accurate and scene-setting descriptions. These beckon the discriminating traveler to a variety of interesting lodgings."
—-Norman Strasma, publisher of *Inn Review* newsletter

The "Recommended Country Inns" series is designed for the discriminating traveler who seeks the best in unique accommodations away from home.

From hundreds of inns personally visited and evaluated by the author, only the finest are described here. The inclusion of an inn is purely a personal decision on the part of the author; no one can pay or be paid to be in a Globe Pequot inn guide.

Organized for easy reference, these guides point you to just the kind of accommodations you are looking for: Comprehensive indexes by category provide listings of inns for romantic getaways, inns for the sports-minded, inns that serve gourmet meals . . . and more. State maps help you pinpoint the location of each inn, and detailed driving directions tell you how to get there.

Use these guidebooks with confidence. Allow each author to share his or her selections with you and then discover for yourself the country inn experience.

Editions available:
Recommended Country Inns
New England • Mid-Atlantic and Chesapeake Region
The South • The Midwest • West Coast
Rocky Mountain Region • The Southwest
also
Recommended Romantic Inns
Recommended Island Inns

Recommended
COUNTRY INNS™
The South

Alabama • Arkansas • Florida • Georgia
Kentucky • Louisiana • Mississippi
North Carolina • South Carolina • Tennessee

Fourth Edition

by Sara Pitzer
illustrated by Duane Perreault

A Voyager Book

The Globe Pequot Press

Old Saybrook, Connecticut

Library of Congress Cataloging-in-Publication Data

Pitzer, Sara.
    Recommended country inns. The South / by Sara Pitzer ;
illustrated by Duane Perreault. — 4th ed.
        p. cm.
    "A Voyager book."
    Includes indexes.
    Contents: Alabama — Arkansas — Florida — Georgia — Kentucky —
Louisiana — Mississippi — North Carolina — South Carolina —
Tennessee.
    ISBN 1-56440-089-1
    1. Hotels, taverns, etc.—Southern States—Guidebooks.
    2. Southern States—Description and travel—1981- —Guidebooks.
    I. Title.
    TX907.3.S68P58   1992; aa21 08–17–92
    647.947501—dc20   92-29446
                                                          CIP

Manufactured in the United States of America
Fourth Edition/First Printing

Contents

Indexes

A Few Words about
Southern Inns

Diversity thrills me. I look for it. Visiting inns in the South, I found it in abundance. Southern hospitality is not just one way of behaving. It ranges from thigh-slapping camaraderie at the kitchen table of a rural inn to the white-gloves graciousness of a Mississippi plantation. Whether or not you have a good time visiting inns in the South depends almost entirely on your choosing those places that are in line with your personal tastes. I have described as accurately as I can what goes on in each inn listed in this book. Please *use* these descriptions. If you are a reserved person who likes privacy, or if you are looking for a place to spend time in seclusion with someone, don't go to an inn where the emphasis is on group activities or where I have said that the innkeeper likes to be closely involved with guests. If you like the amenities of civilization, don't go to a place I have described as rustic.

The inn scene has changed tremendously since we published the first edition of this book in 1987. For one thing, inns have become popular. Staying at them isn't a novel idea for most people anymore. By and large, they've also become better in terms of the features we've come to want when we travel—private baths, hot water, professionalism of operation, better accommodations for handicapped people, and accepting credit cards, for instance. In other words, inns are trying to respond to market demand. You, of course, are the market. The inns aren't the only observers of this phenomenon.

In response to the growing popularity of inns, travel clubs that once treated inns strictly as "mom-and-pop motels" and rarely included them in their travel guides have established an inn category. After due inspection and approval, many inns are now being included in the guides, often with ratings of several stars or hands or diamonds.

The inspections and requirements an inn must meet before such guides accept them are rigorous and standardized. It means the bathrooms of such places will be reliably clean and the toilet paper folded into a triangle. An escape from standardization, however, is what drove some of us into searching for inns in the first place. As a traveler, one of the main ways you can keep a wave of sameness from overtaking the inn world too is by letting innkeepers know specifically what you like about their facilities and what doesn't matter. If you truly want the most expensive little bottles of shampoo and hand lotion (known as "amenities" in the hospitality business), say so. If you think they're beside the point, say that, too. One of the best inns in the South will never make it into a standardized guide. In each of its bathrooms you'll find a full-sized bar of Ivory soap. Period. No little baskets and bottles. The issue here isn't whether these things are good or bad but whether they matter to you or not. You must speak up or the formal check-sheet of a guide rating will decide for you.

As you travel, you are bound to find some wonderful inns that are not in this guide. That's not because I'm discriminating against them; it's either because I haven't been able to visit yet or because I don't know about the place. If you find a must-not-miss inn, let me know. And, in spite of my best efforts to choose only very stable inns for this book, occasionally an inn changes, declines in quality, and disappoints a reader. I hope it won't happen to you, but if it does, let me know about that, too. A lone author can't cover a territory as large as the South perfectly. Your comments and questions are invaluable in guiding my travels.

Have fun,

Sara

About This Inn Guide

Working on the theory that most of us know our alphabet better than our geography, I have arranged the listings in this book alphabetically. The ten Southern states are listed in alphabetical order, as are the towns within each state and the inns (by name) within each town. The maps at the beginning of each chapter show you where the inns are, geographically.

The initial *S* stands for Sara and indicates a highly idiosyncratic observation about something I liked.

Caveats

Rates: Often they are complicated, and they change. I have tried to indicate general ranges here, but you should always discuss rates when you make reservations. They may have gone up, or, it happens, you may qualify for a discount that you don't know about.

Forms of payment: Innkeepers love cash. Every inn in this book will gleefully accept your folding money or traveler's checks. These days, most inns accept Visa and MasterCard, as well as personal checks. Some accept other credit cards, too. I have mentioned under "Rates" if an inn does not accept credit cards or personal checks; nevertheless, when you are making your reservations, it is always a good idea to ask because, as with everything else, these things change, sometimes without notice.

Children: Life used to be so simple. An inn could specify whether children were accepted or not and could even specify what ages were appropriate to the inn. A couple of legal discrimination-against-children battles have changed that. Therefore, in these guides we usually mention children only when an inn welcomes them especially. That doesn't change the fact that some inns are not suited to small children. Some have priceless fragile antiques that could be destroyed by one toddler's misstep; others have lofts, balconies, mountaintop locations, and other features that make the places downright dangerous for children. Moreover, some inns don't have cribs or extra beds to accommodate a child in a room with adults. Don't ever just show up with a child at an inn. It's simply not fair to you or the child or the innkeeper. Talk it over when you call for reservations.

Pets: In the South, few inns accept pets. There's a good reason for this. The long warm season and frequent humidity of the South please fleas as much as sunbathers, and infestations are a recurrent problem, even in well-maintained homes with pets. I've noted in the preliminary matter of an inn's write-up if pets are accepted, but there are only a few; you really can't travel with your pets and stay at inns in the South.

Smoking: More and more inns are restricting smokers in some way. Some inns permit smoking in guest rooms but not in public areas; some inns permit just the reverse. Some inns offer nonsmoking rooms on request. Many inns now do not allow smoking inside at all. These are listed as a "no smoking inn" under the category "Rooms" in the preliminary write-up. There also is an index listing these inns. If smoking, its presence or absence, is important to you, ask about it when you make reservations. Smoking policies are definitely in a state of flux.

Wheelchair access: Increasingly, inns are finding ways to accommodate wheelchairs, but in some old buildings what they are able to do is limited. Where I have noted "L" in the index, you can get into some parts of the inn, but not all. Discuss your particular needs with the innkeeper. Inns for which I do not mention wheelchairs at all are not equipped to handle them.

Air conditioning, television, and telephones: Most inns in the South are air-conditioned these days, so I've mentioned only those that are not. The only ones that don't have air conditioning are those at high altitude, where you sleep under blankets even in July and are more apt to be looking for a heater than a cooler. As for television and telephones, there's absolutely no consistency. Some inns have one or the other, some both, some neither. I've listed that information about each inn in the category "Rooms" in the preliminary matter.

Booze: The laws about serving alcohol in the South vary from state to state and from county to county within the states. You can drive the better part of a day in some states—North Carolina, Kentucky, and Arkansas especially—and never get out of dry counties. Some states, such as South Carolina, sell no alcohol on Sunday, except in "open" tourist areas. Others, like North Carolina, don't sell alcoholic beverages until after 1:00 P.M. Some inns, in such states as Tennessee, are in areas that forbid the sale of liquor by the drink but allow the sale of bottled liquor, even though they are in dry counties. I have tried to indicate what to expect at each inn, but if an evening cocktail or wine with dinner is important to you, I suggest that you travel with your own supply. Make sure that you understand the inn's policy before taking alcoholic beverages into any public area. In the South, we use the phrase "brown bagging" to mean bringing spirits of your own into a public place like a restaurant.

Reservations: Make them. You go to inns for personal attention and the feeling of being a special guest. Your responsibility is much the same as it would be if you were going to visit friends. You don't show up without warning.

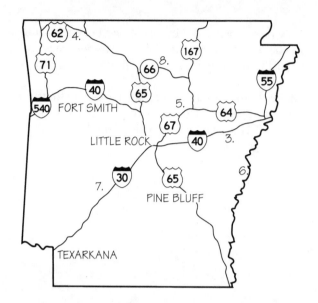

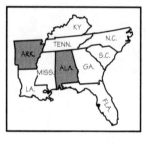

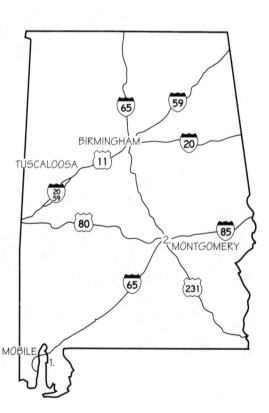

Alabama and Arkansas

Numbers on map refer to towns numbered below.

Mershon Court
Fairhope, Alabama
36532

Innkeeper: Susie Glickman
Address/Telephone: 203 Fairhope; (205) 928–7398
Rooms: 4; all with private bath. No smoking inn.
Rates: $65, single; $69, double; $55, corporate single; continental break-
fast.
Open: Year-round.
Facilities and activities: Swimming pool, gazebo, bicycles. Nearby: restaurants,
bay fishing off pier, beaches, antiques and boutique shops.

Fairhope is a little coastal resort town at Mobile Bay known
mostly to a few people who have been vacationing here for years. It
also has a significant permanent population, of the slow-and-easy-
laid-back variety. If you don't know about it, you can zip back and
forth between Pensacola, Florida, and Mobile, Alabama, on the
Interstate and never see this coastal gem.

So how does Susie Glickman, whose speech tells you at once
that she's not a Southern Magnolia, know about it?

Fannie Flagg told her.

And the story behind that is that Fannie and Susie became
close friends during the ten years Susie was working in California as
personal secretary to Dolly Parton. When Fannie found out that
Susie was planning a career change and wanted to run a small inn
in a quiet little town, she told Susie, "Go to Fairhope."

Here Susie was able to buy Mershon Court, already set up and running as a bed and breakfast inn. The place is bright and cheerful, with casual furnishings in lots of pretty pale colors. In the breakfast alcove, a bank of windows looks out over the pool and yard. Guests eat at a glass table that adds to the feeling of brightness. (Susie's breakfast specialty is muffins with a hole in the middle, like tiny bundt cakes.)

Susie's new; the furnishings are mostly new; the house has been around for a while. It was built in 1900 by Fairhope's first physician, Dr. Mershon. Local people have filled Susie in on the history of the house and on everything else in Fairhope.

They've made Susie one of their own, which isn't hard to want to do because she's lively and personable, but they've found they can only go so far with Susie, who has a fondness for T-shirts and comfortable pants. Susie tells the story of one local friend who was trying to help her get herself together for a local social function that called for clothes a bit more formal. Apparently it wasn't going well, because the friend looked at Susie and said, "I don't know if I can make a Southern Magnolia out of a California Raisin or not."

And that's why it's fun to stay at Mershon Court.

How to get there: From I-10, take Highway 98 into Fairhope, staying on Alternate 98 when you come to it. It runs directly to Fairhope Avenue. Turn right.

Red Bluff Cottage
Montgomery, Alabama
36101

Innkeepers: Anne and Mark Waldo
Address/Telephone: 551 Clay Street (mailing address: P.O. Box 1026); (205) 264–0056
Rooms: 4, plus 1 children's room; all but children's room with private bath, television on request. No smoking inn.
Rates: $55 to $65, double; single $5 less; full breakfast. Inquire about special arrangements for children. No credit cards.
Open: Year-round.
Facilities and activities: Guest refrigerator and coffee maker, children's fenced-in play yard, gazebo. Nearby: restaurants, Alabama State Capitol, historic sites, Jasmine Hill Gardens, Montgomery Museum of Fine Arts, Alabama Shakespeare Festival Theatre.

Red Bluff Cottage is a new building, built especially as a B&B inn. The guest rooms are all on the ground floor, with the kitchen, dining room, living room, den, and music room on the second floor, which makes the guest rooms quiet and the public rooms exceptionally light and airy, looking out over the yard and gardens.

The flower gardens are an important part of Red Bluff Cottage; guest rooms are filled with fresh flowers, and seasonal blooms adorn the breakfast table. Anne has been a passionate gardener for years, an especially rewarding activity in Montgomery's climate where it's moist and warm most of the year. When I visited, her border, full of intertwined patches of pink, white, yellow, and blue, looked like Monet's garden.

The Waldos' personal passions influence the look of the rooms inside the inn as well. In the music room, a harpsichord, a piano, and a recorder testify to the talent in the family—no guarantee that you'll hear a little concert during your stay, but it does happen.

In the guest rooms, you see furniture that's been in the family for years: the bed Anne slept in as a child, an antique sleigh bed that was her great-great-grandmother's, a spread crocheted by Mark's grandmother, and an old leather trunk from his great-aunt in Wisconsin, which contained invitations to fireman's balls dated 1850.

But artifacts of family past don't mean much unless you enjoy the present family. I enjoyed these people so much that I hung around longer than I should have.

Mark was the rector of an Episcopal parish in Montgomery for almost thirty years. During these years, the Waldos raised six children, all of whom keep in touch regularly. They have funny tales of those tumultuous times, including one about driving away from a rest stop in the van one vacation and not noticing that a child had been left behind until a routine "count-off" revealed that number three was missing.

After Mark's retirement, the Waldos became innkeepers because they wanted to keep new people coming into their lives. How can Mark and Anne fail? People who love flowers and books and music and can raise six kids and still be enthusiastic about taking in more of the human race must be genetically inclined to be innkeepers.

How to get there: Take exit 172 off I–65. Go toward downtown (east) on Herron Street 1 block. Turn left on Hanrick Street. Parking is on the right off Hanrick by the inn's rear entrance.

Great Southern Hotel
Brinkley, Arkansas
72021

Innkeepers: Stanley and Dorcas Prince
Address/Telephone: 127 West Cedar; (501) 734–4955
Rooms: 4; all with private bath, television, and wheelchair access.
Rates: $38, single; $44, double; room service breakfast. Advance arrangement required for children.
Open: Year-round.
Facilities and activities: Lunch and dinner in Victorian Tea Room for guests and public Monday through Saturday, wheelchair access to dining room, brown bagging permitted. Exercise room and sauna, banquet room for 200. Nearby: birding and picnicking, Louisiana Purchase Park, historic Helena homes open for touring, Ozark mountains.

The first note I wrote down about the Great Southern Hotel was, "Big, big, big lobby."

Surely, I thought, there's a better way to describe that lobby. I asked Dorcas how *she* thinks of it. "Well, it's really big," she said.

The pink marble in the area of the desk is emphasized by a pink fleur-de-lis pattern in the wallpaper. The expanse of floor seems even larger because of the geometric repetition of the mosaic tile. When you look up—15 feet up, to be exact—you get the same feeling from the pressed-tin pattern of the ceilings.

In its heyday, the hotel had sixty-one rooms. The four rooms open now for guests are on the first floor of the three-story building. The Princes live in a suite on the second floor. When the renovation is complete, they plan to have thirty-five rooms available for guests.

Even with just four rooms, they're developing an interesting clientele. One elderly couple comes once a month. Around midday Saturday, they eat at a favorite restaurant specializing in catfish and then check into the hotel. Dorcas takes snacks to them in their room in the afternoon.

Another couple, who had honeymooned at the hotel in the early fifties, recently held a family reunion here, where it all started.

Because they have only four rooms to rent, the Princes have concentrated on the dining room. People drive long distances to eat here. I learned about the place from a friend in Memphis who offered to meet me here for a meal.

The entrees change from day to day, but you can expect to find anything from lamb chops to seafood St. Jacques, along with Arkansas rice (a specialty), several vegetable casseroles, a soup-and-salad table, and a table full of varied desserts. I found the shrimp in a sauce of Monterey Jack cheese and capers irresistible. For dessert, there is a chocolate torte rich enough to fill you for days.

On Easter Sunday and Mother's Day, the hotel serves wonderful gourmet brunches, lasting from 10:00 A.M. until about 3:00 P.M., that attract people from the cities in every direction.

How to get there: From I–40, take Route 49 south into the middle of Brinkley. In the same block as the library and the police station, turn left onto Cedar Street. The street dead-ends at the hotel.

S: *Dorcas and Stanley have become deeply involved in buying and saving the old train station across the street and in getting the neighborhood listed as a National Historic District.*

Dairy Hollow House:
Century Inn and Restaurant
Eureka Springs, Arkansas
72632

Innkeepers: Crescent Dragonwagon and Ned Shank
Address/Telephone: 515 Spring Street; (501) 253–7444 or (800) 562–8650
Rooms: 3 in the Farmhouse, 3 suites in the Main House; all with private
bath, 2 with Jacuzzi.
Rates: $115 to $175, single or double, full breakfast delivered to rooms in a
basket. Two-day minimum stay on weekends.
Open: Year-round.
Facilities and activities: Dinner at the Restaurant at Dairy Hollow (seven
nights a week in season; weekends only off-season) for guests and
public. Reservations preferred, one seating nightly at 7:00 P.M., brown
bagging permitted. Wheelchair access to restaurant. Fireplaces, 700-
gallon outdoor hot tub. Nearby: restaurants; within walking distance of
most Eureka Springs tourist attractions and historic sites.

If I had to put a label on it, I'd call this place "sophisticated
bucolic." Nature took care of the bucolic with a hillside full of trees
and wildflowers. Crescent's striking sense of color has a lot to do
with the sophistication.

Dairy Hollow House started as a restored Ozark farmhouse painted a creamy peach and trimmed in deep teal. It has grown to include
a second building that is now the main house, where three suites, the
restaurant, and a central, front-desk check-in area are housed.

I slept in the Iris Room, which got its name from the predominant color of its decor. The blue quilts on the beds are handmade. The window blinds are woven in shades of blue from fabrics Crescent chose to coordinate with the quilt.

Every room and suite has a fireplace trimmed in local "Eureka limestone." The recently renovated Main House is decorated as the original Farmhouse is, with antiques, fresh flowers, and eye-catching colors, including a turquoise that sounds unlikely until you see how well it works.

You haven't had the full Dairy Hollow experience unless you have dinner in the restaurant. The food is fresh and regional, but regional with a contemporary twist. Crescent and Ned call it Nouveau 'Zarks. They received an Inn of Distinction award from Uncle Ben's Rice for being named a Top Ten Country Inn three years running.

When I was there, I had a cold cucumber mousse that I tried later to duplicate at home, followed by a spinach-pea-mint soup, a grapefruit salad with black olives and scallions, a layered Italian crepe torte made with several cheeses and tomatoes, fresh vegetables, and Augusta's Fall Down Cake for dessert. I don't know if they call the cake that because Augusta tried to bake one and it fell or because she ate it after such a meal and *she* fell down.

So many people asked for Crescent's unusual recipes that she and a cooking colleague wrote the *Dairy Hollow House Cookbook*, with more than four hundred recipes and a lot of commentary about Eureka Springs. And the *Dairy Hollow House Soup and Bread Cookbook* has just come out. You can duplicate many of the dishes served at Dairy Hollow House, but if you eat that way too often, you'll end up "Zarked" for sure!

How to get there: Starting from the historic downtown area of Eureka Springs, take the old historic loop (old 62B, Spring Street) past the post office and all the other houses. Go just over 1 mile to where Spring Street curves sharply toward the original inn. The main house, where guests check in, is at the intersection of Spring Street and Dairy Hollow Road.

Heartstone Inn
and Cottages
Eureka Springs, Arkansas
72632

Innkeepers: Iris and Bill Simantel
Address/Telephone: 35 Kingshighway; (501) 253–8916
Rooms: 10, plus 2 cottages; all with private bath.
Rates: $58 to $105, full breakfast. Inquire about winter discounts.
Open: Year-round except from mid-December through mid-January.
Facilities and activities: Massage/Reflexology therapist available by appoint-
ment. Located in the historic district, within walking distance of down-
town Eureka Springs tourist activities. Nearby: restaurants.

The Heartstone Inn gets its name from a large, flat, vaguely
heart-shaped stone that the Simantels found on the property. They
play with the heart theme, using the phrase "Lose your heart in the
Ozarks" and a heart-shaped logo in their brochure. The doors have
heart-shaped welcome signs. The stone that justifies it all rests in
the front garden, surrounded by flowers.

As far as I'm concerned, the Simantels have such heart they
could use the theme even without the stone.

They came to the Ozarks from Chicago to become innkeepers.
They love Eureka Springs. They love their inn. They love their
guests.

The inn is pretty. It's an Edwardian house, painted pink, with a white picket fence and lots of bright pink geraniums and roses all around.

Most of the rooms are furnished with elegant antiques, though a couple are done in country style. By the time you read this, there will be a new luxury Jacuzzi suite of special elegance, too. The fairly steady addition of such outdoor niceties as decks and a gazebo means there are always glorious places for special gatherings such as weddings.

But I think the attractiveness of the inn comes not so much from its pretty artifacts as from what those things reflect of Iris and Bill. For example, in the dining room I admired a Pennsylvania Dutch hex sign in which tulips and hearts make up the pattern. Iris said that the sign stands for everything they believe in and explained the symbols for faith, hope, charity, love of God, and smooth sailing. Then she kept the moment from getting too solemn by pointing to a print of yellow irises on the other wall. She said, "That's so I remember who I am in the morning."

In the living room, she keeps a collection of ceramic English cottages and ceramic pieces decorated with pictures of cottages. She says that it's how she keeps in touch with the fact that she's English in spite of having lived in Chicago.

The Simantels have been enjoying a good bit of "discovery," applause from magazines and newspapers and other innkeepers for doing such a good job. The praise, Iris says, has not gone to their heads. They are still keeping their prices moderate, because they don't want to attract snobs who go to places only because they are expensive. Not that Bill and Iris could be snobs if they wanted to. That Simantel humor bubbles too close to the surface.

When Iris was talking about the elaborate breakfasts they serve, she said that guests feel pampered by breakfasts including strawberry blintzes, coffeecake, and several kinds of fruit. As part of making breakfast special, she said that they dress up in long prairie dresses to serve it. "Well, Bill doesn't wear a prairie dress," she said. "That would be too special."

How to get there: From the west, take the first 62B exit off Route 62: From the east, take the second 62B exit. Follow 62B through town until it becomes Kingshighway.

Oak Tree Inn
Heber Springs, Arkansas
72543

Innkeeper: Freddie Lou Lodge
Address/Telephone: Highway 110 West; (501) 362–7731 or (501) 362–8870
Rooms: 6, plus 4 lakeside condos and 4 lakeside cabins; inn rooms have private whirlpool baths, 5 with fireplace; condos have televison, some with wheelchair access. No smoking in inn, but allowed in condos and cabins.
Rates: $50 to $80 per room; $10 less Sunday through Thursday; condos and cabins $100 to $130, with 2-night minimum stay; full breakfast and evening dessert.
Open: Year-round.
Facilities and activities: Swimming pool, hot tub, tennis courts. Nearby: restaurants, area noted for fall foliage and spring dogwood, 45,000-acre Greers Ferry Lake, rainbow- and brown-trout fishing on Little Red River.

Freddie Lou has made big changes at Oak Tree Inn since my first visit there, adding the lakeside condos and cabins to accommodate more people and putting in such niceties as the new swimming pool, hot tub, and tennis courts. The rooms are still decorated to suit a variety of tastes—Victorian, country, oriental—and the baths are all equally luxurious with their whirlpools. Magnificent old oak trees near the inn provide shade for a patio.

When you arrive, you'll find in your room a typed list of interesting things to see in the area and a list of recommended restaurants, including information about the kind of food served and the kind of dress appropriate at each. Freddie Lou visits all the local restaurants each year before she makes her list to be sure that each restaurant is still worth recommending.

Freddie Lou says that she left television out of the guest rooms of the inn deliberately, as a result of her marriage-counseling background. She says she wants the inn to be a place where couples can come to be together and talk without the distractions—including television—of daily routine. She does, however, have television in the lakeside condos, for those who just can't give up the habit.

A step more out of the routine: In the evening, Freddie Lou will serve you a treat—homemade pie or cake or something like her special piña-colada dessert. And in the morning she'll serve you the kind of breakfast that could make lunch obsolete. It might be eggs Benedict, or waffles and scrambled eggs, or a spectacular baked high-rise pancake with fresh fruit.

Sometime after breakfast or before dessert, be sure to look around outside, where nice flower borders thrive. In addition to lovely roses and money plants, I found big, healthy strawberry plants growing in with balsam and some impatiens.

How to get there: State Highway 25 goes into Heber Springs. From 25, take Highway 110 west to the inn.

S: *Heber Springs has a population of less than 5,000. It's the kind of place where strangers wave and passing cars will stop so that they won't get in the way if you're taking a picture.*

Edwardian Inn
Helena, Arkansas
72342

Innkeeper: Jerri Steed
Address/Telephone: 317 Biscoe; (501) 338–9155
Rooms: 12; all with private bath. Pets accepted with advance arrangement.
  Wheelchair access.
Rates: $44 to $60, single or double, continental breakfast. $10 each extra
  person. Children free.
Open: Year-round.
Facilities and activities: Conference room. Nearby: restaurants, antiques
  shops, Delta Cultural Center, Mississippi Riverfront Park; St. Francis
  National Forest with two lakes for hiking, fishing, and swimming.

A very rich man built the Edwardian Inn for his family home
in 1904. And even though he went broke, lost it, and a lot of bad
things happened to it over the years, it is perfectly obvious (now
that the restoration is done) that it is a fabulously expensive building.

Everyone notices the woodwork first. The first floor has something called *wood carpeting*. It was parqueted in Germany from strips
not more than 1 inch wide, mounted on canvas, and shipped to
Helena in rolls. The wainscoting on the walls is elaborately carved.
Barleytwist balusters adorn the banister of the oak stairway.

The rooms are correspondingly lovely, with high ceilings and
outstanding period antiques. Many businesspeople stay here regularly because each room has a comfortable modern bath, lots of

space, and places to open up a briefcase, spread out papers, or even set up a portable computer, existing in surprising harmony with the fine old furnishings and restored mantels, mirrors, and candelabra.

There is a second-floor sitting room in addition to the downstairs common rooms.

But what really keeps the Edwardian Inn from being just another fancy house or splendidly appointed hotel is the presence of Jerri Steed. While I was there, she took a number of calls, some from family and some from guests. You couldn't have told from her tone and interest which was which.

Jerri has great credentials for innkeeping. She knows antiques from having had her own shop. She knows about taking care of people from having raised a family. She enjoys mingling with guests. And she cares for the inn as though she owned it.

In the morning, guests have homemade rolls, whatever fruit is fresh in season, and coffee in the sunny little latticed breakfast room. Jerri takes pride in serving breakfasts that are not ordinary and in adding special touches, such as using real cloth napkins.

How to get there: Take 49B into Helena and follow it up a hill directly to the inn, which is painted deep yellow.

S: *Even though the inn is right in town, you can see tame birds, 'coons, and squirrels playing outside the kitchen window.*

Stillmeadow Farm
Hot Springs, Arkansas
71913

Innkeepers: Jody and Gene Sparling
Address/Telephone: 111 Stillmeadow Lane; (501) 525–9994
Rooms: 4; 2 with private bath, 2 can be rented as a suite. No smoking inn.
Rates: $40, single; $50 to $70, double; continental breakfast. Personal
checks or cash only.
Open: Year-round.
Facilities and activities: Antiques shop, hiking trails, herb garden, Mountain
Brook Stables, Inc. on premises. Nearby: restaurants, Hot Springs bath-
houses, Hot Springs National Park, and lakes Catherine, Hamilton, and
Ouachita.

We have to start with the obvious question: What's a reproduction 1740 post-and-beam saltbox furnished with early country
antiques doing in Arkansas? Simple. Jody and Gene are not home-
sick New Englanders; they're natives of Arkansas who happen to
like saltboxes and country antiques.

They're neat people who decided to get away from the pres-
sures of working in the nine-to-five world. They make their living
now with the inn and by selling antiques in their adjacent shop.

The inn is a delight to be in. It is filled with sturdy, comfortable
antiques. The four-poster bed in my room was covered with a crocheted white bedspread. An old painted blanket chest stood as a
bedside table.

Downstairs, Jody and Gene have set aside a parlor especially for guests, where you can have a fire in the fireplace when the weather's right.

At breakfast, they share another sitting and dining area that has a table at a big window looking out over the woods and meadows. It's all true New England, with herbs hanging to dry and a braided rug in front of another brick fireplace. Jody has acquired some good old wooden kitchenware, pottery, and baskets. After breakfast, we talked around the table for a long time, then moved to the couch in front of the fireplace for a long time more.

We had much to talk about. Jody is expanding her herb garden. Gene knows detailed history of the Hot Springs thermal baths. Their son just bought his very own backhoe. A guest in her nineties who had been there to look around carried two canes—one for walking and one with a handle so heavy that it seemed it must be for defense. Oh, and Jody and Gene hoped that darned woodpecker hadn't awakened me trying to take out his own reflection in the bedroom window.

We traded recipes and kid stories and what-it-used-to-be-like-to-work-in-the-real-world stories. We talked about several good restaurants nearby and how surprisingly good the Moo Shu Pork is at the Hunan, given that Chinese food isn't overly appreciated in the South. Probably we'd all still be talking if we hadn't had other things we needed to do.

A young couple on a fishing trip, who shared a lot of the talk with us, must have felt as fully at home as I did because Gene noticed that they had made their bed before leaving. Even though the bed still had to be stripped for clean sheets, it seemed like a special gesture. Gene grinned and looked sentimental when he saw it. "Will you look at that? Just look at that. Now isn't that something, though?" he said.

How to get there: The inn is 5 miles south of Hot Springs, off State Highway 7. From Highway 7, go east on Highway 290 about 1 1/2 miles to the Stillmeadow Farm sign. Follow the signs down the drive another 1/2 mile to the inn. Jody will send a map when you make a reservation.

Williams House
Hot Springs National Park, Arkansas
71901

Innkeepers: Mary and Gary Riley
Address/Telephone: 420 Quapaw; (501) 624–4275
Rooms: 6; 2 sometimes share a bath, 2 are suites, 2 have private bath. Pets accepted in one room with advance arrangement.
Rates: $55 to $90, full breakfast.
Open: Year-round. Sometimes closed in January, depending on weather.
Facilities and activities: Nearby: restaurants, art galleries, National Park hiking trails, Hot Springs thermal baths, Oaklawn Park Race Track, 3 lakes for boating, fishing, and swimming; golf.

Mary says that guests want good beds and good breakfasts and that her inn is popular because she provides custom-made beds and excellent food. I think there's more to it than that.

Start with the building. You won't find many Victorian brownstones in Hot Springs. The doctor who built it in 1889 had the stone hauled in. In the ensuing years, it's been through some hard times, but the Rileys have refurbished it well. You can't help being impressed by the turret and tower with notched battlements on the outside and the lovely woodwork and the black marble fireplace inside.

But, to me, the real attraction is Mary. Take her attitude about the antique piano, for example. She can't play it. She tried and tried and couldn't master it, but she loves the sound of its music, so she keeps it tuned and encourages as many guests as possible to play it. She has even talked the staff into playing. She told one of the maids, "I'll clean; you play."

You find Mary's touch again in her collection of houseplants, massed in all the windows with good light. They're well grown, and her selection includes plants that serious growers cultivate out of special interest. No decorator plants maintained by a contract gardener here.

Mary will do whatever she can to accommodate guests with special needs. She's been known to get up at 5:00 A.M. to make sure that a guest had a good breakfast before leaving to catch a flight. ("I won't say I *liked* it, but I did it.")

I don't know what she served for that 5:00 A.M. breakfast. Under normal circumstances, her breakfasts go way beyond run-of-the-mill bacon and eggs. She knows that lots of people actually like bacon, grits, and eggs, so she always offers those, but she also alternates a variety of daily special entrees, ranging from eggs Benedict to pecan waffles. The day I was there, breakfast included a quiche made with peppers, bacon, and Swiss cheese.

Another nice extra is a sheet that she prints up for guests entitled "How a Thermal Bath Is Taken in Hot Springs National Park." It tells you exactly what happens. In addition, she keeps ice and jugs of mineral-spring water in a refrigerator at the bottom of the stairs outside the kitchen so that you can sip the waters even if you don't go to the baths.

How to get there: From the north on I–40, take Route 7 and follow it into Hot Springs. This is a drive of about two hours, longer than it looks on the map, because the road winds through mountains. In Hot Springs, turn right off Route 7 onto Orange Street. Go 3 blocks to the corner of Orange and Quapaw, where you will find the inn. From the south on I–30, take Route 7 22 miles into Hot Springs and stay on 7 until you come to Orange. Turn left onto Orange and go to Quapaw.

Commercial Hotel
Mountain View, Arkansas
72560

Innkeepers: Todd and Andrea Budy

Address/Telephone: Court Square (mailing address: P.O. Box 72); (501)
269–4383

Rooms: 8; 4 with private bath, some with wheelchair access. No smoking
inn.

Rates: $38 to $55, double; single $5 less; breakfast included. Children under
6 free.

Open: Year-round. November through March by reservation only.

Facilities and activities: HearthStone bakery and mini-bookshop. Nearby:
restaurants, Blanchard Springs Caverns, Ozark Folk Center, swimming
in Sylamore Creek, many mountain-music programs.

Todd and Andrea have started an unusual diary at the Commercial. They are asking for entries from people who stayed at the
hotel in earlier times. I love the results.

One entry reads, "Vera and Laren Waggoner honeymooned
here January 1, 1920." Another man wrote that he boarded here in
1929 for $5 per month, with meals. And a woman wrote that it was
nice to see the lobby clean and white—she remembered that it
always used to be thick with cigar and cigarette smoke.

The entries are accumulating—from a traveling salesman who
stayed here regularly during World War I, from vacationers who
stopped only a few times but always loved the place, and from peo-

ple who stayed here for one reason or another as children and have not been back until now.

The inn they are remembering isn't elaborate now. Never was. Never presumed to be. When the Budys took it over, it was a battered old boardinghouse, like a fat lady in a tight corset, structurally sound but sagging at the edges. In restoring it and returning it to operation as an inn, they added such niceties (or should I say necessities?) as central air conditioning and heat, lots of nice pale-blue carpeting, and good clean paint. They kept the original furniture and iron beds. Today they're antiques.

Of the two baths that the four upstairs rooms share, one is antique, the other modern, so you can get clean with either nostalgia or dispatch. The other four rooms have private showers.

I haven't mentioned the bakery yet. Leaving it out would be wrong. Mike Warshauer, the owner and baker, says the bakery is famous for "four or five blocks around or wherever the odor wafts." Sainted magnolias, but that stuff is *good*. Andrea says the hotel has stairs available to work off the bakery's effects. The stream of traffic to the bakery was steady the day I was visiting. In addition to all the traditional bakery goodies that you should just rub directly onto your hips, the bakery serves unusual sandwiches with soup for lunch. The hotel's breakfast goodies come from the bakery.

How to get there: From the east, follow Highway 9, 5, and 14 to where it becomes Highway 5 and 14 (Main Street). Go to Court Square and turn right. From the west, Highway 66 goes into Mountain View directly to the square. From the north, Highway 9 goes to the square. The hotel is on the corner across from the square.

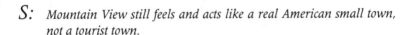

S: *Mountain View still feels and acts like a real American small town, not a tourist town.*

Florida

Numbers on map refer to towns numbered below.

The 1735 House
Amelia Island, Florida
32034

Innkeepers: Gary and Emily Grable
Address/Telephone: 584 South Fletcher; (904) 261–5878 or (800) 872–8531
Rooms: 6 suites; all with private bath and television.
Rates: $55 to $125, single or double, continental breakfast. $5 each additional person.
Open: Year-round.
Facilities and activities: Cooking and laundry facilities, beachfront. Nearby: restaurants, downtown historic Fernandina Beach shopping and sightseeing, boating from the marina.

You don't find many places like The 1735 House at the beach these days. It's a Cape Cod–style inn, directly facing the ocean, furnished with antiques, wicker, neat old trunks, and some bunk beds just right for kids.

Maybe there will be no room at the inn, and you'll stay instead in the lighthouse. Its walls are covered with navigation maps. As you enter, you can either step down into a shower-and-bath area or take the spiral stairs up to the kitchen. A galley table and director's chairs make a good spot for playing cards, chatting, or ocean gazing, as well as eating. The stairs keep spiraling up to a bedroom with another bath, and finally up to an enclosed observation deck, which is the ultimate spot for ocean views.

Wherever you stay, in the evening all you have to do is tell the staff what time you want breakfast and they'll deliver it right to your room in a wicker basket, along with a morning paper.

The physical setup is uncommon, but the staff have the true inn spirit. They'll give you ice, towels for the beach, bags for your shell collection or wet bathing suit, and just about anything else you need. All you have to do is ask. I was recuperating from the flu during my visit, and they even gave me a box of tissues!

The staff are full of helpful recommendations about good eating places, of which there are many on Amelia Island, too. The Down Under Seafood Restaurant, under the Shave bridge on A1A, is in keeping with the nautical mood of the inn and the lighthouse. The seafood is all fresh from the Intracoastal Waterway. There's a boat ramp with a dock, and the atmosphere is correspondingly quaint. You can enjoy cocktails and dinner.

If staying at The 1735 House gets you in the mood for more inns, you're welcome to browse through a large, well-used collection of books about inns in the office.

How to get there: Amelia Island is near the Florida/Georgia border. Take the Yulee exit from I–95 onto Route A1A and follow the signs toward Fernandina Beach. The inn is on A1A.

The Bailey House
Fernandina Beach, Florida
32034

Innkeepers: Tom and Diane Hay
Address/Telephone: 28 South Seventh Street (mailing address: P.O. Box 805); (904) 261–5390
Rooms: 4; all with private bath and television. No smoking inn.
Rates: $65 to $95, single or double, extended continental breakfast.
Open: Year-round.
Facilities and activities: Bicycles available. Nearby: municipal golf courses, lighted tennis courts, beaches, antiques malls; within walking distance of restaurants and shops in the historic downtown area and the City Marina.

Unlike some antique-filled Victorian inns, The Bailey House has a homey, lived-in feeling. You feel that it would be okay just to walk in and sit down.

The Hays have a fine collection of Victorian antique furniture, but they've arranged it carefully so that no room seems too full and you never feel as if you're bumping into knickknacks everywhere you turn. Consequently, you're able to give a lot of attention to some special pieces. I was charmed by the working pump organ, and I mentally conjured up all kinds of stories about the old wicker bath chair. And the ficus trees in the parlor and entryway fit in so perfectly that I felt they'd been growing there at least a hundred years.

Each of the four guest rooms has its own special features: a walnut plantation bed with an 8½-foot-high headboard, from Mississippi, in the Rose Room; an antique footed tub (and separate shower) in the Country Room; and towels and sheets coordinated with the color scheme in each room. Tom jokes that the towels are the luxury size that "make your suitcase hard to close."

Breakfast is spread on the marble-topped buffet in the dining-room bay window for guests to help themselves to in the morning. In addition to the usual coffee, juice, fruits, and pastries, the Hays feature bran muffins with nuts and raisins and honor all requests for the recipe.

Fernandina Beach has had good food for a long time, and in recent years some great new places have been added. For lunch, Bretts, an old favorite, serves salads, soups, good breads, and pasta creations. Snugg Harbor is a popular favorite these days for seafood, and the Beech Street Grill, kind of a coastal bistro, receives the Hays' special, enthusiastic recommendation. An added bonus—all these restaurants are within walking distance of the inn.

How to get there: From I-95 or U.S. 17, take Route A1A to Amelia Island. Stay on A1A. In Fernandina Beach, A1A becomes Eighth Street. Turn left on Centre Street and left again on Seventh Street. The Bailey House is on the left corner at Seventh and Ash streets.

The Seaside Inn
Fernandina Beach, Florida
32034

Innkeeper: Bill Conrad
Address/Telephone: 1998 South Fletcher Avenue; (904) 261–0954
Rooms: 10; all with private bath.
Rates: $65 to $75, single or double, breakfast not served. Inn especially suited for children. Personal checks not accepted.
Open: Year-round.
Facilities and activities: Lunch (weekends March through November) and dinner in Sliders Restaurant. Lounge, ocean beachfront. Nearby: historic Fernandina Beach and Fort Clinch shopping and sightseeing, more than 100 holes of golf, tennis, deep sea fishing and boating from the marina, horseback riding on beach.

The Seaside Inn has changed hands since I first visited here; but except for some small changes, the same slightly wacky atmosphere, simple but pleasant oceanfront rooms, and good food remain the same.

In the guest rooms, the furniture has been painted to match the colors on the stenciled walls. In the upstairs hall, odds and ends from auctions, the things we now call "collectibles," keep your eyes busy.

The energy and high good humor of the place come, I think, from the staff, who are young, local, and having a lot of fun working here. What they lack in polish they make up for in exuberance! When I had lunch outside, just a few feet from the beach and ocean, I was served by a college-aged waiter who practically danced as he placed a sandwich of fresh shrimp, melted cheese, lettuce, and onion in front of me.

The Sliders Restaurant gets its name from oysters. Raw oysters used to be called "sliders" (oh, gross), and beautiful *fresh* raw oysters in season are a feature of the restaurant, along with a lot of other excellent seafood and some imaginative offerings such as Creole-style black beans and rice, a smoked-fish dip, and Grouper Verde— grouper topped with spinach, lemon pepper butter, and Parmesan cheese. The best seller is Crepes Amelia, shrimp, scallops, and crab-meat in light crepes.

How much you enjoy The Seaside Inn depends greatly on timing your stay according to the kind of activity you like—or don't like. During the week, the place is quiet, pleasant, almost placid. On weekends, however, top-notch bands of the kind that appeal to the twenty-five to forty-five-year-old age group entertain in the Sliders lounge. The place rocks until the wee hours. If you're not a rocker, stay during the week; if you're born to boogie, try a weekend.

How to get there: Take I–95 to the Amelia Island/Fernandina Beach exit. Travel 14 miles east to Amelia Island on A1A. After crossing the bridge, turn right at the second traffic light onto Sadler Road. The inn is about 1 mile down Sadler Road, on the ocean.

S: *Most of the building in this stretch of beach consists of homes and condominiums rather than hotels or motels, so the beach is pleasantly without concessions.*

Chalet Suzanne
Lake Wales, Florida
33859

Innkeepers: Carl and Vita Hinshaw
Address/Telephone: U.S. Highway 27 (mailing address: P.O. Drawer AC);
    (813) 676–6011; for reservations, (800) 288–6011
Rooms: 30; all with private bath, television, and telephone, 3 with Jacuzzi.
Rates: $95 to $185, single or double, full breakfast. Pets $20 extra.
Open: Year-round.
Facilities and activities: Lunch, dinner, wheelchair access to dining room.
    Cocktail lounge, wine cellar open for sampling, gift shop, antiques
    shop, ceramics studio, swimming pool, lake, soup cannery, air strip.
    Nearby: golf, tennis, fishing, tourist attractions of central Florida.

   Chalet Suzanne releases a photograph for publicity along with
this caption: "Through wrought-iron gates one can view the unlikely hodgepodge of towers, turrets, and gables that ramble in all directions." Well, yeah, that too.
   Everyone who writes about the place falters under the burden
of trying to describe what they've seen—a collection of whimsical,
odd buildings asssembled over a number of years by Carl Hinshaw's
mother, who got into innkeeping and the restaurant business trying
to keep body and soul together after being widowed during the
Great Depression. I've seen the words "Camelot," "phantasmago-
ria," "fairy tale," "magical," in the reviews of writers trying to cap-
ture the mood of the place. Any and all will do. Staying here is a

great giggle for anyone who doesn't like too many straight lines, who enjoys walks and walls that tilt, and who appreciates the kind of humor represented by a potted geranium atop the ice machine.

I stayed in the Orchid Room, a roughly octagonal space where sherry and fruit were set out on a small table between two comfortable chairs. Live plants and fresh flowers were scattered throughout the room and its bath, and the furniture was painted various shades of aqua, cream, and deep orchid. The bath had black and gray tile and an improbable little bathtub of brick-colored ceramic tile. The tub was really too straight up and down to sit in; I used the shower and afterward appreciated finding a blow dryer to try to tame my hair. Although I saw signs of wear on the carpet and some of the furniture, everything was clean and comfortable and quiet.

Chalet Suzanne is famous for its award-winning restaurant, in which the tables are all set with different kinds of china, silver, and glasses collected by the Hinshaws over years of travel. Carl's Romaine soup, Vita's broiled grapefruit garnished with chicken livers, and the shrimp curry are all much-extolled selections, so I tried them all with a nice house wine dispensed in generous servings. I enjoyed everything, including being served by waitresses in costumes that looked Swiss in the Swiss dining room, where European stained-glass windows provide a focal point.

A waitress told me that Carl Hinshaw's soups—which have become so popular that he started a cannery on the premises for people who want to take soup home—have made it to the better gourmet shops and even to the moon with the *Apollo* astronauts— not necessarily in that order.

So there you are, in a wacky, unreal environment, eating multistar-winning food that must be famous by now on the moon, served by waitresses dressed like Snow White, and you're sleeping in a room that looks as though it came out of a Seven-Dwarfs coloring book . . . how are *you* going to describe it? I give up.

How to get there: Chalet Suzanne is 4 miles north of Lake Wales on Highway 27. Signs clearly mark the turns.

Inn by the Sea
Naples, Florida
33940

Innkeeper: Caitlin Maser
Address/Telephone: 287 Eleventh Avenue South; (813) 649–4124
Rooms: 6; 4 with private bath.
Rates: $45 to $120, single or double, tropical continental breakfast. Inquire about discounts for long stays.
Open: Year-round.
Facilities and activities: Fishing rods, beach cruiser bicycles. Nearby: walk to restaurants, art galleries, shops; 7 miles of white-sand beaches, golf, tennis, shopping, greyhound race track, Everglades National Park.

Inn by the Sea is a beach house for vacationers and sometimes a lodging place for travelers who come to Naples on business. It's hard to see how they could remain in a business frame of mind staying here, though. The building of wooden cove siding is surrounded by tropical plants—coconut palms, bougainvillea, an orange tree, and luxuriant specimens of many plants we barely keep alive in pots on the windowsill farther north. Inside, the casual decor, which includes wicker and cheerful floral print fabrics, complements the heart-of-pine floors and cypress and pine ceilings and feels light and cool.

Ceiling fans turn lazily, making the air conditioning more effective and adding to the tropical atmosphere. On cooler days, you can open windows in the guest rooms and enjoy a great cross-breeze. I stayed in the Captiva Room, which looked especially refreshing with green-and-white-striped walls and drapes against white-eyelet bedclothes. Because it was cool outside, I kept the windows open and dropped off to sleep feeling the breeze and listening to the night sounds of summer peepers.

In the morning, I spent time looking at the inn's art—seascapes, beach scenes, birds—mostly done by local artists, much of it for sale to guests.

The "tropical" breakfast emphasized all the local fruits that simply never seem to taste as good outside southern Florida; everyone at the table had seconds.

Part of the importance of this house is that it preserves another of Naples's old homes. (Each guest room is named for a local island.) Although there are new condominiums on one corner, the neighborhood ambience is still of Old Naples.

How to get there: From I–75, take exit 16. Bear right to Goodlette Road. Turn left and follow Goodlette Road 4 miles to its end. Turn right onto Highway 41. Continue toward the beach to Fifth Avenue South. Turn left on Third Street South to Eleventh Avenue South. The inn is on the corner.

New World Inn
Pensacola, Florida
32501

Innkeeper: Janice Crawford
Address/Telephone: 600 South Palafox Street; (904) 432–4111
Rooms: 14, plus 2 suites; all with private bath, telephone, and television. Wheelchair access.
Rates: $65 to $100, double; single $10 less; continental breakfast on Saturday, Sunday, Monday. Inquire about weekend, group, and special rates.
Open: Year-round.
Facilities and activities: Restaurant serves continental breakfast daily, lunch Tuesday through Friday, dinner Monday through Saturday; closed Sunday. Full bar, closed Sunday. Fax machine, banquet accommodations, catering. Located in Pensacola's historic downtown waterfront. Nearby: beaches, shopping.

Let's talk food first. I don't think I've ever had a bad meal in Pensacola or along the coast of the Florida panhandle, but some restaurants unquestionably treat the good seafood and fresh produce more elaborately than others. New World Restaurant, companion to New World Inn at New World Landing, is one of Pensacola's more elegant dining places. The menu corresponds. How about Snapper Chardonnay, with julienne vegetables and cream? Definitely special.

My friend Rich Pahalek, who lives in Pensacola, watched New World Landing come to life. He's one of several people who raved to me about the way the history of the site has been preserved.

Originally it was a box factory, built on the waterfront for convenient shipping. As interest in historic restoration and preservation grew in Pensacola, the way old warehouses were being handled all along the East Coast and especially in Charleston, South Carolina, influenced this restoration.

The hotel reflects Pensacola's history. That's more complicated than you might think, because five flags have flown over Pensacola: French, British, Spanish, American, and Confederate.

Thus, each of the inn's rooms is named for a famous person in Pensacola's history and decorated to fit that person's nationality, using Baker reproductions of Spanish, French, English, and American furniture.

The three dining rooms of New World Restaurant have been handled similarly: The Barcelona Room has a Spanish decor, the Pensacola Room is decorated with huge photographs of the city, and the Marseille Room reflects French influence.

The days when travelers were willing to accept below-par accommodations to stay at small, historic inns seem about gone, and New World Inn is definitely part of the new wave of small hotels that provide not just adequate but luxurious rooms within their historic walls.

They're in step, too, with the trend toward lots of personal (dare I say European-style?) service. If you become a repeat customer, you can expect to be greeted by name when you appear. And, no matter how picky you are, the staff will try to accommodate you. One staff member recalls changing rooms for a guest three times before she decided she was satisfied. Then they provided extra pillows and blankets and, finally, coffee at 4:00 A.M. They did it all with a smile. If your requests are more reasonable, imagine how kindly *you'll* be treated!

How to get there: The inn is at the corner of Palafox and Cedar, 1 block south (toward the waterfront) of Main. Ask for a map when you make reservations.

Casa de la Paz
St. Augustine, Florida
32084

Innkeepers: Sandy and Kramer Upchurch
Address/Telephone: 22 Avenida Menendez; (904) 829–2915
Rooms: 4, plus 2 suites; all with private bath and television. No smoking inn.
Rates: $65 to $115, single or double, continental breakfast. Extra person in room, $10. Two-night minimum stay on weekends. Advance arrangements needed for children.
Open: Year-round.
Facilities and activities: Nearby: walk to most St. Augustine historic sites; restaurants, tour carriages and trolleys, beaches.

The Upchurches have created a beautiful inn. They started with a fine building, the only remaining example of pure Mediterranean Revival architecture from the turn of the century in St. Augustine. It has ornate iron molding and barrel-tile roofing.

Inside, the sun porch with huge arched windows, black-and-white tile flooring, white walls, and white wicker furniture, accented with lush green hanging baskets and foliage plants, feels so bright and airy and spacious that you scarcely distinguish between the outside and the inside. "That's the feeling we're trying to create all through the house," Sandy said, "cool, uncluttered, and clean."

Part of that effect in the guest rooms comes from handmade piqué blanket covers in geometric, scroll, or lace patterns, used instead of heavy comforters. "After all, this is the South," Sandy said. The beds are made up with 100 percent cotton sheets, and six feather and down pillows to a bed! If you're a very big person, you might decide to displace a couple of pillows for the night.

In the dining room, the spacious effect comes partly from a Federal bulls-eye mirror hanging at the far end of the room. It's been in Kramer's family for years and has thirty-five balls, indicating the number of states in the Union at the time the mirror was made. It faces French doors at the opposite end of the room, reflecting the view overlooking Matanzas Bay.

You'll probably eat your breakfast in this room. The designation "continental" doesn't really do breakfast justice. Although the inn doesn't always serve eggs, when they do appear, a delectable version is a casserole of eggs whipped with cream cheese and baked with spinach, mushrooms, green onions, and Swiss cheese. All the inn's breads are homemade and baked in such variety that even if you stay for a week, you won't get the same breakfast twice.

How to get there: From I–95, take State Road 16 to A1A into the city, where A1A becomes Avenida Menendez. The inn is just past Hypolita Street.

S: *During their visits, many guests find the presence of the Upchurches' young daughter, Sydney, a bit of lagniappe.*

Casa de Solana
St. Augustine, Florida
32084

Innkeeper: Faye McMurry

Address/Telephone: 21 Aviles Street; (904) 824–3555

Rooms: 4 suites; all with private bath and television, some with fireplace, some with balcony. Wheelchair access.

Rates: $125, single or double; full breakfast, decanter of sherry, and chocolates. Extra person in room, $10.

Open: Year-round.

Facilities and activities: Bicycles provided for touring St. Augustine. Nearby: restaurants and all historic sites and tourist activities of St. Augustine, beaches, marinas.

Maybe the idea of staying in one of the oldest homes of America's oldest city sounds to you as if it would be interesting and educational but uncomfortable. But then you haven't reckoned on Faye. She loves history and old homes enough to have given up a career as a juvenile-court lawyer in Virginia to buy and renovate a 1763 Colonial home and turn it into an inn, but she loves creature comforts, too. To suit her, the inn had to be comfortable and glamorous as well as historic.

Her guest suites are decorated with marble, brass, and cut glass. Breakfast is served in an elaborate formal dining room at a mahogany table, on exquisite old family china. Faye's lavish breakfasts always include fresh fruit, eggs, meat, breads she bakes herself, and classy little touches such as molded butter pats. She uses different molds to fit the season or a special occasion.

Despite all this elegance, guests treat Casa de Solana like a second home. While I was there, a young woman breezed in, said she was all ready for the wedding but was more interested in sun than in nuptial plans, so she ran out into the courtyard, where she threw herself full-length onto the grass and lay with nose and toes pointed up, absorbing springtime sun. (I should add that should you decide to get married while you're at the inn, Faye is empowered to perform the ceremony.)

The walled courtyard muffles sound and blocks out a view of the sidewalk, so you do feel protected from the tourist bustle of St. Augustine when you want to be. But part of the fun of St. Augustine is taking in the historic spots and trying as many different spots for dinner as you can get to.

At breakfast, Faye's guests often sit around discussing where they went the night before for dinner. She makes personal, blunt recommendations and also offers a page-and-a-half-long listing of good restaurants in the area. She and her husband, Jim, like to send guests to the Mediterraneo, where they often go themselves. They got so excited telling me about the Flounder Belle Meunière that we all ended up consulting the restaurant's menu to be sure that the sauce did indeed include shrimp *and* mushrooms. And as I left, they were warming up a friendly argument about whether the veal Marsala or the flounder was better.

How to get there: When you make reservations, Faye will send you a high-lighted map with directions for getting from I–95 to U.S. 1 into St. Augustine to Aviles Street.

Kenwood
St. Augustine, Florida
32084

Innkeepers: Mark, Kerrianne, and Caitlin Constant
Address/Telephone: 38 Marine Street; (904) 824–2116
Rooms: 12, plus 1 3-room suite; all with private bath. No smoking inn.
Rates: $55 to $85, double; $125, suite; continental breakfast.
Open: Year-round.
Facilities and activities: Swimming pool. Nearby: restaurants, St. Augustine
historic sites and tourist activities, short drive to ocean beaches.

Kenwood gets better and better. The story is interesting. A number of years ago the building languished as a dilapidated boarding house. It was purchased by owners whose specialty was renovation, and they set about restoring it to soundness and safety, named it Kenwood, and started modest operations as an inn. When they went on to their next project, the new owners continued improving the property and ran Kenwood in their own laid-back style until health problems eventually forced them to give it up.

Then the Constant family entered the scene. Mark and Kerrianne were innkeepers in New England who, like so many visitors, got the St. Augustine I-wanna-stay bug. Caitlin, their daughter, was too young to do much innkeeping in New England, but she's rapidly growing into it all in St. Augustine. Kenwood is definitely a family project now.

The Constants are adding even more improvements at Kenwood. They've redone the courtyard and gardens to include a great variety of tropical plants and lots of colorful blooms. The swimming pool sits in the newly landscaped area like a summertime jewel.

Mark and Kerrianne brought many of their favorite antiques from New England and have mixed these antiques with comfortable couches and chairs in cool greens, creams, and rose. I especially like the way they've arranged furniture into several groupings so that people can gather in any one of several places at any time. While I was there, I found three different, animated conversations going on. I almost did myself in trying to get involved in all of them at once.

We had a lot of conversation at breakfast, too, inspired mostly by Kerrianne's unusual offerings. We got into much "what do you think this is?" and "oh, taste this, it's marvelous" as we nibbled our way through several generous trays full of goodies. I especially liked the sweet potato muffins and the strawberry butter.

When we weren't talking about food, we were asking Kerrianne questions about her family in New York and, this sounds awful, we were cracking up at how she could turn what should have been disastrous episodes into funny stories. It tells you something about Kerri's style that she did all this casually dressed in something loose and cool, with bare feet.

Mark's approach is relaxed, too. I kept trying to move from the entrance to a far corner of the living room without walking on an especially lovely, pale oriental carpet. Mark kept laughing at me and saying that in Connecticut everyone walked over it with slush on their boots.

How to get there: From I–95 south, exit to Route 16 east. At the end of Route 16, turn right onto San Marco Boulevard. After the fifth set of lights, bear right at immediate fork onto Marine Street. The inn is 2 blocks on the right. From I–95 north, take exit 94 to Route 207. At the end of Route 207, turn left onto Route 1 North. At the first set of lights, turn right onto King Street. At the end of King Street, turn right and bear right at immediate fork onto Marine Street. The inn is 2 blocks on the right.

Bayboro House
St. Petersburg, Florida
33701

Innkeepers: Gordon and Antonia Powers
Address/Telephone: 1719 Beach Drive Southeast; (813) 823–4955
Rooms: 4; all with private bath and television. No smoking inn.
Rates: $69 to $79, double, continental-plus breakfast. Inquire about weekly
    and monthly rates.
Open: Year-round.
Facilities and activities: Beach chairs and towels. Nearby: restaurants, ocean
    beach, Salvador Dali Museum, Sunken Gardens, Busch Gardens, Uni-
    versity of South Florida Bayboro Campus.

Bayboro House generates stories that tell you as much about
staying here as a room-by-room description.

Seems relatives of the man who used to own the house held a
reunion here. Gordon and Antonia were excited because they
thought it would be a sentimental occasion and also an opportunity
for them to learn more about the house and family. The old owner
was C. A. Harvey. The family knew that he had died in 1913, but *no
one* knew what his name was. C. A. was it.

The family had included C. A.'s very old family servant, Olivia,
in the party. She hobbled in leaning on a black and gold cane,
repeating, "Thank you, Lord. Lord, thank you for letting me come
into this house one more time." But she didn't remember anything
about how the house used to be.

42

All the Powerses learned was that the original light fixtures are still in the house.

Then there's the story about Herb Hiller, a respected travel writer who specializes in Florida. He was at Bayboro House, moving from room to room, sitting on one antique chair after another, taking notes furiously. He sat on the red fainting couch, and then finally he moved to the porch and sat on the swing. His eyes seemed suddenly unfocused and wide with amazement. He said, "Why, this could be Florida a hundred years ago."

Yet another story is about guests who checked into Bayboro House and left their kids with neighbors—not neighbors from back home, but neighbors of the Bayboro House. "The neighborhood has been good to us," Gordon said.

What it all comes down to is a nice old Victorian house built shortly after 1900, filled with the antiques and odds and ends that Gordon and Antonia have collected over the years: the fainting couch that Hiller made famous, marble-topped tables, quilts, the inevitable player piano, and all the doilies, dollies, and dishes that used to catch the Victorian fancy. The inn is run by friendly, accommodating people in a friendly, visually unremarkable neighborhood. It's directly across the street from a beautiful part of Tampa Bay, close enough to walk barefoot to the beach in the kind of area that usually gives way to whatever waterfront high-rise project comes along first.

"It's amazing that the house is still there. Who knows how long we'll be here?" Gordon said.

It's worth trying while Rod Serling still controls the horizontal and the vertical!

How to get there: From I–275, take exit 9. Go south on Fourth Street South to Twenty-second Avenue South; turn left and go 5 blocks to Tampa Bay, then left onto Beach Drive SE.

S: *The new Suncoast Dome is just five minutes away.*

The Homeplace
Stuart, Florida
34994

Innkeeper: Jean Bell
Address/Telephone: 501 Akron Avenue; (407) 220–9148; after 5:00 P.M., (407) 286–6751
Rooms: 3; all with private bath. No smoking inn.
Rates: $65 to $85, double; "Florida-style" continental breakfast, predinner drinks and hors d'oeuvres; complimentary beverages, and fresh fruit.
Open: Year-round.
Facilities and activities: Swimming pool, heated spa, bicycles, tandem bike, small-boat access docking. Nearby: restaurants, waterfront activities, sailing, ocean beaches, shopping centers, tennis, racquetball.

The first thing I saw at The Homeplace was a framed slate on the front porch bearing the greeting "Welcome, Sara Pitzer." It sounds like a small thing, but you'd be amused at how good it makes you feel.

Jean Bell was waiting to take me on a whirlwind tour of an inn so full of interesting odds and ends that you could explore it for a week. When the inn first opened, one local newspaper writer speculated that Jean was making up at the inn for not having had a playhouse as a child. Jean's husband, Jim Smith, is a developer who saved the house from bulldozers by moving it from its original location into a vacant spot in Creekside Commons. Then Jean took over. The energy and distinctive taste she has poured into the place amaze me.

She has haunted antiques shops, yard sales, flea markets, and the neighbors' homes, gathering everything from old toys (remember those wooden pecking chickens on a board?) to *old* empty cans with labels still on to stock the Hoosier cabinet in the kitchen. Jean did library research, consulted with a woman who lived in the home originally, and studied old Sears catalogs to learn how to furnish the 1913 Victorian rose-colored frame house as it would have been when it was built. She refinished the antiques she found and cleaned up the old kitchen utensils herself.

Of the guest rooms, I especially liked Opal's Room, named in honor of a woman who donated several personal items for it. The oak bed is covered with a crocheted bedspread; a treadle sewing machine that looks as if it would still work holds a picture of Opal's family and her diary, and late nineteenth-century clothes dress a seamstress form in the corner.

Downstairs, a sun porch furnished with white wicker looks out on the patio, swimming pool, and spa, which are surrounded by a display of hibiscus, citrus, bottle brush, and bougainvillea that is lush even for Florida.

Unless you want breakfast in bed, the patio is a nice place to eat breakfast, which Jean carries over on a tray from the kitchen of her own house across the street. You never know what she'll bring: maybe hard-boiled eggs wrapped in colored cellophane and tied with a bow; exotic treats such as mango-nut bread, made from old Florida recipes; and always fresh fruit from the trees in the yard. Jean is using some turn-of-the-century recipes from her old cookbooks. Whatever it is, you know it'll be good and, like Jean, lots of fun. She said, "I try to do something special for each individual. I want people to come here to have fun." More fun are her "Victorian Hangups," small, lacy gift items she's created. Now her son calls her "the Doily Mom."

How to get there: From I–95, take the State Road 76 exit in Stuart. Follow State Road 76 east into town, where it becomes Colorado Avenue. Turn left on Fifth Street and go 3 blocks to Akron Avenue. Look for the Creekside Commons sign at the parking lot.

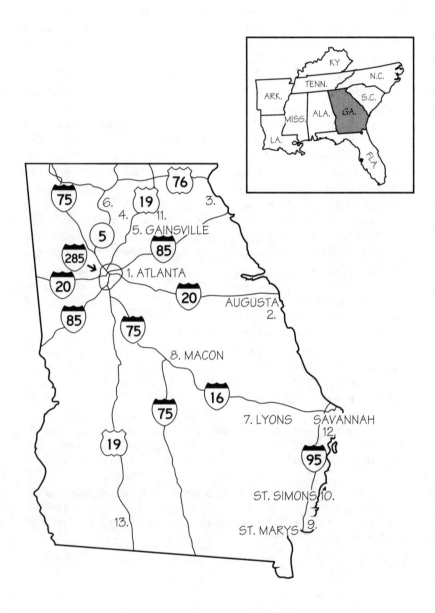

Georgia

Numbers on map refer to towns numbered below.

Beverly Hills Inn
Atlanta, Georgia
30305

Innkeeper: Mit Amin
Address/Telephone: 65 Sheridan Drive Northeast; (404) 233–8520
Rooms: 18, plus 5 suites; all with private bath, small kitchen, telephone, and television.
Rates: $59 to $74, single; $74 to $120, double; $80 to $120, suites; continental breakfast.
Open: Year-round.
Facilities and activities: Nearby: restaurants, shopping centers, department stores, art galleries, museums, theaters, historic sites.

Being at the Beverly Hills Inn with guests from as far away as Italy, Sweden, and Venezuela makes me feel sophisticated, international-jet-setty-glamorous, and a little superior to all the poor people staying in one of those Atlanta hotels of chrome and glass with fast-talking bartenders, slow-running elevators, and hear-through walls.

At the Beverly Hills, the interior walls are brick, so thick you couldn't hear the Cleveland Symphony if it were playing Beethoven in the next room. That's because the building was originally an apartment complex. When the original remodelers converted it to an inn, they kept the little kitchens in the rooms and decorated the rooms with antiques, oriental fabrics, and sunny colors.

I liked the larger-than-usual space with room for a couch or extra chairs. It felt bright and attractive and very private. The kitchens don't call you to cook, really (no visitor should bother to cook in a city as full of fine restaurants as Atlanta), but it's great to have a place to chill a bottle of wine, warm a baby bottle, or brew a cup of tea.

In the winter, breakfast is served in a sunny white-brick room decorated with plants and overlooking a garden patio. In good weather, breakfast moves right out to the patio. Guests sit around in the sun, reading their papers and striking up conversations with one another. It's friendly and casual. In chilly weather, a pleasant solarium brings sunshine to your morning paper.

At the end of the day, you can spend some time chatting or reading in the library hoping, if you're no more talented than I, that someone will play the baby grand piano for a while. As dinner time approaches, Mit will ask you what kind of food you like and whip out his copy of *Cuisine Atlanta* to help you decide which of the ten restaurants within walking distance or the scores more a short drive away will be exactly what you're in the mood for.

How to get there: From downtown Atlanta, drive north on Peachtree for about fifteen minutes. Turn right onto Sheridan Drive. From I–85 south, take the Peachtree exit. Turn left. Continue going about fifteen minutes to turn right onto Sheridan. The inn is about ¹/₂ block on the right.

Shellmont
Atlanta, Georgia
30308

Innkeepers: Ed and Debbie McCord
Address/Telephone: 821 Piedmont Avenue Northeast; (404) 872–9290
Rooms: 4, plus 2-bedroom carriage house; all with private bath, carriage house with television and telephone.
Rates: $70 to $85, single; $80 to $100, double; continental breakfast.
Open: Year-round.
Facilities and activities: Located in historic midtown Atlanta. Nearby: restaurants, historic sites, city shopping areas, cultural activities.

It's taken the McCords a lot of undoing to get back to historic basics. Until Ed and Debbie bought it, their classic Victorian home had been in the same family since it was built in 1891. As generations of a family will do, earlier inhabitants had papered and painted many layers over the original walls and wood and plaster ornamentation. But now, when you stay here, you can see it as it was originally designed and built.

The family that owned it kept records and photographs showing the original decor, including colors, wallpaper patterns, and elaborate stenciling. The McCords have replicated everything that they couldn't restore.

The outside of the house is blue, green, and yellow. Inside are a mind-boggling number of Victorian touches. For instance, there's a weird little room called the "Turkish Room," which isn't really Turkish at all but is done in a style that Victorians imagined must be Turkish. At the foot of the stairs is a good-sized choir stall with room for an organist and singers to entertain assembled guests. Above the stall are five elaborate stained-glass windows that Ed and Debbie believe are by Tiffany, though they're still trying to verify it.

Shellmont has been listed as a City of Atlanta Landmark Building, one of only thirty-three, and it is on the National Register of Historic Places.

But fascinating as all this is, especially if you're interested in history and architecture, the real fun of staying at the Shellmont is the time you spend with Debbie and Ed. The amount of attention they give guests is pretty much up to the guests. But if you'd like to sit in front of the fire in the Turkish Room and do needlework and chat, Debbie will whip out her stitchery and join you in a minute.

Ed, a native of Atlanta, can entertain you endlessly with stories about the city and with suggestions on where to go for food, shopping, and sightseeing.

One of the restaurants Ed and Debbie recommend for dinner is the Abbey. It's in an old church building, within walking distance, and specializes in veal, venison, and seafood.

I wish I'd been here to see the couple who honeymooned at the inn and returned a year later to share their anniversary celebration with Debbie and Ed with a champagne picnic—including pieces of their original wedding cake, frozen—on the floor.

For your own creature comforts, the McCords have added an ice maker and a coffee/hot water area as well as a phone just for guests in an upstairs nook.

How to get there: From I–75/85 north, exit onto International Boulevard. Turn right onto Piedmont. Go north 1 mile to the inn. From I–75/85 south, exit onto North Avenue. Turn left. Cross the bridge over the expressway and continue about a mile to Piedmont. Turn left onto Piedmont. The inn is on the corner of Piedmont and Sixth.

Oglethorpe Inn
Augusta, Georgia
30901

Innkeeper: Fran Upton

Address/Telephone: 836 Greene Street; (404) 724–9774

Rooms: 19; all with private bath, television, and telephone, some with whirlpool and fireplace, some with refrigerator. Pets accepted with advance arrangement.

Rates: $60 to $125, single or double, full Southern breakfast. Inquire about long-term discounts, children's rates, and special indulgence packages.

Open: Year-round.

Facilities and activities: Hot tub in garden, gas grill for cookouts. Nearby: restaurants, historic sites, walk to central business district, Savannah River.

The inn comprises *three* buildings: two Victorian houses that are about one hundred years old and a carriage house. Each of the buildings has its own special features. The main Victorian, with the "Oglethorpe" canopy, is a dusky rose frame-and-shingle building that snuggles into the mature landscaping; the house next door has an antique stained-glass window in which a damaged top has been perfectly matched and replaced by a local stained-glass artist; the cheerful pink carriage house offers some smaller, less expensive rooms.

Staying in any of the rooms brings you individualized service that probably ought to be called pampering. If you ask for a wake-up call in the moring, coffee and a newspaper will be delivered.

Breakfast in bed? Oh, slothful traveler, you got it. With champagne? Oh, decadent vacationer, it's yours. Heavy cream in the coffee and eggs Benedict? Hey, chubs, are you sure you want to go this far? Well, they'll go through with it if you do.

And don't think it has to be an anniversary or a honeymoon. Because the inn is so close to the central business district, many people in Augusta on business stay here regularly, and the inn is used to handling long stays. Do you suppose these businesspeople stay here, in the comfort of antique-furnished rooms, sip a complimentary cocktail, spend a little time in the hot tub, avail themselves of the breakfast pampering, then return home affecting a look of fatigue and say, "Hi, honey. Boy, it was a hard trip"?

How to get there: From I–20, take Washington Road exit. Go straight. The road becomes Calhoun and then Greene Street. The inn is on the right.

Telfair Inn
Augusta, Georgia
30901

Innkeeper: Lee Edwards
Address/Telephone: 326 Greene Street; (404) 724–3315 or (800) 241–2407
Rooms: 78 in 16 restored houses; all with private bath, television, and telephone, some with fireplace, some with whirlpool.
Rates: $75 to $185, double, coffee. Breakfast extra. Inquire about rates for singles, seniors, and children.
Open: Year-round.
Facilities and activities: Dinner. Cocktail lounge, conference facilities, pool, hot tub, lighted tennis court. Nearby: walk to the Savannah River, the central business district, Port Royal, the Riverwalk, many historic sites; walking tours, museums.

Telfair is an unusual combination of entrepreneurial business sense and a passion for historic restoration. Telfair is a project of The Upton Company (as is Oglethorpe Inn) that has been in process since the early 1980s. All the buildings that make up the inn fill a block in Olde Towne, a village of historic buildings restored for a variety of uses by people convinced that preserving the city's old buildings can be economically rewarding as well as socially significant. The inn's buildings all back up on a private interior parking area.

Lee Edwards, who has consulted on the restoration of many Victorian homes and helped set up many inns, says that Telfair is

54

the first and largest "cluster inn" in America. Each building has its own special features: hardwood floors or a sun porch or interior brick walls or unusual woodwork. But, of course, you can stay in only one room at a time, and that's what should interest you most. Rooms throughout are furnished with antiques and some reproductions, attractive spreads, drapes, and carpets, and comfortably modern bathroom facilities, including Jacuzzis in some baths.

The rooms in the Telfair Concierge House are the luxury accommodations, where you have the advantage of a concierge staff to do everything from arranging transportation and meetings to receiving and sending fax messages. The staff are uniformly pleasant and helpful here, as well as in the rest of the inn.

No matter what room you stay in, you're just a few steps away from dinner in the inn's restaurant. You'll need a reservation, because the restaurant seats just twenty-six.

When I first arrived at Telfair, I found Lee Edwards in a chef's apron, supervising activities in the kitchen, because in addition to being an expert on inns and restoration, he's a chef. He explained to me that "pulled" barbecue duckling simply meant that the meat was pulled off the bones before being served. And he said that for his money, one of the best things on the menu is creamed peppered grits, even if you don't like grits. Generally, the food is a kind of combination of Low Country and European styles, those rich and tasty dishes you might as well just sit in, seeing as how that's where they end up anyway.

How to get there: From I–20, take the Washington Road exit. Go straight onto Calhoun, which eventually becomes Greene. The inn is between Fourth and Third streets on Greene Street, approximately 6 miles from I–20.

Glen-Ella Springs
Clarksville, Georgia
30523

Innkeepers: Barrie and Bobby Aycock

Address/Telephone: Bear Gap Road, Route 3 (mailing address: Box 3304);
(404) 754–7295 or (800) 552–3479

Rooms: 16 rooms and suites; all with private bath, some with fireplace and
television, some with wheelchair access.

Rates: $75 to $135, single or double, continental breakfast and full breakfast
Saturday. Inquire about discounts for weeknights and stays of more
than 3 nights.

Open: Year-round.

Facilities and activities: Dining room, with wheelchair access, open to guests
and public most days; reservations requested; available for private parties; brown bagging permitted. Gift shop, conference room. Swimming
pool, 17 acres with nature trails along Panther Creek, herb and flower
gardens, mineral springs. Located in northeast Georgia mountains near
historic sites. Nearby: restaurants, golf, horseback riding, boating, rafting, tennis, hiking.

I think I'm in love!

Usually country inns are elegant or they are rustic. This one-
hundred-year-old place is both. The suites are beautifully finished
and furnished, with fireplaces; refinished pine floors, walls, and
ceilings; local mountain-made rugs on the floors; whirlpool baths;
and such niceties as fresh-cut pansies floating in crystal bowls.
Some of the less-expensive rooms are simpler, though perfectly

comfortable, with painted walls and showers in the bathrooms.

The fireplace in the lobby is made of local stone, flanked with chintz-covered chairs.

An especially nice swimming pool, surrounded by an extra-wide sun deck that seems posh enough for any Hyatt hotel, overlooks a huge expanse of lawn that ends in woods. Both the pool and the lawn are great for kids.

The dining room is what I would call "subdued country," but there is nothing subdued about the food. It is simply spectacular—some of the best I've had anywhere in the South.

Because I sat with a large group for dinner, I had an opportunity to taste a wide assortment of entrees and appetizers. I remember scallops wrapped in bacon served in a light wine sauce; chicken livers in burgundy wine; fresh trout sautéed and then dressed with lime juice, fresh herbs, and toasted pecans; and halibut with Jamaican spices. I sampled desserts the same way and gave my vote to the homemade cheesecake.

The story here is that Barrie, a wonderful cook, had wanted a restaurant for a long time. But the Aycocks also wanted to work and live away from the city. They bought Glen-Ella even though the old hotel needed a tremendous amount of renovating.

They figured that here Barrie could have her restaurant, and since the inn was so far out in the country, lots of guests would spend the night. They do. And lots of other guests, who come for longer stays just to be in the country, enjoy the added pleasure of five-star quality food.

The latest is that the Glen-Ella gift shop has the *Glen-Ella Cookbook,* with some of the inn's best recipes, for sale. You can order it by calling or writing the inn.

And now one more bragging point for Barrie and Bobby. The hotel has been added to the National Register of Historic Places.

How to get there: Go 8⁷/₁₀ miles north of Clarksville through Turnerville on U.S. Route 23/441. Turn left at the Glen-Ella sign on to New Liberty–Turnerville Road and continue for 1 mile to the next Glen-Ella sign at Bear Gap Road, which is a gravel road. Turn right. The inn is about 1¹/₂ miles on the left.

Mountain Top Lodge
Dahlonega, Georgia
30533

Innkeeper: David Middleton

Address/Telephone: Old Ellijay Road (mailing address: Route 7, Box 150); (706) 864–5257

Rooms: 13, including 2 suites, in 2 buildings; all with private bath, 2 with sitting area, refrigerator, private deck, gas-log fireplace, and whirlpool tub; some with wheelchair access.

Rates: $65 to $125, double; single $10 less; full country breakfast.

Open: Year-round.

Facilities and activities: Meeting rooms, sun deck with oversized heated outdoor spa. Located in the North Georgia mountains, near historic sites in Dahlonega. Nearby: restaurants, antiques and craft shops, gold panning, rafting, hiking, fishing.

This is a *new* country inn—a new cedar lodge built to age gracefully in the woods. Its most striking feature, when you first see the place, is the marvelous 14-foot-wide deck wrapped around the building, looking directly into the woods.

Inside, you feel as though you've stepped into a page from *Country Living* magazine. The guest rooms are furnished with pine furniture, country-style antiques and accessories, and mountain crafts. The beds have dust ruffles, and quilts hang on the walls.

The room I like best is decorated with many toys from David's childhood. Framed on the wall is this motto:

Look at life
through a child's unclouded view
and find in it
everything miraculous and new.

To this adult eye, the old toys, a Lionel engine caboose, worn trucks and cars, a little mouse made by a guest, and a rag doll with mouth and eyes stitched in sequins all look magical and new.

In the cathedral-ceilinged great room, tongue-in-groove pine panels the walls. A Vermont Castings stove, the kind on which you can open the doors to watch the fire, warms the area in winter, making this the spot where guests congregate to talk or play games or read.

The mountain scenery in this part of North Georgia takes my breath away. If you stay here, you should plan to spend some time walking and driving in the mountains. I particularly enjoy the seasons of spring flowers and fall foliage, but these mountains (and this inn) really don't have a bad season.

For relaxing outdoors, I loved the gazebo swing in the woods, next to the rock garden and a trickling fountain and quietly flowing stream. And next trip I'm going to arrange to have a picnic in one of the picnic areas Dave's created.

As far as David is concerned, the inn's hospitality is an important supplement to its glorious setting. Many guests return whenever they want to retreat for a few quiet days. David tries to offer friendly little touches without imposing too much activity or attention on guests who'd rather be alone.

Breakfast, however, is a sharing time when everyone indulges in generous amounts of ham, sausage, eggs, grits, fruit and juice, and muffins or divine biscuits, the secret of which is soft flour.

How to get there: From Dahlonega, take 52 West for 3¹/₂ miles. Turn right on Siloam Road. Go ¹/₂ mile, turn right on Old Ellijay Road. The road ends at the inn's entrance.

The Dunlap House
Gainesville, Georgia
30501

Innkeeper: Rita Fishman
Address/Telephone: 635 Green Street; (404) 536–0200
Rooms: 9; all with private bath, telephone, and television, some with fireplace, some with wheelchair access.
Rates: $65 to $95, single or double, continental breakfast.
Open: Year-round.
Facilities and activities: Nearby: restaurants, Helen and tourist activities, North Georgia mountains, Lake Lanier, Quinlan Art Center.

If you want to feel like a Very Important Person, a queen maybe, or president of Some Big Company, stay here. The Dunlap House staff don't even aspire to be folksy or intimate. They cater especially to business travelers, and everything is geared to providing every service you can imagine without making demands on guests to be chatty or personable in return. I would expect to be greeted, "Good evening, Ms. Pitzer," not "Hi, Sara." If you've ever traveled tired or wanted absolute calm without the intrusion of other people's personalities, you'll understand.

Dunlap House is an elegantly renovated 1910 house listed in the National Register of Historic Places. The furnishings are period reproductions that include many pale pine pieces, so that the overall effect is bright and light, not the heavy darkness we sometimes associate with historic homes.

In the front lobby area, comfortable chairs with good lights are just right for sitting a few minutes to read the paper. A few small round tables with chairs farther back make a good place to have a social drink in the evening if you bring your own. And the white wicker–furnished porch is my choice of locations for the continental breakfast of fruits, berries and cream, and apple spice muffins. Some people prefer breakfast on a tray in their room, but I like being outside with those healthy ferns and ficus plants.

As for dinner, Randolph's on Green Street is a neighboring restaurant in an old English Tudor–style house with a solid granite foundation and exposed beams in the living room. The offerings include standards such as prime rib of beef and fresh Georgia trout, as well as some more elaborate continental entrees, including veal prepared a couple of different ways.

While you're out eating entirely too well, the staff at the inn are busy freshening your room, polishing your shoes, pressing your suit, taking care of your laundry, making sure there's a clean terry robe in the room, and if you've asked for it, arranging to accommodate your special dietary needs at breakfast. They'll also call cabs, book flights, and take care of just about any other details that come up.

How to get there: From I–985, take exit 6 to Gainesville. Stay on the same road to the corner of Ridgewood Avenue and Green Street. Turn left at the light and park behind the inn.

※

S: *The Fishmans, new owners, have restored the magnificent pocket doors leading to the original front parlor.*

The Woodbridge Inn
Jasper, Georgia
30143

Innkeepers: Brenda and Joe Rueffert
Address/Telephone: 411 Chambers; (404) 692–6293
Rooms: 12; all with private bath, telephone, and television. Pets welcome.
Rates: $40 to $72, single or double, breakfast not served. Children free.
Open: Year-round.
Facilities and activities: Lunch on Wednesdays and Sundays, dinner every
night, beer and wine available, brown bagging permitted for cocktails.
Swimming pool. Nearby: short drive to restaurants; tennis and golf;
Amicalola Falls State Park hiking; Carter's Lake swimming, sailing, and
fishing; Amicalola River and Talking Rock Creek white-water canoe-
ing.

I went to the restaurant early. A cheery man with a black
mustache was digging flower beds around the front porch of the
inn. Seeing my camera, he said, "Take my picture," and struck a
bunch of comic poses.

While I was tasting a wonderful seafood chowder that the
waitress had recommended and eating crackers topped with a
homemade cheese-spread from a crock on the table, I asked who
the funny man working out front was.

"That's Joe, the owner and the chef," my waitress said.

Made me nervous. How was he going to cook my dinner if he
was outside with a shovel? Especially something as out-of-the-

ordinary as venison fillet in a pepper-and-cognac sauce or sweet-breads with mushrooms?

Not to worry. I finally decided on the sautéed sweetbreads and somehow Joe got back into the kitchen and shortly produced the best calf sweetbreads I've ever tasted. They were lightly browned and delicately crisp on the outside, perfectly moist and tender inside, mixed with whole sautéed mushrooms that were still firm and juicy, and a splash of light wine sauce. Everything was so good that I ate slowly for a long time.

I almost hated to leave the dining room to go to my room. The dining room is in a historic old hotel that was built in the mid-1800s. The guest rooms are in a separate, newly built lodge a few steps away on the side of a hill with a magnificent view of the mountains.

The lodge is a contemporary wood building that blends grace-fully into the landscape. The rooms have either patios or balconies, depending on whether you're on the first floor or on one of the other two floors. Inside they're quiet and simple but luxurious, with ceiling fans and vanities with tops of local marble. My room had spiral steps going up to a sitting area with a pull-out bed that could accommodate children if you wanted to bring them.

How to get there: Jasper is in the mountains, about an hour-and-a-half drive north of Atlanta. From the south, take I–75 to 575; then follow the signs into Jasper. From the north, take U.S. 53 off I–75 into Jasper. In Jasper, go north on Main Street. Cross over a small wooden bridge on the right and go into the parking lot.

ð

S: *The inn doesn't serve breakfast, but Joe and Brenda have begun a thoughtful courtesy for guests. There are facilities for making your own coffee in each room.*

Robert Toombs Inn
Lyons, Georgia
30436

Innkeeper: Ellie Phillips
Address/Telephone: 101 South State Street; (912) 526–4489
Rooms: 11, plus 7 suites in inn and annex; all with private bath, telephone, and television.
Rates: $28 to $50, single or double, breakfast. $5 each additional person. Children under 12 free.
Open: Year-round.
Facilities and activities: Continental breakfast weekdays for guests only; restaurant open to the public for dinner Monday through Saturday; full bar service. Americana Furniture Showroom and other shops in Robert Toombs Square, a renovated turn-of-the-century business complex. Nearby: Georgia mountains.

Anyone who thinks Small Town America has vanished hasn't been to Lyons, Georgia. Lyons is the kind of town where everybody waves to the sheriff and the sheriff even waves to strangers. It's the kind of town where merchants stick their heads into each other's stores to say "mornin' " and ask about the new gran'baby.

Anyone who thinks you can't find a good inn and good food in such a town hasn't been to the Robert Toombs Inn. The late-1800s building has been beautifully renovated since its earlier incarnations as the Elberta Hotel and as Mrs. Wen's Boarding House. The foyer is large and sunny; fresh white plaster walls set off beautiful wood floors; a gas-log fireplace provides a focal point in the lobby.

Because the owners, Wallace and Rose Ann Clary, also own the Americana Furniture Showrooms, the inn's rooms are furnished in high-quality traditional and Colonial pieces from there. The rooms are as comfortable and pleasant as your own bedroom.

The food in the restaurant is modestly priced and very good. You can always go the traditional route with prime rib or a steak, or you can get fancy with an entree like Chicken Cordon Bleu, or you can eat traditional Southern with fried catfish and hush puppies. For dessert, I can't imagine having anything but the hot fudge cake, but *you* might prefer apple pie a la mode.

What charms me is that in the context of these urban-quality accommodations and meals, small-town informality and exuberance flourish. The manager was showing everyone a stack of photographs taken at a baby shower the staff held in the inn for one of the waitresses. While we talked, a chef brought a salad of Vidalia onions and feta cheese into the office for opinions. We all tasted and pronounced the salad wonderful except that it needed a touch more salt.

Someone told me a story about how an older woman spent several weeks at the inn because her husband had been hospitalized with a heart attack while they were visiting in Lyons, and the innkeeper simply adopted the woman and took care of her like family.

Maybe you can't find that small-town spirit everywhere, but at the Robert Toombs Inn in Lyons, Georgia, it's a way of life.

How to get there: The inn is in Robert Toombs Square on Highway 1 in the center of town.

1842 Inn
Macon, Georgia
31201

Innkeeper: Phillip Jenkins

Address/Telephone: 353 College Street; (912) 741–1842; reservations (800) 336–1842

Rooms: 22; all with private bath, telephone, and television, some with whirlpool and fireplace, some with wheelchair access.

Rates: $65 to $95, double; single $10 less; continental breakfast and other inn courtesies.

Open: Year-round.

Facilities and activities: Beverages from bar at nominal charge, meeting rooms. Nearby: restaurants, easy access to Macon Historic District walking tours, Cherry Blossom Festival in March.

I deliberately sought out the 1842 Inn because so many people, travel writers and inn guests alike, recommended it to me as a place where everything's been done right. I agree.

It all started with a strong-minded owner who was determined to get the restoration done right, then work on service. The new owner and manager has taken it from there.

When you start with a Greek Revival antebellum house of this beauty, it's hard to see how anyone could go wrong; but when the earlier owners bought the property, the house had passed its glory years, was divided into apartments, and had fallen into disrepair.

Such a building has a continuing life (life implies growth and change), as its fortunes wax and wane over the years. Originally it was smaller, with only four columns. About the turn of the century, the house was enlarged, columns were added, and elaborate parquet floors were laid over the original heart pine floors.

Now, fully restored, this main house is connected by a courtyard to a Victorian cottage that was moved from Vineville Avenue to the rear of the inn and refurbished to provide additional rooms. One wonders: In another generation, what next?

When you stay at the 1842, you may find the history interesting, but if you're like me, you want to know more about your creature comforts. They're all here, including full handicap facilities, blackout linings in the draperies for late sleepers, and walls that are insulated to keep your room quiet. Some rooms have a second television set in the bathroom so that you can watch while you enjoy the whirlpool.

The furnishings are a mix of fine antiques, period reproductions, oriental rugs, and luxurious towels and linens. The beds are all king- or queen-sized period reproductions with custom-made mattresses.

The inn offers all the services of a fine European hotel: continental breakfast delivered to your room with flowers and a paper, evening cocktails and brandy, turn-down service with mints on the pillow, and shoe shines while you sleep. Moreover, the inn has begun winning coveted awards from other inn guides—which shall remain nameless in *this* guide!

And just to bring it all back to everyday reality, I'll tell you that when I learned Dr. Joyce Brothers had stayed here and wanted to know where to get the same sheets, I went through a whole closetful with the maid trying to guess which ones Dr. Brothers had admired.

How to get there: From I–75, take exit 52 to Forsyth Street. Turn left on College Street.

Riverview Hotel
St. Marys, Georgia
31558

Innkeeper: Jerry Brandon
Address/Telephone: 105 Osborne Street; (912) 882–3242
Rooms: 18; all with private bath and television.
Rates: $40, single; $50, double; includes tax and continental breakfast.
Open: Year-round.
Facilities and activities: Breakfast, lunch Monday through Friday, dinner;
wheelchair access to restaurant. Lounge (closed Sunday), self-guided
tours of St. Marys historic district. Nearby: Crooked River State Park
and King's Bay Submarine Base, hour's drive to Okefenokee Swamp,
best access to Cumberland Island by ferry.

You can't tell an inn by its name. I've seen places called inns
that were motels, and here's a place called a hotel that's really an
inn. Sitting on the banks of the St. Marys River, across the street
from the ferry to Cumberland Island National Seashore, the
Riverview has a sitting room, a veranda with rockers, and an old-
fashioned lobby with big brown-and-white tiles on the floor. The
rooms are furnished, without frills or ruffles, with heavy country-
style furniture.

The Brandon family renovated the 1916 building in old-time
style and furnished it with simple country furniture appropriate for
the campers, bikers, and hikers who tend to gather in St. Marys.

If you are here before a ferry is scheduled to leave for Cumberland Island, the lobby will probably be full of knapsacks and back-packs, whose owners are eating in Seagle's Restaurant in the hotel, along with everybody else in town.

The restaurant has been renovated with wood siding, Irish green accents, a gallery for local artists, and some original brick walls exposed for the old-fashioned flavor.

The food is fantastic! I thought the stuffed shrimp were surely the best thing possible until I tasted the fried rock shrimp, which are sweeter than regular shrimp and were fried in a delicate homemade batter resembling tempura batter.

After dinner, I got to talking with Jerry and learned that before he took up innkeeping, he'd been a chemist and a tournament bridge player. He got involved with the Riverview Hotel because it was a family place and he wanted to continue the tradition. If you really want to make his day, show up asking for a fourth for bridge. At least that used to make his day. But Jerry is now the mayor of the town and so busy that he's harder to pin down than he used to be. Still, it never hurts to try.

If you're just exploring Georgia, you'll like St. Marys. It's historic but handles its tourism in a low-key way. The local people don't get all gussied up for it.

How to get there: From I–95, take Route 40 east straight into St. Marys and down to the water. The inn is on the right.

S: *For a special day, you can arrange to have Seagle's pack you a picnic lunch basket to take to Cumberland Island or Okefenokee or the state park.*

Little St. Simons Island
St. Simons Island, Georgia
31522

Innkeeper: Debbie McIntyre

Address/Telephone: St. Simons Island (mailing address: P.O. Box 1078); (912) 638–7472

Rooms: 2 in main lodge with private bath; 4 in River Lodge, all with private bath; 4 in Cedar House, all with private bath; 2 in Michael Cottage share bath.

Rates: $200, single; $350, double; all meals, wine with dinner, island activities, and ferry service. Minimum two-night stay. Inquire about longer-stay and off-season discounts.

Open: March through May and October through November for individuals; June through September for groups only.

Facilities and activities: Bar in lodge; collection of books about native birds, plants, animals, and marine life; swimming pool, stables, horseshoes, ocean swimming, birding, naturalist-led explorations, beachcombing, shelling, fishing, canoeing, hiking.

This is truly a special place. It is a 10,000-acre barrier island still in its natural state except for the few buildings needed to house and feed guests. You can get there only by boat.

When my husband and I visited, we felt welcomed as though we'd been visiting there for years.

I still marvel at how much we did in a short time. The permanent staff includes three naturalists. One of the naturalists loaded us into a pickup truck and drove us around the island to help us get oriented. We walked through woods and open areas and along untouched ocean beaches. I saw my first armadillo. I gathered more sand dollars than I've ever seen in one place before. We saw deer, raccoons, opossums, and more birds than I could identify. Serious bird-watchers plan special trips to Little St. Simons to observe the spring and fall migrations.

We rode horseback with one of the naturalists. I was scared to death because I'd never been on a horse before, but they got me up on a mild-mannered old mare, and she plugged along slowly. By the end of the ride, I almost felt as though I knew what I was doing.

We canoed out through the creeks. When a big wind came up, I had a notion to be scared again, but the naturalist directed us into a sheltered spot where we could hold onto the rushes until the weather settled; then we paddled on.

When we weren't out exploring the island, we sat in front of the fire in the lodge, chatting with the other two guests and inspecting the photographs on the walls. They're standard hunting-camp pictures; rows of men grinning like idiots and holding up strings of fish, hunters with rifles grinning like idiots, and people climbing in and out of boats grinning like idiots.

One of the best meals we had while we were there was roast quail, served with rice pilaf and little yellow biscuits. As I polished off an unladylike-sized meal and finished my wine, I realized that *I* was grinning like an idiot. After dinner, with no thought of television, I retired to the comfortable bed in a simple, pleasant room and fell asleep instantly, still grinning.

How to get there: When you make your reservations, you will receive instructions on where to meet the boat that takes you to the island.

S: *The inn has added such creature comforts as nice bathrooms and handy ice machines, but these all rest lightly and inoffensively in the natural scene.*

The Stovall House
Sautee, Georgia
30571

Innkeeper: Ham Schwartz
Address/Telephone: Lake Burton Road (mailing address: Route 1, Box 1476); (404) 878–3355
Rooms: 5; all with private bath, 1 with wheelchair access.
Rates: $40, single; $70, double; continental breakfast. Children under 4, free; children ages 4–18, $11. Personal checks or cash only.
Open: Year-round.
Facilities and activities: Dinner, Sunday brunch, brown bagging permitted, wheelchair access to dining room. Located in the Northeast Georgia mountains. Nearby: lakes, rivers, creeks, waterfalls, and state parks for fishing, hiking, rock climbing, snow skiing (in season).

This place reminds me of the farm where I grew up—rolling fields, a huge vegetable garden, a big white house with the kind of front porch people really sit on, and a lively assortment of kids and animals.

Ham is a zany, enthusiastic innkeeper who has brought a home of the 1800s back to life by restoring, renovating, decorating, and then welcoming guests as family. He says that he wants the place to feel like home away from home.

Not that many of us have homes with mantels and doors handmade of walnut, working fireplaces in all the downstairs rooms, heart-of-pine floors, and an original telescoping bed (the first Hide-A-Way) made in 1891.

Ham's particular genius is being able to blend his passion for restoration with a sense that history is about living, not about museums. Stovall House is on the National Register of Historic Places and has won two important awards for restoration. But you enjoy the inn not for its awards but for how it feels to stay here.

To give you an idea of how special the place seems to some guests, one man made a weekend reservation and confided to Ham that he planned to give his girlfriend an engagement ring while they were there. Another guest liked the place so well that she worked the Stovall House logo in needlepoint for Ham. Guests often plan birthday and anniversary celebrations here.

Just being in a room can be a celebration. In some of the upstairs rooms, you can go to sleep watching stars and wake up to see the sun rise through skylights strategically placed in the dormers.

Even though people celebrate romantic milestones at the inn, you don't have to live on love alone while you are here. The food is good—and fresh!

Some of the vegetables come from that huge garden I mentioned. The menu features homemade soups, fresh vegetables fixed in as many different ways as Ham and the staff can think of, and such delicacies as poached trout.

For brunch, I had a ham-and-cheese phyllo—a splendid concoction of Swiss cheese and diced ham wrapped in leaves of Greek pastry and baked until the cheese melted and the pastry turned brown. I had a mixed green salad that was crackling crisp, served on a cool plate, and lightly flavored with an herb house dressing.

How to get there: Sautee is 5 miles east of Helen, Georgia, on Highway 17. At the Sautee Store, turn onto Highway 255 (Lake Burton Road). Drive about 1¹/₂ miles. The inn is on the right.

S: *Ham is deeply involved behind the scenes in the restoration of the old Nacoochee School, which dates back to the 1800s, and its development as an arts and community center. He says that in a few years the center will, itself, be a reason to visit the area.*

Ballastone Inn
and Townhouse
Savannah, Georgia
31401

Innkeepers: Richard Carlson and Tim Hargus
Address/Telephone: 14 East Oglethorpe Avenue; (912) 236–1484 or (800)
 822–4553
Rooms: 24; all with private bath, telephone, television, and VCR; some with
 fireplace and Jacuzzi, some with wheelchair access. Small pets accepted.
Rates: $95 to $145, single or double; $175, suites; continental-plus break-
 fast, afternoon tea, and sherry on arrival.
Open: Year-round.
Facilities and activities: Full-service bar, landscaped courtyard. Located in
 Savannah historic district. Nearby: restaurants, antiques shops, Savan-
 nah riverfront, historic sites.

The Ballastone Inn is the kind of place that indulges the whims
and idiosyncrasies of even the most crotchety traveler. I was
impressed when I saw the good humor and ease with which the
staff carried in extra luggage, rearranged schedules, and hastened
check-in for a group of what I considered unusually demanding
guests.

Such other nice things the staff will do for you include serving
your breakfast at whatever time you choose, either in your room,
in the double parlor, or in the courtyard, and arranging everything

from restaurant reservations and theater tickets to sightseeing tours and airline flights. They'll even polish your shoes if you leave them outside your door at night.

Like many old buildings in Savannah, the inn has been restored with special attention to authenticity, using Scalamandré fabrics and Savannah Spectrum colors. The colors were developed by chipping old buildings down to the original paint and matching it.

The most impressive thing about the inn is the absolute faithfulness with which the fabric, carpet, and eighteenth- and nineteenth-century furniture and art have been combined to fit the period of the house.

The Townhouse, built as a private residence in the 1830s, is the city's oldest building south of Liberty Street. It, too, has been beautifully restored. The Townhouse accommodations are larger, with separate sitting rooms and private kitchens.

If you stay in the Townhouse, you will receive a daily basket of gourmet items, including wine, with which to prepare early breakfast or late brunch whenever you want it.

Whichever building you stay in, you have twenty-four-hour concierge service and off-street parking.

How to get there: Take I–16 east to its end in downtown Savannah, where it merges into Montgomery Street. Turn right at the second stoplight onto Oglethorpe Avenue. Go 4 blocks to Bull Street. The inn is next to the Juliette Gordon Low House.

The Eliza Thompson House
Savannah, Georgia
31401

Innkeeper: Lee Smith
Address/Telephone: 5 West Jones Street; (800) 348–9378
Rooms: 25; all with private bath, telephone, and television.
Rates: $88 to $108, per room; deluxe continental breakfast and daily wine-and-cheese reception.
Open: Year-round.
Facilities and activities: Located in the Savannah historic district. Nearby: restaurants, antiques shops, Savannah riverfront, historic sites.

My friends Jim and Vicki Kefford discovered this inn and wrote to tell me about it in a letter so charming that I obtained their permission to use it here.

Sara, have we got an inn for you—Eliza Thompson. We visited. The place is full of antiques and old southern charm plus telephones and color television in the rooms. Real nice.

Right down the street, Mrs. Wilkes', the darndest lunch spot, five tables that seat eight people each, laden with fried chicken (non-greasy), at least six fresh vegetables—carrots, okra, collards, sweet potatoes, mashed potatoes, corn-bread stuffing, green beans, and limas. Plus sausage, beef tips, and a bowl of spaghetti. Then there's the muffins, three kinds. Pitchers of iced tea and for dessert a tray passed around with three or four varieties of pies and custards.

Are you ready for this? After eating, patrons are reminded to take their plates to the kitchen. All this for $7.50, pay after you return from the kitchen.

When I talked to them later, Jim and Vicki mentioned also the courtyard, which has been landscaped with Old South formality, including fountains; then they told me about the parlor, where guests may sip sherry and relax with one another after the day's activities. When I visited, I found the opportunity to talk with other guests especially pleasant at the end of the day.

The mix of guests is interesting—travelers like Jim and Vicki en route to farther places, tourists exploring Savannah, and an increasing number of men and women who find inns more congenial than motels when they're in Savannah on business. It makes for good conversation.

If you like Civil War lore, you'll be interested in hearing about how Eliza Thompson (the house was built for her in 1847), a beautiful red-haired widow, entertained here in traditional gracious Southern style and feared that Sherman would destroy her home when he marched into Savannah.

How to get there: From the north, exit from U.S. 17A; turn left onto Oglethorpe. Go to the second light and turn right on Whitaker. Go to Jones and turn left. From I–95, take I–16E and then the Montgomery Street exit. Immediately turn right (at the Civic Center) onto Liberty. Take Liberty to the first stoplight at Whitaker. Go right on Whitaker for 3 blocks, then turn left on Jones. A *small* sign identifies the inn.

The Forsyth Park Inn
Savannah, Georgia
31401

Innkeepers: Virginia and Hal Sullivan
Address/Telephone: 102 West Hall Street; (912) 233–6800
Rooms: 9, plus 1 cottage; all with private bath, television, and telephone, some with Jacuzzi and working fireplace.
Rates: $60 to $145, single or double, continental breakfast and evening wine.
Open: Year-round.
Facilities and activities: Located in Savannah historic district, opposite Forsyth Park. Jogging, tennis courts, playgrounds for children, picnic area, and touch garden for the blind in the park. Nearby: restaurants, historic sites, Savannah riverfront, historic lighthouse, forts, and beaches.

I'm pleased to have The Forsyth Park Inn back in this guide. When I first visited here, I liked the inn and its location in the historic district across from the park, but it fell upon hard times and was closed for a while. Virginia and her son, Hal, bought the inn and reopened it March 1, 1988. They're doing a great job, and being here is once again a pleasure.

You can find more opulent inns in Savannah, but none more friendly. Hal and Virginia serve good wine chilled in a silver bucket at their nightly social hour when guests really do join them in the parlor or on the patio to chat. Moreover, Hal and Virginia are good at providing the little favors that sometimes make the difference between an okay stay and a really comfortable one.

Here's an example. I spent the night at the inn on the Friday before St. Patrick's Day, a wild-and-woolly weekend in Savannah. I was amused to see how excited the Sullivans were about St. Patrick's Day, and I enjoyed their enthusiasm but didn't share it. I just wanted to get out of town early Saturday morning before all the commotion started, way before people were thinking about breakfast, so I told the Sullivans I probably would be gone before they were even up. Before I went to bed, they brought me a tray with a percolator, filled and ready to plug in, a croissant and a couple of muffins, and three pieces of fresh fruit. Next morning, I was on the road before sunrise, fed and full of coffee and feeling very, very good about Hal and Virginia as innkeepers.

Meanwhile, back at the inn, I found the rooms much as they had been under previous ownership, done in period furnishing with four-poster king- and queen-sized beds and (glory) windows that you can actually open if you want to. Some of the rooms have interesting fireplaces and antique marble baths.

A new addition that I enjoyed is the grand piano, which really does get played, tucked under the staircase.

My visiting on St. Patrick's Day weekend taxed Virginia and Hal's skills in recommending eating places that wouldn't be packed to the gills with partying Irish, but that had a positive side because in the course of the conversation I discovered that they know Savannah intimately.

How to get there: At Savannah, take the U.S. 16 exit off I–95. Go north on Montgomery Street to Liberty. Turn right on Liberty. Continue to Whitaker, which is one-way. Follow Whitaker to Hall Street. The inn is on the corner.

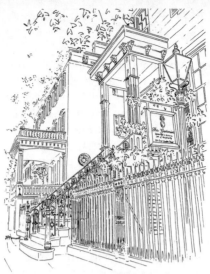

The Gastonian
Savannah, Georgia
31401

Innkeepers: Hugh and Roberta Lineberger

Address/Telephone: 220 East Gaston Street; (912) 232–2869 or (800) 322–6603

Rooms: 11, plus 2 2-room suites; all with private bath, fireplace, television, and telephone, rooms with wheelchair access.

Rates: $98 to $225, single or double, full sit-down Southern breakfast or silver-service continental breakfast in your room, afternoon tea, and wine and fresh fruit on arrival.

Open: Year-round.

Facilities and activities: Sun deck, hot tub, off-street lighted parking, garden courtyard. Nearby: restaurants, carriage tours of historic district, Savannah Riverfront shops.

I first heard about The Gastonian from Jeff Simpson, a student in a class I was teaching at the University of North Carolina in Charlotte. Jeff said that he'd read about the inn and decided to check it out when he visited Savannah. He couldn't afford to stay there but stopped in anyhow, and he was treated to a full tour with commentary by Hugh Lineberger. That's what's special about The Gastonian. It's also astonishingly elegant—I'll tell you more about that—but, more important, the Linebergers are here, personally, involved in the daily activities of the inn and its guests. Often an inn of this opulence turns out to belong to absentee owners, or to a group of owners who hire a staff to run the place. A staff may be perfectly competent, but it's not the same as being in an inn with innkeepers who've poured their passion into the property. And that sure describes Hugh and Roberta.

It's not just passion they've poured in, but also money—a million and a half of their own and $900,000 of the bank's, Hugh says, calling it a poor investment but a "hell of a love affair."

How could you not love it? The inn comprises two 1868 historic buildings sitting side by side and a two-story carriage house, joined by a garden courtyard and an elevated walkway.

The guest rooms are filled with English antiques, exotic baths, Persian rugs, and fresh flowers. The most outrageous bath is in the Caracalla Suite (named for a Roman emperor); it has an 8-foot Jacuzzi, sitting on a parquet platform draped with filmy curtains, next to a working fireplace. The fixtures here are of solid brass. In another room, they are of sculptured 24-karat gold. Each bath is unique and styled to complement the theme of its room—French, Oriental, Victorian, Italianate, Colonial American, or Country. All the inn's water runs through a purification system, which means, Hugh says, that you have to go easy on the bubble bath.

The public rooms are equally lavish, furnished with English antiques, satin damask drapes, and Sheffield silver. This kind of thing can easily be intimidating, but not when you're under the same roof with the Linebergers, who figure that having raised five daughters, a history-laden inn is a retirement pushover and jolly good fun at that. "It beats standing around with a golf club in my hand," Hugh says.

How to get there: From I-95, take I-16 to Savannah. Take the Martin Luther King exit and go straight onto West Gaston Street. The inn is at the corner of East Gaston and Lincoln streets.

Magnolia Place
Savannah, Georgia
31401

Innkeeper: Ron J. Strahan
Address/Telephone: 503 Whitaker Street; (912) 236–7674; outside Georgia, (800) 238–7674
Rooms: 13; all with private bath, television, and telephone, 6 with Jacuzzi.
Rates: $89 to $195, single or double, continental breakfast, high tea, and evening cordial.
Open: Year-round.
Facilities and activities: Hot tub, VCRs and film library. Located in Savannah historic district, overlooking Forsyth Park, which offers jogging, tennis courts, playground for children, picnic area. Nearby: restaurants, easy access to major businesses and corporate offices, within walking distance of riverfront.

This inn has a verified ghost who's been known to open and close doors and make other noises in distant rooms, turn on televisions and air conditioners, and move things around. According to legend, the ghost of Magnolia Place is the original owner, a cotton magnate who lost his fortune when the boll weevil hit and who committed suicide by falling down the steps. Some staff members say the ghost is a strong and positive presence.

But I tell about the ghost mainly for fun, because the real attraction of Magnolia Place is in its exotic furnishings, your luxurious accommodations, and the top-notch service of the staff.

Some examples: A hot tub in the backyard, Jacuzzis and gas fireplaces in some of the rooms, English antique furnishings, and prints and porcelains from around the world. The butterfly collection in the parlor is famous.

The parlor, where high tea with imported teas, wine, and benne seed cookies is served in the afternoon, used to be a ballroom. Its fireplace is rimmed with tiles from Portugal, hand painted to look as though two rose trees rise from pots at floor level and "grow" up so that their bloom-laden branches nearly meet under the mantel. Around the room, artfully placed pieces of Japanese cloisonné and Chinese porcelains catch your eye.

The international touch extends to the staff, for although they are local and can tell you about the area from an insider's view, they speak English, French, and Spanish, and can provide interpreters for Japanese if necessary.

In any language, if you ask for a dinner recommendation, one place they'll mention is Elizabeth on Thirty-Seventh, a well-known gourmet restaurant in a turn-of-the-century home nearby.

While you're at dinner, the staff at the inn are busy turning down your bed and placing hand-rolled truffles and cordials in your room, checking on your supply of Neutrogena amenities, and handling any personal requests you've made for extra service.

Personal attention like this attracts corporate and international travelers and celebrities, discreetly unidentified, as well as tourists. Best I can figure, the ghost hangs around, too, because he can't find such good service anywhere else.

How to get there: From I-95, take I-16 east onto Montgomery Street. Turn right on Liberty Street and then right on Whitaker. Coming from Charleston, take 17 north over the Talmadge Bridge. Immediately turn left on Oglethorpe and follow it to Whitaker. Turn right on Whitaker. Park behind the inn.

S: *The staff can arrange private tours of Savannah if you'd rather not be herded along with a group.*

Susina Plantation Inn
Thomasville, Georgia
31792

Innkeeper: Anne-Marie Walker
Address/Telephone: Meridian Road (mailing address: Route 3, Box 1010);
(912) 377–9644
Rooms: 8; all with private bath. Pets accepted with advance arrangement.
Rates: $150, double; $115, single; full breakfast and dinner with wine. Children under 6 free. No credit cards.
Open: Year-round.
Facilities and activities: Lighted tennis court, swimming pool, fishing pond, jogging trails. Nearby: antiques and gift shops in Thomasville, golf, 22 miles to Tallahassee, Florida.

I've known only two Swedish women in my life. One is Anne-Marie Walker, the other a woman called Mrs. Carter. Mrs. Carter was the second-best cook I've ever encountered. Anne-Marie is the first.

The night I was here, Anne-Marie served dinner on English bone china to a total of six guests at a 12-foot-long antique table. Anne-Marie decides what to prepare according to the quality and availability of ingredients. The other guests had already eaten here the night before, and as we sipped our wine and chatted before dinner, they talked mostly about the previous night's meal, which included an eggplant appetizer they all raved over. My dinner lived up to the advance praise. It was one of the best meals I've had anywhere, not because it was elaborate or exotic, but because every item was perfectly prepared. A green salad with feta cheese practically crackled with crispness on chilled plates. The appetizer, zucchini boats with shrimp, tantalized us with herb flavors we couldn't quite identify. The loin of pork served with a mustard sauce was juicy and tender inside, browned and crusty outside. The potatoes were browned and just crispy enough to give your teeth something to notice before getting to the mellow insides. And we had all the big Swedish biscuits we could eat. Anne-Marie has an exceptionally good white table wine that complemented everything: Chateau Elan vin blanc. She gets it from Atlanta.

All this feasting took place in the dining room of an 1841 Greek Revival plantation home hidden back on a country road on 115 acres dotted with live oaks and the requisite Southern Spanish moss.

The mansion has eleven fireplaces, a spiral staircase, and wide center halls in true plantation style. The rooms are huge, furnished with antiques and oriental rugs. My room had a claw-footed tub with an added shower in the bath and a four-poster canopied queen-sized bed. The wallpaper, draperies, and spread, all in a deep blue floral pattern, matched. My windows looked out into the tops of old live oaks. To me, the place had the slightly worn and settled feeling of a big old home rather than the spit shine of a tour building buffed by a large staff. Having come from a series of staff-polished, impersonal inns, I found the change comforting.

I found that in addition to being a first-class cook, Anne-Marie is a flexible, accommodating innkeeper. Three of the guests, women traveling together, had gotten their schedules confused and arrived at Susina a day early. Fortunately, it was the middle of the week and not too busy, so Anne-Marie was able to settle them into rooms and make them dinner. She did it so well that before they left they presented her with a large antique china serving platter that looks right at home on her dining-room buffet.

How to get there: Susina is on the Meridian Road, 12 miles south of Thomasville and 22 miles north of Tallahassee. Follow Susina signs off Route 319.

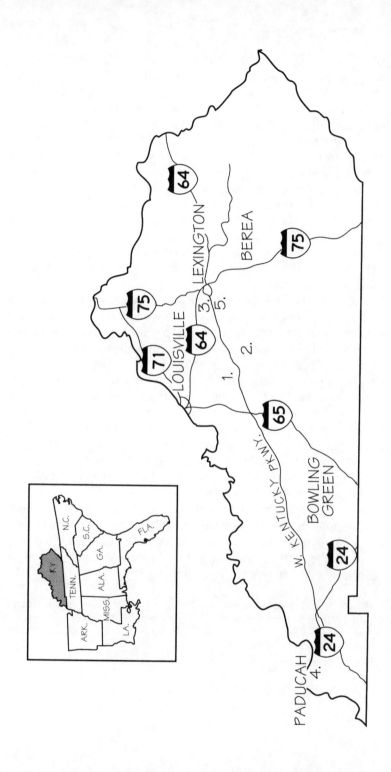

Kentucky

Numbers on map refer to towns numbered below.

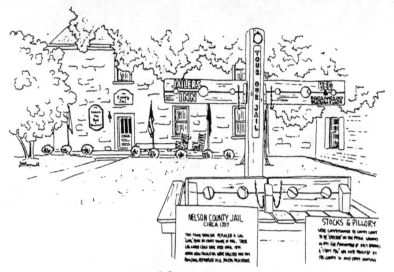

Jailer's Inn
Bardstown, Kentucky
40004

Innkeepers: Fran and Challen McCoy
Address/Telephone: 111 West Stephen Foster Avenue; (502) 248–5551
Rooms: 5; all with private bath, 2 with wheelchair access, 2 with television.
Rates: $55 to $70, double or single, continental breakfast.
Open: Year-round.
Facilities and activities: Nearby: restaurants, whiskey distilleries, My Old Kentucky Home State Park, Bardstown Historical Museum, Shaker Village.

"I guess I'm sentenced to life imprisonment," Fran McCoy likes to say. Considering that she owns the old country jail, how could she resist that line?

The inn was a jailer's residence until 1987. Fran and Challen purchased it in June 1988 and opened the prison section for tours almost right away. At that time, they didn't know it had been built by Fran's great-great-uncle. The front building, known as the "old" jail, was built in 1819 of native limestone. It had two cells and an "upstairs dungeon" for prisoners. The stone building behind this, built in 1874, was known as the "new" jail. Once it was operating, the front building became the jailer's home.

Fran and Challen turned the "old" jail into an inn decorated with antiques and oriental rugs, except for the former women's cell, which is done entirely in prison black and white and contains the three original bunks. The floor is tiled in a black-and-white geometric pattern, the mirror over the sparkling white sink has a white frame, and a picture on the white brick wall has a black frame. Fran says she loves it. Well, I'm sure it's better than it was.

A much prettier room, the favorite of many guests, is the Garden Room, which looks out over the courtyard and is decorated in aqua green with wicker and wrought iron and lots of flowers. (The courtyard is a favorite spot for eating a breakfast of fresh pastries and fruits every morning.) The garden-room bedspreads are cross-stitched quilts in floral patterns.

The Victorian Room, a feminine room with flowered wallpaper, a tall-mirrored vanity, lace-edged bed covers, and old-fashioned flowered hats on a stand in the corner, pleases guests, too.

Fran, who did all the decorating herself, takes obvious pleasure in the results. When she talks about it, though, it comes out sounding strange: "I just love my jail," she says.

How to get there: The inn is just off Court Square in downtown Bardstown. Highway 31-E runs directly to the square.

Beaumont Inn
Harrodsburg, Kentucky
40330

Innkeepers: C. M. (Chuck) and Helen W. Dedman
Address/Telephone: 638 Beaumont Drive; (606) 734–3381
Rooms: 33; all with private bath, telephone, and television. No-smoking
rooms available.
Rates: $70 to $95, double; single $15 less; breakfast.
Open: Mid-March to mid-December.
Facilities and activities: Lunch and dinner. Swimming pool, tennis courts,
shuffleboard, gift shops. Nearby: boating, fishing, and swimming on
Herrington Lake; golfing; Keeneland Race Track; Shaker Village; Old
Fort Harrod State Park.

Harrodsburg is in the heart of Kentucky's horse country, an
area crammed with historic sites and gorgeous scenery, but the
truth is that a lot of people go to the Beaumont Inn mainly to eat.
The inn's food and service are famous.

When I made my dinner reservation, I had a choice of a 6:00
P.M. or a 7:30 P.M. seating. I chose the earlier one. A bell rang right
on the hour to announce dinner, and I was immediately shown to a
table with my name on it. I ordered roast beef, although I was
tempted by the country ham, which is aged two years, and decided
to begin with a cup of cream of celery soup, because the appetizer
was included in the cost of the meal. And from that point on, it
seemed to me that the food kept coming for more than an hour.

After I'd eaten a salad of Bibb lettuce with Roquefort dressing, the waitress brought my plate of roast beef and a trayful of serving dishes from which she served me mashed potatoes and gravy, limas, corn pudding, and mock scalloped oysters. Nobody seemed to know what was in the mock scalloped oysters, but the taste was so convincing that the people at the next table, who didn't hear the word *mock*, never did realize that they weren't eating the real thing. As I ate, the waitress returned several times to offer seconds and refill the basket of biscuits. For dessert, I had a crisp meringue shell filled with vanilla ice cream and fresh strawberries. And while I was reflecting on the enormous quantities of food being served in the dining room, the innkeeper came to the table to make sure I'd had enough to eat.

I saw a nice thing happen. The waitress at another table found out that a gentleman at that table was celebrating a birthday dinner; she brought him a bagful of extra biscuits to take home—her gift.

It seemed to me that I'd barely had time to stroll around the grounds admiring the lush greenery and take a quick look at some of the antiques inside the inn after dinner before I got sleepy. Then it was breakfast time, and the whole incredible flow of food started all over again, with an overwhelming number of choices, including a stack of the lightest, tastiest batter corn cakes I've ever sunk a tooth into.

How to get there: In Harrodsburg, turn left off South Main at the United Presbyterian Church onto Beaumont Avenue and then right onto Beaumont Drive.

Shaker Village of Pleasant Hill

Harrodsburg, Kentucky
40330

Innkeeper: Ann Voris
Address/Telephone: 3500 Lexington Road; (606) 734–5411
Rooms: 81 in 15 buildings; all with private bath, television, and telephone. Inn especially suited for children.
Rates: $42 to $80, single; $52 to $90, double; breakfast extra.
Open: Year-round except Christmas Eve and Christmas Day.
Facilities and activities: Breakfast, lunch, dinner open to guests and public by reservation. Shaker Village preserves 33 original nineteenth-century buildings as they were used by the community of Shakers living in the village; they are open for tours. Craft shops, Shaker craft and farming demonstrations. Nearby: cruises on the *Dixie Belle* riverboat.

"That's the closet," Ann Voris said. We were in one of the guest rooms and she was pointing to a strip of heavy pegs along the wall. The Shakers hung everything, from their clothes to their utensils and chairs, on such pegs. Guests at Shaker Village do the same.

The rooms are furnished in the same sparse, simple style of the Shakers: rag rugs; streamlined, functional furniture; trundle beds; plain linens. Only the modern bathroom, telephone, and television set in each room make it different than it originally would have been.

Like other communities of plain people, the Shakers made up in the bounty of their table for what they lacked in knickknacks. The Shakertown menu, which says, "We make you kindly welcome," does the same. Shakers, wherever they lived, adopted the food of the area. In Kentucky, this means fried chicken, country ham, fried fish, roast beef, and large sirloin steaks. Fresh vegetables (some from the garden on the premises) and salads are passed at the table, as are breads from the bakery. The smell of baking bread distracts you much of the day at Shaker Village. And for dessert, Shaker lemon pie tops off everything. It's an unusual lemon pie, made with a double crust and whole sliced lemons, plus eggs and sugar, because the Shakers didn't waste anything—not even lemon peels.

Although the meal is bountiful, the dining rooms in the old Trustees' House resemble the guest rooms in their simplicity. The wood floors are polished and clean but unadorned. The tables and chairs are typical, functional Shaker design, and the place settings are plain white dishes. For me, it added up to a fascinating, almost-insider's view of unusual people whose way of life is almost gone except in this re-creation.

How to get there: The entrance to Shaker Village is off U.S. Route 68, 7 miles northeast of Harrodsburg and 25 miles southwest of Lexington. Signs mark the drive clearly.

S: *Many special events, including weekends of Shaker music and dance, are held during the year. You can write for a yearly calendar to help you plan a trip according to your interests.*

Scottwood
Midway, Kentucky
40347

Innkeepers: Dale and Ann Knight Gutman
Address/Telephone: 2004 East Leestown Pike; (606) 846–5037
Rooms: 3, plus guest cottage; 2 upstairs rooms share 1 bath, all others with
    private bath, 2 with fireplace, all with television and VCR. No smoking
    in inn.
Rates: $80 to $90, single or double, full breakfast.
Open: Year-round.
Facilities and activities: Formal rose garden, nature path, bird-watching. Near-
    by: Kentucky Horse Park Race Course, historic sites, Shakertown.

Scottwood is an early (about 1795) Federal-style Kentucky
brick house set among green fields, near a creek, across from a
horse farm. Dale and Ann want guests to think of it as a place to
which they can escape for periods of retreat and rest.

Just being inside takes you from your ordinary life. Dale has
painted a fanciful mural of local houses and farms (in the Rufus
Porter style, he says) that sweeps up the stairwell and into the hall.
It serves as a lighthearted introduction to outstanding antiques
throughout the house. The Gutmans have been collecting antiques
for fifteen years and came to the inn business well prepared to furnish their rooms. Their folk art collection especially pleases guests.

The common room, done in period antiques, reminds you of a
New England keeping room. Dale painted the ash floors in this

room like a red-and-beige checkerboard, "the way it *should* be in New England," he said.

In the living room the focal point is a large red English architectural cupboard that houses an outstanding china collection.

In addition to whatever time you spend here admiring the antiques collections, reading, and walking outside, consider experimenting with photography. The flowers, the nature trail, the creek, and the nearby horses represent enough possible subjects to keep a photographer busy for a lifetime. Dale says some guests come for just that.

Since you're staying in a Kentucky house, you can reasonably expect a Kentucky breakfast. Dale's the cook. He prepares varied menus, trying to include some healthful choices, and he says, "something not so healthful" every day. Traditional favorites include country ham, spoon bread, fruits, and pancakes.

My discerning friend Howard Wells discovered this place and convinced me it was worth writing about. He liked everything about Scottwood, especially Dale and Ann. Their involvement is what makes everything work, he says, because "they're enjoying themselves." It has the sound of a blessing.

How to get there: From I–64 take the Midway exit. The inn is 1½ miles east of I–64.

Paducah Harbor Plaza
Bed and Breakfast
Paducah, Kentucky
42001

Innkeeper: Beverly Harris
Address/Telephone: 201 Broadway; (502) 442–2698
Rooms: 4 share 2¹/₂ baths; all with telephone.
Rates: $35 to $60, single or double, full breakfast. Extra person in room $5.
Open: Year-round.
Facilities and activities: In downtown Paducah, across from Market House
  Museum, Yeiser Art Center, and Market House Theatre. Nearby: One
  block from Tennessee and Ohio Rivers. Riverboat cruises; restaurants,
  Museum of the American Quilters' Society, about two dozen antiques
  shops.

The old brick building operated as a hotel from the time it was
built, about 1903, until the 1950s. Today its restoration is a major
project in downtown Paducah's redevelopment. The restoration of
the building probably will continue for some time. For now, the
second floor is finished and houses the Paducah Harbor Plaza Bed
and Breakfast.

On the exterior, one of the most impressive features of the
five-story building at the corner is its detailing in sandstone and yellow pressed brick. Longer and more narrow than today's brick, this
unusual fire-treated brick is extra hard, and it's no longer made.

From inside the building, you can appreciate the leaded stained-glass windows, original copper ceilings, marble columns, and ceramic tile floors, all of which have been restored with a lot of love and labor on the part of the Harris family.

The guest rooms all have 10-foot ceilings, original windows, tongue-and-groove hardwood painted floors, and ceiling fans. The rooms are decorated with period antiques and antique quilts from Beverly's family.

Quilting is important to Paducah. The American Quilters' Society holds shows and special events here, sponsors workshops and lectures, and maintains the Museum of the American Quilters' Society. The museum is a 30,000-square-foot facility, which gives you some idea how much attention quilts receive here. Beverly plans to continue using quilts in her decorating theme as she enlarges the bed and breakfast. Even now the family quilts in the guest rooms are accompanied by other handmade quilts and pillows donated by guests who have enjoyed their visits in Paducah Harbor Plaza.

Guests invariably like the bright, cheery Broadway Room. It has huge bow windows and overlooks the market area and the Ohio River. The room serves as a common gathering place with a television set and a VCR for guests. It is also where Beverly serves breakfast, which includes homemade blueberry muffins, sausage, quiche, fresh fruits, and a choice of juices, coffee, and tea. You eat at a long, elegantly set oak table with place mats done in a quilt pattern. Live plants and fresh flowers add the final fillip.

How to get there: The inn is at the corner of Second and Broadway streets in downtown Paducah.

Shepherd Place
Versailles, Kentucky
40383

Innkeepers: Marlin and Sylvia Yawn
Address/Telephone: 31 Heritage Road; (606) 873–7843
Rooms: 2; both with private bath, television available on request. No smoking inside.
Rates: $60, single; $56, double; $70, three; full breakfast.
Open: Year-round.
Facilities and activities: Pond with ducks and geese. Nearby: restaurants, Lexington, Shakertown.

On five rural acres in the middle of Bluegrass Country, the Yawns keep fifteen sheep. Don't go thinking lamb chops, though; you'd have it all wrong. These sheep are for guests to enjoy watching and petting, for shearing, and for loving. Their wool, as far as Sylvia is concerned, is for spinning and knitting. She shears the sheep only once a year, even though twice a year is possible, so that the wool will be longer and more suited to her handcrafts.

If you spend time here, you're bound to learn about the sheep, to want to see Sylvia spin, and probably to buy some yarn or order a hand-knit sweater for yourself. In this situation the choices are so personal that you can even request a sweater from Pearl's or Abigail's or Sabrina's wool, and Sylvia will see that the appropriate yarn is set aside to knit your sweater. Obviously you won't get it in a week or two, but a garment so uniquely your own seems worth waiting for.

In busy times you might have to wait to book a night at the inn, too, but the experience, like a sweater of Sabrina's wool, is worth the wait.

To give you an idea, an old-fashioned swing sways on the porch. The downstairs parlor once had French doors. These have been converted to floor-to-ceiling windows that let in a glorious amount of light. The light is picked up by 12-inch-high baseboards painted white. Spice brown walls keep the overall effect from being glaring. Queen Anne–style chairs are set off by formal English sofa lamps, and a red-and-blue oriental rug unifies all the room's elements.

The guest rooms are uncommonly large, 20 feet by 20 feet, with bathroom facilities fitted into alcove rooms in their corners.

As pleasing as all this is, the real kick comes from Sylvia's pleasure with it all. In every way she's thrilled with being an innkeeper in her old Kentucky home. She's proud of the smooth gleam of interior paint Marlin (who used to be a professional painter) has accomplished. She enjoys cooking huge breakfasts, which often include Kentucky ham and such delicacies as whole wheat pancakes with walnuts. She loves the sheep and working with their wool. And, most significant of all, she enjoys the guests. "We get such *good* guests. We have a bulletin board full of cards and letters they send after they've been here," she said, "This is all even neater than I thought it would be. It's a real blessing."

How to get there: Coming from Knoxville on I–75, take exit 104 onto the Lexington Circle; from Cincinnati, take exit 115. From the Lexington Circle take exit 5B onto U.S. 60. Drive 6 miles to Heritage Road and turn left. The inn is at the corner of U.S. 60 and Heritage Road.

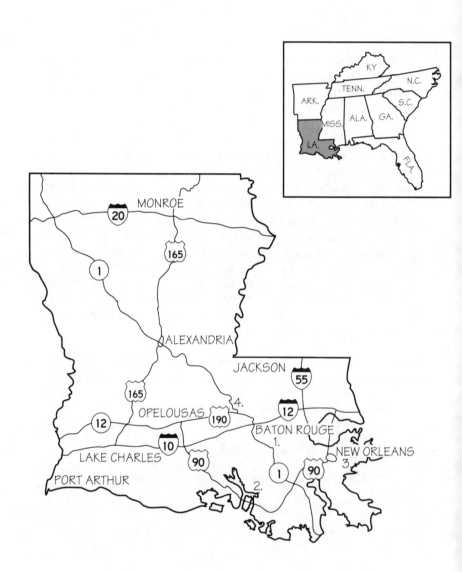

Louisiana

Numbers on map refer to towns numbered below.

Tezcuco Plantation
Burnside, Louisiana
70725

Innkeeper: Debra Purifoy

Address/Telephone: Burnside (mailing address: 3138 Highway 44, Darrow, LA 70725); (504) 562–3929

Rooms: 16 cottages; all with private bath and television, some with kitchen and fireplace. Pets welcome.

Rates: $45 to $185, single or double, tour of plantation house and grounds, bottle of wine, and full Creole breakfast. $20 for each extra adult, $7.50 for each extra child.

Open: Year-round except Thanksgiving Day, Christmas Day, and New Year's Day.

Facilities and activities: Antiques-and-gift shop. Nearby: restaurants, plantation tour homes and historic sites, Mississippi River.

Tezcuco Plantation tries to give guests a feeling of what it would have been like to live on a working sugar plantation in the 1800s. The original plantation house is an antebellum raised cottage (cottages were a lot bigger in those days) built about 1855 from cypress grown and cut on the property and from bricks made in the plantation's kiln.

The original outbuildings, long since gone from the grounds, have been replaced by moving in appropriate ones found on other plantations.

The overnight cottages are restored slave quarters, doubtless improved since slaves lived in them, with ruffled curtains, air conditioning, antique furnishings and artifacts, pecky cypress paneling, and the work of Louisiana artists on the walls.

Altogether there are thirty buildings on the plantation now, including a children's playhouse, a greenhouse and potting shed, and an old shop with antique tools and a printing press.

Guests sit in rockers on the porches of the little cottages, chatting back and forth from cottage to cottage in the old-time way.

For dinner, the people at Tezcuco will certainly suggest that you drive a couple of miles to Lafitte's Landing Restaurant next to the Sunshine Bridge on the Mississippi River, where John D. Folse, a chef much admired in the area, serves up wonderful, rich, and well-seasoned gourmet meals in his historic building.

Also, by the time you read this, a restaurant should be open on the grounds.

How to get there: Tezcuco is between Baton Rouge and New Orleans, near I–10. Coming from the north or the south on I–10, take exit 179 onto L.A. 44 south to Burnside. The plantation is 1 mile north of Sunshine Bridge on L.A. 44. Write for brochure with map.

Madewood
Napoleonville, Louisiana
70390

Innkeepers: Keith and Millie Marshall
Address/Telephone: 4250 Highway 308; (504) 369–7151; for reservations, call
10:00 A.M. to 5:00 P.M.
Rooms: 5 in mansion, 1 cabin and 3 suites in the Charlet House; all with private bath, some with wheelchair access. Inquire about pets.
Rates: $90 to $159, single or double. Charlet House and cabin accommodations include continental breakfast and wine and cheese on arrival. Mansion rooms include full breakfast and dinner. No personal checks.
Open: Year-round except Thanksgiving Eve and Day, Christmas Eve and Day, New Year's Eve.
Facilities and activities: Dinner. Nearby: Mississippi River tour boats and tours of plantation homes.

Madewood feels like a house in the country—a fancy one, admittedly, a Greek Revival mansion with six white columns, but a house in the country nonetheless. Irises grow around the sides of the porches; you can see fields in each direction; pear trees on the property produce fruit for the inn, and the parking area is shaded by established old trees.

The mansion itself is filled with antiques, oriental rugs, and crystal chandeliers, and it has recently been painted and completely refurbished, but Madewood still feels like a home rather than a museum.

Upstairs, one room has been preserved as a dressing room—

bathroom, complete with an old scoop-shaped metal bathtub that would have had to be filled and emptied with a bucket. It makes you appreciate the modern bathrooms now available to guests.

And old clothes are displayed in some of the tour bedrooms, laid out and hanging as though someone were just about to put them on.

You get a simpler sense from the rooms in the old slave cabin, a rustic little building with a working fireplace and tufted quilts on the beds.

Wherever you stay, be sure you arrange to have Thelma cook dinner for you. She's one of those cooks who can tell you exactly what's in a dish—she just can't give you exact amounts. She stirs things until they "feel right" and cooks them until they "look right." Her menu includes chicken pies and shrimp pies, gumbos, corn bread, green beans, bread pudding, and Pumpkin Lafourche. Pumpkin Lafourche is a casserole of apples, raisins, pumpkin, sugar, butter, nutmeg, cinnamon, and vanilla, and don't ask in what proportions or for how long or at what temperature Thelma bakes it. Just enjoy.

Dinner includes wine and an after-dinner drink in the parlor, where there's one of the tiniest old pump organs I've ever seen.

How to get there: From I–10, take exit 182, cross Sunshine Bridge, and follow Bayou Plantation signs to Highway 70, Spur 70, and Highway 308. The inn faces the highway.

❀

S: *At the rear of the house, the original open-hearth kitchen for the plantation home is still intact, set up with odd tables and chairs, an antique washing machine, and assorted pieces of cooking equipment so that you can imagine what it must have been like when meals for the family and guests were prepared there.*

Hotel Provincial
New Orleans, Louisiana
70116

Innkeepers: Clancy, Verna, and Bryan Dupepe; Bryan Dupepe, Jr., general manager

Address/Telephone: 1024 Chartres Street; (504) 581–4495; outside Louisiana, (800) 535–7922

Rooms: 97; all with private bath, telephone, and television, some with wheelchair access.

Rates: $90 to $130, single or double, breakfast extra. Children under 17 free in same room with parents.

Open: Year-round.

Facilities and activities: Honfleur Restaurant open 7:00 A.M. to 10:00 P.M. for guests and public, bar, wheelchair access. Swimming pool, free off-street parking. Located in the French Quarter 2½ blocks from Jackson Square. Nearby: restaurants, antiques shops, jazz, historic tours, aquarium.

Good things happened to me here. Obviously an inn with ninety-seven rooms isn't a cozy little hostelry just like home. But the outdoor patios and courtyard around the pool are magic. Every time I sat down, I met somebody interesting who was in the mood to talk. Sitting by the pool (really nice), for instance, I got into conversation with a woman from California who is publishing a book of recipes from a woman's art club. The members used to meet weekly to take turns posing for the group to practice painting nudes and to eat a gourmet lunch. The lunch recipes are illustrated with paintings done by the clubwomen during those meetings. You just don't get into conversations like that in my home town.

I found the people who work at the inn equally chatty. I was sitting at an odd hour, cooling off with a cold imported beer in the dining room—a pretty little room with plaid fabric and lots of framed and lighted travel posters on the walls—when I got into a conversation with one of the staff about the restaurant's food. Next thing I knew, she was plopping a bowl of creole gumbo in front of me, along with a scoop of rice and a piece of hot French bread, instructing me to taste it and see if it wasn't the best thing I'd ever put into my mouth. Well, it was.

While I was sampling gumbo, a couple came in, excited because they had eaten at a restaurant called Honfleur in Europe and wanted to compare this one with it.

This Honfleur seats about sixty or seventy people, serves three meals a day, and offers room service. It's supervised by a master chef whose offerings range from French bistro to New Orleans specialties. It's become a favorite with local people.

That, combined with the fact that the hotel has been in the Dupepe family since its opening more than three decades ago, gives it a wonderfully nontouristy feeling.

The hotel is a collection of low buildings, townhouses, slave quarters, and old business buildings—nothing high-rise—unified by restoration and courtyards. The rooms have high ceilings and imported French furniture or New Orleans–Creole antiques, as well as the modern amenities of a luxury hotel.

How to get there: The inn is in the French Quarter. Chartres is between Royal and Decatur. The inn is on Chartres between Ursulines Street and St. Philip.

Lafitte Guest House
New Orleans, Louisiana
70116

Innkeeper: John Maher
Address/Telephone: 1003 Bourbon Street; (504) 581–2678 or (800) 331–7971
Rooms: 14; all with private bath and telephone, television on request.
Rates: $69 to $135, single or double, continental breakfast.
Open: Year-round.
Facilities and activities: Off-street parking. Located in the French Quarter.
    Nearby: restaurants, antiques shops, jazz, historic tours.

When Lafitte was built in 1849, it was a single-family home. Today, as a guest house, it still feels more like a home than a hotel. I attended a meeting in the parlor, and I swear that something about the Victorian furniture, oriental rugs, and elegant red velvet draperies made us all more cooperative than we would have been in an ordinary meeting room.

The guest rooms are decorated in period furnishings and have a kind of low-key calm that is a refreshing retreat from the outside activity of the Quarter. Many of them have the original black marble mantels over their fireplaces. Several have four-poster beds with full or half testers. The rooms in the main house are somewhat larger than those in the slave quarters and have simpler furnishings, but they have exposed brick walls that lend another kind of charm to a room, and, if anything, the sense of privacy is even greater in these rooms.

I especially liked the staff I met here. Their approach is informal; instead of a conspicuous desk for checking in, they use an unobtrusive antique table set well back in the hall so that when you come in the front door you see the Victorian parlor before you see anything resembling a hotel front desk. It was busy that week, yet everyone had time to answer questions and provide helpful little extras.

New Orleans has so many good restaurants that recommending just one seems wrong. The inn staff all know a lot about city restaurants and tours and will talk to you about your own particular tastes, then make suggestions about where to eat and what to do. You can also exchange experiences and recommendations with other inn guests during the daily cocktail period from 5:00 to 7:00 P.M. over wine and hors d'oeuvres. And, as if that weren't enough, you'll also find a book of menus to browse. If this seems like a lot of emphasis on food, it is. As John Maher, the innkeeper, says, "Some people come just to eat!"

How to get there: The inn is in the French Quarter. Bourbon Street is between Dauphine and Royal.

S: *It was exciting to walk up and down Bourbon Street in the evening, full from a good meal, listening to the different music coming from each establishment along the way and enjoying the high spirits of the tourists and performers as they acknowledged each other.*

St. Ann/
Marie Antoinette
New Orleans, Louisiana
70130

Innkeeper: Stephen V. De Ferrari
Address/Telephone: 717 Conti Street; (504) 525–2300 or (800) 535–9111; fax
(504) 524–8925
Rooms: 60; all with private bath, telephone, and television.
Rates: $95 to $135, single; $115 to $175, double; $295 to $495, suites;
breakfast extra.
Open: Year-round.
Facilities and activities: Breakfast patio, swimming pool, bar, valet parking.
Located in the French Quarter. Nearby: restaurants, antiques shops,
jazz, historic tours.

The minute I got into the little lobby here and saw deep-green
plush carpeting, mirrored walls, and crystal chandeliers, I started
looking around for wealthy dowagers accompanied by young
heiresses. I think I spotted a few, sitting around and looking elegant, but most of the guests were businesspeople and tourists like
me.

The restaurant, which serves only breakfast, sets the tone. It
has a wall of brick painted white, pink marble floors, peach table-
cloths, and silver trays. A long wall of windows looks out onto a

brick patio with tropical plants and a fountain, also set up for serving breakfast. You could order juice and croissants or go for something more impressive—poached eggs on creamed spinach with artichoke bottoms and hollandaise sauce, maybe.

In keeping with the lobby and restaurant, the bar has brass-topped tables, white painted chairs, and panels of stained glass in the ceiling. There's more brasswork in the elevators. I saw a lot of people busy polishing brass early in the morning.

The guest rooms are elegant, too, with French Provincial dressers and desks, some brass beds, and luxuriously modern bathrooms.

At dinner time, for a complete contrast, you can go next door to the Olde N'awlins Cookery, a simple restaurant with plain tables, bare floors, and the kind of Cajun and Creole cooking people line up for. My choice was deep-fried soft crabs, but the barbecued shrimp, served in a big bowl of barbecue juice for dipping bread into, is probably the favorite dish of repeat customers. The waiter, who turned out to be an expatriate New Yorker who moved because he got tired of being cold, has made it a personal mission to teach tourists that barbecued shrimp in New Orleans has nothing to do with cooking on a grill or spit Yankee style.

There we all were, tourists and dowagers alike, breaking the legs off crabs and peeling the shells off shrimp, then licking the juice from our fingers before returning to the elegance of the St. Ann for an after-dinner drink in the Cypress Bar.

How to get there: The inn is in the French Quarter. Conti Street is between Bienville and St. Louis, in the block between Bourbon and Royal.

623 Ursulines
New Orleans, Louisiana
70116

Innkeepers: Jim Weirich and Don Heil
Address/Telephone: 623 Ursulines Street; (504) 529–5489
Rooms: 7 suites; all with private bath, television, and small refrigerator.
Rates: $60 to $70, single or double. Breakfast not served. Personal checks, travelers checks, or cash.
Open: Year-round except the last 2 weeks in August.
Facilities and activities: Located in the French Quarter. Nearby: restaurants, antiques shops, jazz, historic tours.

Visiting with Jim and Don was pure fun. The way they explain it, Jim loves to talk and Don likes to clean, so for a time we sat chatting as Don polished some leather and brass, grinning from time to time, while Jim knocked off one witticism after another.

I loved their inn. Each suite comprises sitting room, bedroom, and bath. The rooms are simple, immaculately clean, and so quiet that guests have been known to ask if they were the only people there, when in fact the house was full. (Jim says that it's quiet because the inn is surrounded by museums.) Rather than furnish the rooms with antiques, Jim and Don have selected the kind of contemporary furniture that provides comfort without calling attention to itself. I found the effect relaxing.

You enter the rooms from a fenced-in private patio that is spectacular. It still has the original old brick paving, laid in an intricate pattern and shaded by the biggest magnolia tree imaginable, right here in the heart of the city. Azaleas blooming in huge pots line one side, along with roses, gardenias, crotons, and a surprising collection of bromeliads attached to the brick wall.

Scattered in with all these tropical plants, a goodly number of orchids were blooming profusely. I could have spent hours here looking at all the plants and admiring how well they are grown.

Breakfast is not served at the inn. I said, "What's the matter, doesn't anyone like to cook around here?" That's when they showed me the Croissants d'Or, a French-pastry shop next door. In the morning, guests go over in their bathrobes, choose goodies from a mouth-watering display, and carry them back to the flowered courtyard to enjoy with their complimentary morning newspaper. I don't think I'll ever forget the blackberry-currant mousse I had.

How to get there: The inn is in the French Quarter. Ursulines is between St. Philip and Gov. Nicholls. The inn is on Ursulines in the block between Royal and Chartres.

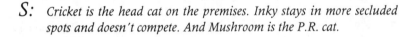

S: *Cricket is the head cat on the premises. Inky stays in more secluded spots and doesn't compete. And Mushroom is the P.R. cat.*

Terrell House
New Orleans, Louisiana
70130

Innkeeper: Harry Lucas

Address/Telephone: 1441 Magazine Street; (504) 524–9859 or (800) 878–9859

Rooms: 9; all with private bath, telephone, and television, carriage house rooms with wheelchair access.

Rates: $65 to $110, single or double, continental breakfast and evening cocktail.

Open: Year-round.

Facilities and activities: Library of books about New Orleans and Louisiana, secluded courtyard. Nearby: fine restaurants, the French Quarter, the New Orleans Convention Center, the Riverwalk shopping-dining-entertainment center, St. Charles Avenue and the Garden District (where most antiques shops in the city are located), docks for the *Delta Queen* and other riverboats.

Terrell House has everything going for it: architecture, furnishings, location, a skillful innkeeper, and an owner who loves the place.

The house was built in 1858 by a wealthy New Orleans cotton merchant. It has twin parlors, marble fireplaces, gaslight fixtures, guest rooms that open onto balconies, and an outstanding courtyard.

As for the furniture, I'd heard about it from other innkeepers before I even visited. The inn is furnished with an excellent quality collection (much of it rosewood) of New Orleans furniture of the 1850s. Many pieces are by Prudent Mallard. Many of the antiques are family pieces of the Terrell House owner, Fred Nicaud. His mother was born in one of the beds; a spread was crocheted more than a hundred years ago by family members.

But Freddy loves to search out and bring home appropriate antiques, wherever he finds them. He found the Waterford crystal chandelier that now hangs in the dining room in Boston. From Boston, Freddy flew home coach, but the pilot decided to belt such a delicate and fragile piece into a first-class seat.

Freddy also found a full collection of small bedroom furniture, probably doll furniture or salesman's samples, from 1900, that enchants me every time I see it.

During one of my visits, Freddy, practically leaping through the door he was so excited, lugged in a wonderful oriental carpet he'd found. No one ever knows what Freddy's going to bring home next.

Another nice feature of the inn is its location in the Lower Garden District. Although it doesn't look like much when you first drive up, Magazine Street is wonderful—in the process of restoration and full of antiques shops and interesting little stores, as well as about a hundred restaurants. It's quieter than the French Quarter. This is where the local people shop and eat away from the tourist area.

You can get as much or as little advice and attention as you want from Harry Lucas. He knows all about tours, tourist attractions, and interesting spots off the beaten path. Of course he knows all about restaurants, too.

How to get there: From I–10 East, take the Canal Street exit and turn right toward the river. Go 10 blocks to Magazine Street; turn right on Magazine to the 1400 block. From I–10 West, take Poydras Street exit. Go 10 blocks to Magazine Street and turn right to the 1400 block.

Barrow House
St. Francisville, Louisiana
70775

Innkeepers: Shirley and Lyle Dittloff
Address/Telephone: 524 Royal Street (mailing address: P.O. Box 1461); (504) 635–4791
Rooms: 3, plus 1 suite; all with private bath and television, telephone on request.
Rates: $65, single; $75 to $85, double; $95, suite; continental breakfast, wine, and cassette walking tour of Historic District. Full breakfast available at $5 extra per person. Cash and personal checks only.
Open: Year-round except December 22–25.
Facilities and activities: Dinner for guests by advance reservation. Located in St. Francisville Historic District. Nearby: tour plantations and historic sites.

Loosen your girdle and listen to this: crawfish salad, chicken Bayou La Fourche (stuffed with crabmeat), jambalaya rice, pecan praline parfait. Served on good china with sterling silver flatware by candlelight on a flower-decorated table in the formal dining room, under the old punkah "shoo fly" fan. Oh, be still my heart!

I can tell you lots more about Barrow House, and I'll get to it, but how can Louisiana food like that, served with such style, come anywhere but first? You have to arrange for such dinners ahead of time, and you select from a number of different possibilities for each course.

After a meal—next day maybe—you can do penance by jogging down Royal Street with the locals, an enjoyable thing to do even if all you ate the night before was half a Big Mac.

"We want people to have a good time here," Shirley said. And they do. Beyond the food there's the house, an 1809 saltbox with a Greek Revival wing added in the 1860s, that's listed on the National Register of Historic Places and furnished with 1860s antiques.

The gorgeous antiques include a rosewood armoire by Prudent Mallard and a *queen-sized* Mallard bed with a *Spanish moss* mattress. You don't have to sleep in that bed unless you want to, but one man, a doctor with a bad back, said it was the most comfortable bed he'd ever had.

Spanish moss was the traditional mattress filler used in Louisiana for two hundred years. The Dittloffs' informal tour of the house gives you a chance to learn how the mattress was made and to see all the fine antiques.

Similarly, the professionally recorded Historic District walking tour (with Mozart between stops) the Dittloffs wrote guides you from Barrow House to twenty-three historic stops.

Food and antiques and tours matter, but unless good people are involved, it's probably more fun to go to Disney World. This will give you an idea about the Dittloffs. Their inn came to my attention partly through a magazine article on inns in the magazine *Louisiana Life.* Barrow House was included in the article because when a magazine staffer was married in St. Francisville, she dressed for the wedding at Barrow House. By the time she drove off, everybody who should have was crying properly, and Shirley was carrying the bride's train. Shirley was crying, too.

Some people don't want too much personal fuss. Shirley says that she and Lyle have learned to know when guests would rather be left alone. You'll get whatever amount of attention you want— no more.

Shirley said, "It's great to have guests, and when they leave they hug you."

How to get there: Barrow House is behind the courthouse in the St. Francisville Historic District. You will receive a map after you make reservations.

Cottage Plantation
St. Francisville, Louisiana
70775

Innkeeper: Mary Brown

Address/Telephone: Cottage Lane (mailing address: H.C. 68 Box 425); (504) 635–3674

Rooms: 6; all with private bath and television.

Rates: $75 to $100, single or double, coffee delivered to the room and full plantation breakfast, tour of house and grounds.

Open: Year-round except Christmas Eve and Christmas Day.

Facilities and activities: Restaurant seasonal, bar service. Swimming pool, croquet, open spaces for outdoor games, antiques shop. Nearby: historic downtown St. Francisville and tours of many plantation homes.

Many plantation inns claim to take you back into history. I think Cottage Plantation really does. You drive over an old wooden bridge and down a long wooded lane to get here. Once you're on the grounds, you can't hear or see the highway traffic.

All the original outbuildings are still in place and appropriately furnished: milkhouse, school, commissary, smokehouse, horse barn, carriage house (with the old carriage still in it), and some of the slave cabins. The old cemetery is intact, too.

This is still a 400-acre working plantation, so you see livestock and farming activities as a matter of daily routine, not as tourist demonstrations.

The black cat, Tuffie, who sits on a porch rocker waiting to be petted, probably had an ancestor in the same spot a hundred years ago. The galleries surrounding the house look out on old buildings and flower gardens kept much as they were in earlier times.

The guest rooms are more comfortable than anything out of the eighteenth century, though, with good mattresses and modern plumbing. Mary has made a fetish of cleanliness; her staff honors it.

In any century, it's neat to have a prebreakfast pot of coffee delivered to your room on a silver tray with a fragile demitasse cup and a flower. The serious breakfast comes later, in the formal dining room, from where you can see that the original wallpaper has been preserved in the house and some of the furniture still has the original 1830 upholstery.

For dinner, the inn has a restaurant in an old tenant house. Each night the menu features a typical Louisiana dish, such as crawfish cooked in butter and a standard American choice like chicken breasts and rib-eye steaks for less adventuresome diners. The day I was here, fresh Louisiana strawberries were just coming into season, and Mary had baked fresh strawberry pie for dessert.

How to get there: The inn is 6 miles north of St. Francisville, on Highway 61. Turn at the sign onto Cottage Lane and follow it to the inn.

S: *I had a wonderful time with Mary. She loves to talk, she's funny, and she's sensitive to the feelings of other people.*

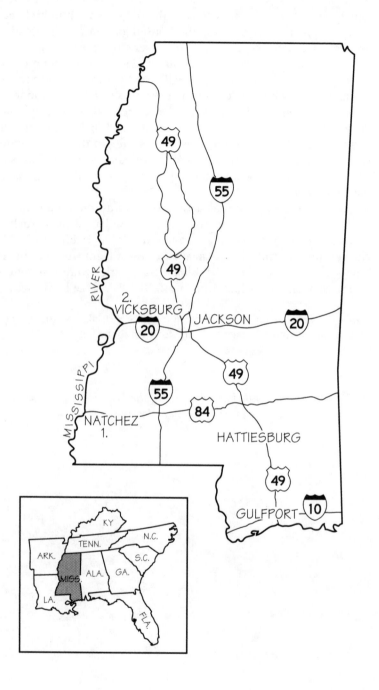

Mississippi

Numbers on map refer to towns numbered below.

Dunleith
Natchez, Mississippi
39120

Innkeeper: Nancy Gibbs

Address/Telephone: 84 Homochitto Street; (601) 448–8500; for reservation calls from outside Mississippi, (800) 433–2445

Rooms: 11, in courtyard wing and on second floor of main house; all with private bath, telephone, television, and fireplace.

Rates: $85 to $130; full Southern breakfast, welcoming lemonade, tour of the house, and snack in room.

Open: Year-round except Christmas Day.

Facilities and activities: Nearby: restaurants, Mississippi riverboat tours, tours of many historic homes in Natchez.

As a gardener who would like to spend much more time with plants, I found special pleasure in the grounds and gardens at Dunleith. Formal gardens are planted in colorful, low-growing flowering plants, and in early spring many thousands of massed tulips come into bloom.

Dunleith is on forty acres of rolling pastureland, which leaves room for refreshing green space as well as for formal garden areas. The plantation has its own greenhouse to provide plants for the gardens as well as for the mansion. Perhaps most delightful of all, an old magnolia tree behind the house has grown so huge that park benches have been arranged under its arching branches where you can sit in the shade and look out over the property. At night the grounds are lighted to give the feel of moonlight.

The lower floor of Dunleith is open for public tours. One of the remarkable attractions is the French Zuber wallpaper in the dining room. The paper was printed before World War I from woodblocks carved in 1855 and hidden during the war in a cave in Alsace-Lorraine. If you look closely, you can see small mildew stains that developed in the cave.

The bed & breakfast accommodations of Dunleith are on the second floor, and in a group of courtyard rooms, away from the public eye.

I got nervous when they said that breakfast is served in what used to be the poultry house; I'm a country girl and I know about chicken coops. But it turned out to be a wonderful, big room, with brick walls and polished wood floors and skylights. The country decor included bright jars of canned hot peppers, and there were flowers everywhere. I thought it was a great place to eat scrambled eggs, bacon, and sausage with cheese grits, biscuits, and pancakes.

The guest-room decor continues the country-and-floral theme with four-poster beds, live plants, and cute little country-store baskets filled with fruit, cheese, and canned juices. The rooms are named after trees. Dunleith is a National Historic Landmark.

How to get there: Highway 81 heading south into Natchez becomes Homochitto Street. Continue about 1½ miles. The plantation is on the left. Write for a map.

Monmouth Plantation
Natchez, Mississippi
39120

Innkeeper: John Holyoak
Address/Telephone: John A. Quitman Parkway (at Melrose) (mailing address: P.O. Box 1736); (601) 442–5852 or (800) 828–4531
Rooms: 8, plus 6 suites, in 3 buildings, 4 cottages; all with private bath, television, and telephone, some rooms with wheelchair access.
Rates: $90 to $165, single or double, full Southern breakfast and house tour.
Open: Year-round.
Facilities and activities: Fixed-price dinner Tuesday through Saturday, honor bar for guests only. 26 acres suitable for jogging, pond, Civil War museum. Nearby: Mississippi riverboat tours, tours of many historic Natchez homes.

At Monmouth Plantation, everything is on a grand scale—restorations, furnishings, gardens, and hospitality. In addition to operating as an inn, Monmouth is one of the mansions in Natchez open year-round for tours, so the staff includes three hostesses, all of whom can give you a mind-boggling amount of information about the history, architecture, and antiques of Monmouth.

As an overnight guest, you're apt to be more concerned with the quality of the rooms than with knowing that the house was built in 1818, that the table in the formal dining room is an Empire piece from New York, or that the water pitchers are made of coin silver. But once you see that the guest rooms are as luxurious as the rest of the house (complete with outstandingly nice, modern bathrooms) you kind of get into the history and elegance and can pretend that you always live this way.

While I was there, I had a chance to meet the owner, Ronald Riches, a young, energetic redhead from California. The place was jumping with activity because they were trying to get some more restoration touches finished by spring in time for the famous Pilgrimage, when many homes are open for public tours. I thought he was one of the workmen and asked what he did. He said that he owned the place; then he thought for a minute. "Actually, I guess this house owns me," he said. Similar passion seems to have infected all the staff.

Ordinarily I'd associate such grand-scale elegance with coldness and formality, but here the staff seem to enjoy one another so much and everybody is so excited about each new project in the restoration that their enthusiasm is almost palpable.

Since my first visit, Monmouth has begun serving five-course candlelight gourmet dinners in the formal dining room, complete with the elegance of ornate silver and fresh flowers. In the Southern tradition, the food is plentiful. I am not sure how anyone who eats it all can find enough room for Monmouth's traditional full Southern breakfast—eggs, grits, sausage, and biscuits—the next morning.

How to get there: From the 61/84 bypass just outside Natchez, turn onto Melrose Avenue and follow Melrose to where it intersects with the John A. Quitman Parkway. You will see the mansion on a small hill. Turn left onto the parkway and then immediately turn left again into the Monmouth driveway.

Weymouth Hall
Natchez, Mississippi
39120

Innkeeper: Gene Weber

Address/Telephone: 1 Cemetery Road (mailing address: P.O. Box 1091); (601)
445–2304

Rooms: 5; all with private bath, some with wheelchair access. No smoking
inn.

Rates: $75 to $80, double; rate adjusted for singles; full plantation breakfast,
house tour, and beverage on arrival.

Open: Year-round.

Facilities and activities: Nearby: restaurants, Mississippi riverboat tours, tours
of many historic Natchez homes.

Gene calls Weymouth Hall a "gem of Natchez" because of its
unique architecture and fine millwork and bridge work, and, most
of all, because of its spectacular view of the Mississippi River. Even
before we had looked around inside, Gene showed me the backyard
of the inn, where guests can sit in the evening to watch the sun set
and the lights come on along the river. "When you've got a view
like this, who cares about the house?" he said.

That's a deceptive line. I've never met an innkeeper more
involved with the restoration and furnishing of a building than
Gene. His collection of antiques by John Belter, Charles Baudoine,
and Prudent Mallard is so impressive that even other innkeepers
talk about it. The rococo furniture in the double parlor looks as

though it had been bought new as a set and kept intact ever since, but Gene spent a lot of time assembling it from wherever he could find it, a piece at a time.

It's worth mentioning that at Weymouth Hall all the guest rooms (which have showers in the private baths) are in the house, not in adjacent buildings or added wings as is the case with some of the larger tour homes. And breakfast is served at a Mississippi plantation table in the main dining room. Gene says that in conversations many guests have said that "living" in the house is important to them.

On a more frivolous note, Gene keeps a player piano from the 1920s, partly to reflect his sense that the inn should be fun, not a museum.

Nor does Gene's involvement stop with the inn and its furnishings. He knows how to entertain guests. He knows the area well and likes to take guests on little personal tours of outstanding old homes in the area. Some guests find these tours more interesting and less expensive than the larger commercial ones available.

You may decide not to leave the property for any kind of tour, however, once you take in the view of the Mississippi River from Weymouth Hall's backyard. It's unquestionably one of the best vistas in Natchez. And the grounds keep getting more pleasing as the shrubbery and gardens mature. Sitting high on the hill catching the breezes and enjoying the view here can be entertainment aplenty, especially if you're with good company.

How to get there: From Highway 65 and 84 (John R. Junkin Drive) on the south side of Natchez, go north on Canal Street as far as you can. Make a left and a quick right onto Linton Avenue and follow Linton Avenue to Cemetery Road. The inn is directly across from the cemetery, on a small hill.

S: *There's nothing spooky about having this cemetery across from the inn. It goes back to 1824. The old ironwork around the cemetery and the inscriptions on the old tombstones are fascinating.*

Anchuca
Vicksburg, Mississippi
39180

Innkeeper: May Burns
Address/Telephone: 1010 First East; (601) 636–4931; outside Mississippi, (800) 262–4822
Rooms: 9; all with private bath, television, and telephone. Family or executive apartment. Small pets welcome.
Rates: $70 to $110, single; $75 to $125, double; breakfast and tour of house. Lowest rates January through February.
Open: Year-round.
Facilities and activities: Swimming pool, hot tub. Nearby: restaurants, Mississippi riverboat tours, historic sites in Vicksburg.

Anchuca is an 1830 Greek Revival–style mansion with a Mississippi state flag flying from the front balcony, from which Jefferson Davis once made a speech. Anchuca gave me the uncanny feeling that the old antebellum life never stopped here.

Little touches do it. The antiques look as though they've been used, not just polished for show. The carpets have obviously been walked on over many years. And in the living room, beside an easy chair, a pair of old wire-rimmed eyeglasses lying next to an open book makes it perfectly obvious that some Confederate figure will be right back to pick up his reading. The player piano plays many foot-tapping tunes.

I think another reason Anchuca feels alive is that although the guest rooms are in the old slave quarters and a turn-of-the-century guest cottage, guests may use the downstairs rooms of the main house until closing time each day. People sit in the chairs. (Some tour homes keep most of the rooms roped off to protect the furniture.) Breakfast is served each morning in the formal dining room under a gas-burning chandelier. A silver-and-Waterford-crystal epergne towers over the center of the table. When I visited, it was heaped with red camellias. I could smell homemade banana-nut bread and coffee being prepared in the kitchen.

The hostess keeps a stack of menus to help you decide where to go for dinner. Like other innkeepers in Vicksburg, she often recommends the Delta Point. For guests who want to sample authentic Southern home cooking, she suggests lunch at the Walnut Hills Tea Room, where the meal is served round-table (family) style. An overwhelming selection of food includes smothered pork chops, chicken and dumplings, six or so vegetables, rice and gravy, slaw, biscuits and corn bread, and a fruit cobbler. I don't mean that's *all* they serve. That's just one sample menu.

How to get there: From I–20, take exit 4B onto Clay. Go to the ninth traffic light. Turn right on Cherry Street. Go 5 blocks and turn right on First East. The inn is on the corner.

Cedar Grove
Mansion–Inn
Vicksburg, Mississippi
39180

Innkeepers: Ted and Estelle Mackey
Address/Telephone: 2200 Oak Street; (601) 636–1605; in Mississippi, (800)
    448–2820; outside Mississippi, (800) 862–1300
Rooms: 9 in the mansion, 2 in the pool house, 8 suites in the carriage house;
    all with private bath, cable television, and telephone, some with patio,
    some with wheelchair access.
Rates: $75 to $140, double; $10 less single; full plantation breakfast, wine
    on arrival, and tour of mansion.
Open: Year-round.
Facilities and activities: Full cocktail service with piano at 5:00 P.M. Swimming
pool and Jacuzzi set in a courtyard with four acres of formal gardens, gaze-
bos, fountains. Nearby: restaurants, Mississippi riverboat tours, historic sites
in Vicksburg.

The place smelled like dried rose petals when I went in. And
just as I was thinking that there was a softness about the atmosphere that most antebellum tour houses lack, I saw the cannonball
lodged in the parlor wall. I saw a patch in the door. I saw a ragged
hole in the parlor floor that had been framed and covered with
heavy glass so that you could see through to the rooms below.

What *is* all this?

"Union gunboat cannonball, from the Civil War," the innkeeper said. "It came through the door and hit the parlor wall. Mrs. Klein, the owner of the house, insisted on leaving it there as a reminder after the war."

And the hole?

"War damage. After the fall of Vicksburg, Grant slept here for three nights. He turned the servants' quarters down below into a Union hospital for his soldiers. The Kleins were in residence at the time."

The innkeepers' familiarity and personal fascination with the history of the house give them little stories to tell about every room of the mansion. Listening to them and knowing that the house is largely furnished with its original antiques adds a human note to the Civil War that I've never gotten from reading plaques in museums or touring military memorials. They even knew that what I thought was a goldfish pond out in the yard actually, back in 1885, had been a catfish holding pond to keep the fish lively until it was time to eat them.

The Mackeys have been working steadily assembling the furnishings, buffing the house, and manicuring the lawns to bring the property up to its pre–Civil War glory. They've done a tremendous amount since I first stopped here a number of years ago, and the place truly looks worthy of the waltzing of Jefferson Davis.

The home was built about 1840 by John A. Klein as a wedding present for his bride. Sure beats a set of Pyrex casseroles!

How to get there: From I–20, take the 1A Washington Street exit. Go north about 2 miles. Turn left onto Klein.

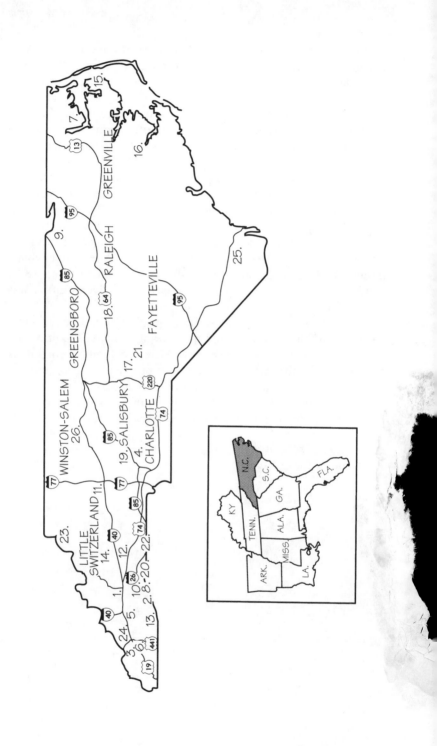

North Carolina

Numbers on map refer to towns numbered below.

Albemarle Inn
Asheville, North Carolina
28801

Innkeepers: Dick and Kathy Hemes
Address/Telephone: 86 Edgemont Road; (704) 255–0027
Rooms: 11; all with private bath, television, and telephone.
Rates: $70 to $95, per room; full breakfast.
Open: Year-round.
Facilities and activities: Swimming pool. Nearby: Biltmore Estate, Blue Ridge
   Parkway, craft and antiques shops, hiking, rafting, golf.

Béla Bartók wrote his Third Piano Concerto while he was at
Albemarle Inn. I'm not suggesting that a stay here will turn you
into a composer, but much about the place does call to mind musi-
cians, artists, and literary gatherings, including the classical and
contemporary music playing in the background.

This building has been restored to its early elegance and is decorated with furniture and accessories that reflect the three years
Dick and Kathy lived in the Far East. You'll find oriental pieces
throughout the inn. You'll also see Kathy's blue-and-white porcelain collection and Dick's needlepoint projects.

To me the most notable feature of the inn is a marvelous
carved-oak staircase with a curved-frame glass window and an
opposing curved balconylike landing. It looks like a setting for the
"balcony scene" from *Romeo and Juliet.* At least one couple has been
married on that spot.

The guest rooms are furnished in various styles, each with a special feature such as antiques or four-poster beds or decorative brass.

Another appealing feature is the inn's nice swimming pool on a grassy landscaped rise. The pool has a wood deck and a gazebo for shade.

Dick and Kathy offer early-evening wine and snacks to give guests a chance to chat with them and with each other. A particularly nice gathering spot is the sun porch. When the windows are open you can hear all kinds of birds singing—the same sound that is said to have inspired Bartok.

How to get there: From I-240 at Asheville, take the Charlotte Street exit. Go north on Charlotte Street about 1¼ miles to Edgemont Road. Turn right. The driveway is marked with a sign.

Cedar Crest
Asheville, North Carolina
28803

Innkeepers: Jack and Barbara McEwan

Address/Telephone: 674 Biltmore Avenue; (704) 252–1389 or (800) 252–0310

Rooms: 10 in main house, plus 2 suites in guest cottage; 10 with private bath, suites with service kitchen and parlor, all with telephone, some with wheelchair access, some with fireplace. Smoking in designated areas only.

Rates: $70 to $120, double; single $6 less; deluxe continental breakfast and afternoon and evening refreshments.

Open: Year-round.

Facilities and activities: English gardens and croquet pitch. Nearby: restaurants, Biltmore House, craft and antiques ·shops; easy access to the Blue Ridge Parkway and mountain activities.

Jack talks of Cedar Crest as a kind of antidote to the Biltmore House, the famous mansion tourists come to Asheville to see. At the Biltmore House, everything is so massive, there are so many rooms, the furniture and art are so overwhelming, that you really can't relate to it. Then you return to Cedar Crest and see work of equal quality, purportedly done by some of the same craftsmen, in something closer to human scale.

Not that Cedar Crest is a modest little cottage. It's an 1890 Queen Anne–style Victorian mansion, so filled with splendid features that I think you'd have to stay about thirty days to see everything. The woodwork, first-generation oak, is elaborate and different in every room: heavy and masculine in the library, for instance, and delicately ornate in the dining room.

Among other features I could absorb during my visit of less than thirty days, I noticed a grand corner fireplace with fluted columns, a beveled mirror, and a gilded cherub. I noticed splendid stained-glass windows in the foyer. In what used to be the maid's room, I noticed a secret closet once used for hiding silverware. I noticed in one bathroom what Jack swears is the largest tub (6 feet long) in Western North Carolina and in another what he says is the smallest tub (4 feet long). I noticed some pencil marks on the door frame of one of the bedrooms indicating the height to which "John" had grown in 1907.

It all would have intimidated me almost as much as the Biltmore House were it not for Jack's enthusiasm and apparently endless willingness to talk about the inn. He has a background in the hotel business and a finely developed sense of hospitality. Being a guest at Cedar Crest goes beyond awe over the features of the building. The best example I can think of, and one I almost missed, is that after the guest-room sheets are laundered, Barbara insists on having them dried on a clothesline in the sun. In this day of automatic dryers, I think a line-dried sheet is almost more of a wonder than a Victorian mansion. The English gardens and croquet pitch are just above what Barbara calls her "Victorian linen garden." The cottage sits just above this area.

Another aspect of the McEwans' hospitality is their willingness to help you find the best place for dinner. Asheville has lots of good food. One of their favorite places to recommend is the Weaverville Milling Company, a restaurant serving veal, steaks, trout, and the like in a building that was a grain mill from 1912 to 1965.

How to get there: Take exit 50 or 50B from I–40 in Asheville. After the exit, stay in the right lane to Biltmore Avenue. The inn is 1¼ miles north of I–40.

S: *Guests truly enjoy the piano in the study.*

Flint Street Inns
Asheville, North Carolina
28801

Innkeepers: Rick, Lynne, and Marion Vogel
Address/Telephone: 100 and 116 Flint Street; (704) 253–6723
Rooms: 8; all with private bath, remote telephone on request.
Rates: $65, single (no single rate on some weekends); $80, double; complete
   Southern-style breakfast and beverages served throughout the day.
   $20 each extra person. Some weekends may require 2-day minimum.
Open: Year-round.
Facilities and activities: Bicycles. Nearby: walk to restaurants and Civic Con-
   vention Center; museums, Biltmore House, Carl Sandburg Historic
   Site, Franklin gem mining, Great Smoky Mountains National Park, Pis-
   gah National Forest.

I smelled cookies baking the minute I walked through the
door. Lynne said she hoped I wouldn't think she was rude as she
excused herself to take them from the oven, and minutes later I
was eating warm chocolate chip cookies and sipping hot spiced
cider. That's how guests are greeted at the Flint Street Inns.

The bedrooms, parlors, and dining rooms are all filled with the
kind of comfortable, turn-of-the-century furniture that reminds
you of visiting a grandparent or favorite aunt in earlier times. Marion made the quilts on the beds, all of which are queen-sized. Here
and there such novel touches as a collection of hats, some 1920s
knickknacks, and a display of 1930s Art Deco collectibles catch your

attention. I especially enjoyed Marion's British tea tiles, a collection she's been building for twenty years.

A number of working fireplaces grace the inns. Sitting in front of one, sipping cider and poring over the menus the Vogels collect from area restaurants to decide where to go for dinner, is my idea of a perfect way to spend an hour late on a chilly fall afternoon.

If you're there in the spring or summer, you'll be enchanted with the way old, old shade trees, old-timey flowers like iris and phlox, bird feeders, and bird baths that actually attract birds recall the times when yards were treated as places to be rather than green expanses to be mowed.

How to get there: Going north on Haywood Street, keeping the Civic Center on your right and passing *over* I-240, Haywood becomes Flint Street. The inns are just beyond the corner of Flint Street and Starnes Avenue, on the left. Turn into the driveway for off-street parking. The Vogels will send you a map when you make reservations.

S: *As the years go by, I hear more and more praise for the Vogels' easy, competent style of innkeeping.*

Grove Park Inn
Asheville, North Carolina
28804

Innkeeper: James France

Address/Telephone: 290 Macon Avenue; (704) 252–2711; for reservations, (800) 438–5800

Rooms: 510, including suites; all with private bath, telephone, and television, some with wheelchair access.

Rates: $115 to $185, single or double; breakfast extra. Rollaways and cribs $20. Children under 16 free when occupying room with parent or adult. Lowest rates January 1 through March 31. Inquire about many special package plans for holidays and sports.

Open: Year-round.

Facilities and activities: Restaurants, bars, lounges, all with wheelchair access. Fitness center with aerobics room, weight room, Nautilus equipment, whirlpools, saunas; shops, indoor and outdoor swimming pools, golf, tennis, racquetball, squash. Nearby: Biltmore Estate, craft and antiques shops, easy access to the Blue Ridge Parkway.

Cozy it ain't. With more than five hundred rooms, the Grove Park Inn sounds more like a small city than an inn. But to North Carolinians, not only is it an inn, it is *the* inn. I lost track of the number of people in North Carolina who said, "If you're writing about inns, have you been to the Grove Park Inn yet?"

So I went. I am, after all, a North Carolinian.

I had a great time.

I think it's an inn.

The story of how the inn was built makes me think of the pyramids. Edwin Wiley Grove, owner of a pharmaceutical firm in St. Louis who had lots and lots of money, liked Asheville so well that he bought a lot of it, including Sunset Mountain. He couldn't find an architect who understood what he wanted, so he got his son-in-law to design and build it, without an architect or a contractor, from boulders hauled off Sunset Mountain. In just under a year, the massive project was finished, but it had taken wagon trains and Italian stonemasons and hundreds of local workers to do it. They fit every stone so carefully that its weathered surface is the only one visible. The inn opened on July 12, 1913.

It's hard to communicate the magnitude of the individual stones or of the entire structure. The building is 500 feet long. The lobby has flagstone floors. It's 120 feet long, almost half the length of a football field. The fireplaces are so big that you can burn 12-foot logs in them. In summer, when there's no fire, kids walk into them to play.

I sat with my husband in front of one of those fireplaces during the winter, with a glass of beer, glad for the warmth of the burning knots. Around me a dozen or so folks, dressed mostly in chinos or woolens with crew-neck sweaters, called requests to the piano player and exchanged the stories of inn guests everywhere about where they'd been and what they'd seen and where to go for dinner.

During the peak season, you can go to three different restaurants without leaving the inn. In the off-season, they're not all open all the time.

How to get there: From I–240 at Asheville, take the Charlotte Street exit (5B). Go north on Charlotte to Macon Avenue. Turn right and follow the signs ⁴/₅ mile to the inn.

The Old Reynolds Mansion
Asheville, North Carolina
28804

Innkeepers: Fred and Helen Faber
Address/Telephone: 100 Reynolds Heights; (704) 254–0496
Rooms: 10; 8 with private bath. No air conditioning in rooms (elevation 2,250 feet).
Rates: $45 to $85, double; single 10 percent less; continental breakfast. No credit cards.
Open: Year-round; weekends only in January and February.
Facilities and activities: Swimming pool. Nearby: restaurants, horseback riding, white-water rafting, hiking, tennis, golf.

The Old Reynolds Mansion is a restored brick antebellum mansion sitting in the middle of an expanse of country gardens, yards, and pines on top of a ridge of Reynolds Mountain. From its wraparound verandas, the view makes you feel that nothing else matters. I don't see how Fred and Helen get anything done with that view to tempt them into rocking and contemplating.

Inside, Helen has decorated with what she calls "comfortable antiques." The front parlor has a fireplace and, hidden behind a shelf full of books and games, a refrigerator in which guests are invited to keep their wine and snacks. Helen also keeps a little library there of menus from all the nearby restaurants to help guests choose a spot for dinner. In the winter, guests eat breakfast in the parlor. (When it's nice out, of course, they eat on the painstakingly restored veranda.)

All the guest rooms on the second floor have working fireplaces. The rooms run along both sides of a wide hall that opens onto the second-floor veranda from where you have the spectacular view of the mountains I've mentioned.

The third-floor rooms have intriguing nooks and crannies that go with alcove windows.

Everywhere you look outside, you see more signs of the work Fred and Helen have done. Their swimming pool, a real, old-fashioned poured-cement pool, measures 25 by 62 feet. But before anybody could swim any laps in it, Fred had to clean out many years' accumulation of gunk and growth, scrub it down, patch it, and paint it. Today, sparkling clean and surrounded by pines and greenery, it's worthy of Hollywood.

Fred saw me admiring the vegetable garden. "Want some zucchini?" he asked. He thought it would be a joke. Nobody he knows wants any more zucchini. When I said I did, he brought me a sack full of squash, all as long as my arm. Behind the garden, a well-tended grape arbor promises grapes in nearly as much abundance. Farther back on the property, the Fabers have begun putting benches among rows of pines to create a shady area for sitting in seclusion.

How to get there: The inn is 4 miles north of downtown Asheville. Take Merrimon Avenue (Route 25 North) past Beaver Lake. Turn right just past the stoplight onto Beaver Street, then turn left up the gravel lane. From Route 19 and 23 North, take Elk Mountain Road, bear to the right, and go left onto Elkwood Avenue at the light. At the next light, turn left and then immediately turn right onto Beaver Street. Turn left up the gravel lane. You cannot see the house from the bottom of the lane.

Richmond Hill Inn
Asheville, North Carolina
28006

Innkeeper: Susan Michel

Address/Telephone: 87 Richmond Hill Drive; (704) 252–7313 or (800) 545–9238

Rooms: 12 in the mansion; all with private bath, television, and telephone, some with showers, some tubs with showers, some with gas-log fireplace. 9 croquet cottages; all with private bath, telephone, television, refrigerator, and fireplace, one with wheelchair access. No smoking in guest rooms.

Rates: $95 to $235, per room, full breakfast. Two-night minimum on weekends in October.

Open: Year-round.

Facilities and activities: Lunch, dinner, Sunday brunch. Beer and wine available. Library, conference facilities, croquet court, nature trails. Nearby: Biltmore House, Folk Art Center, craft and antiques shops, Great Smoky Mountains National Park, Blue Ridge Parkway.

This is a luxurious inn with a heroic saved-from-the-wrecking-ball story. The century-old mansion was the home of a former congressman and diplomat, Richmond Pearson, and his wife, Gabrielle. It was one of the most innovative and elegant homes of its time. But it outlasted the people who wanted to live that way and could afford it. Toward the end, the Pearsons' daughter, Marjorie, then an elderly woman, lived alone in it, using just one room.

In subsequent sales and maneuvering, the building was scheduled to be torn down and then reprieved several times. Many community organizations, including the Preservation Society, campaigned and raised money to try to save the mansion. They also found the Michel family, who were willing to buy and restore it. It was moved, *all in one piece,* to its current spot on the hill. You can begin your stay here by watching a videotape showing the tense moving process.

The building was preserved where possible, and restored or re-created where necessary, with fidelity to the mansion's original state. Much work was done by hand as it would originally have been, rather than with electric tools. Now listed on the National Register of Historic Places, it is considered one of the best examples of a Queen Anne–style mansion remaining. It's a "must see" if you are interested in architecture and preservation.

Because of the fine woodwork, soaring ceilings, and generously sized rooms, the mansion makes a fine inn. Some guest rooms are named for Pearson family members who once lived in them, others for important guests and, on the third floor, for Asheville-connected writers, such as Carl Sandburg. Each writer's room has a picture of the writer and a collection of his or her books.

Also re-creating the past, several hundred of Mr. Pearson's own books have been recovered and placed in the inn library along with books about North Carolina and those by North Carolina authors.

The restaurant reflects the mansion's history in being named "Gabrielle's," after Mrs. Pearson. The food, however, is clearly a product of modern times. Considered American and nouvelle cuisine, it features lighter sauces and more healthful preparation than earlier haute cuisine. I had a seafood chowder with a hint of smoky flavor, salad of arugula and other greens, and roulade of chicken in pimento rosemary coulis. Smoked poultry forcemeat was mixed with vegetables and rolled into a skinless breast of chicken, then roasted in the oven and served with rosemary and pimentos. What a great combination of flavors!

How to get there: From I–240, take the 19/23 Weaverville exit. Continue on 19/23 and turn at exit 251 (UNC–Asheville). Turn left at the bottom of the ramp. At the first stoplight, turn left again onto Riverside Drive. Turn right on Pearson Bridge Road and cross the bridge. At the sharp curve, turn right on Richmond Hill Drive. The mansion is at the top of the hill.

The Inn at Brevard
Brevard, North Carolina
28712

Innkeepers: Bertrand and Eileen Bourget
Address/Telephone: 410 East Main Street; (704) 884–2105
Rooms: 5 in main house, 3 with private bath; 10 in adjacent lodge; all with
   private bath. No air conditioning in main house rooms (elevation
   2,229 feet). All lodge rooms are air-conditioned and have television.
   Smoking allowed only in lodge rooms.
Rates: $59 to $95, per room, full breakfast. Extra person in double room,
   $10. Inquire about off-season discounts and children's rates.
Open: Year-round.
Facilities and activities: Dining room Easter through Thanksgiving. Lunch,
   Sunday only, 11:30 A.M. to 2:00 P.M.; dinner, Friday and Saturday,
   5:30 to 8:30 P.M. Meeting and banquet rooms. Nearby: Brevard Music
   Center, Pisgah National Forest, the Blue Ridge Parkway.

Eileen is Irish. You don't hear a lilt or a brogue in her speech
as much as a briskness. I wouldn't mention it at all except that
when we were talking about the white stucco exterior of the inn,
she told me that in Northern Ireland it is called "pebble dash"
because the finish is applied by dashing it against the outside walls
of the building. That sounds so haphazard that it doesn't seem
appropriate to the way Eileen runs an inn.

Hers is an every-hair-in-place, impeccable-service, just-right-
food kind of place. I knew it the minute I went into the blue-and-
white and pine-paneled porch–dining room for lunch. A young

146

lady who had obviously been carefully trained took my order. The house specialty is poulet bourget, half a fresh pineapple filled with sautéed chicken and fresh vegetables. That's what I would have ordered had it not been for the lobster newburg quiche.

I sipped a glass of white wine as I waited for the quiche, speculating that maybe Eileen had some Irish gremlins on her side out there because exactly at 12:45 the bells in the church next door began playing "My country 'tis of thee . . ." and three women at the next table began to sing along softly. Transcendental little moments like this seldom happen at lunch.

Dinner at the inn has special features, too. Since the Bourgets have a New England background, seafood delicacies from cold northern waters are featured quite frequently on the menu, something you don't see often in the South. Dinner is served by candlelight, making the crystal and silver seem more twinkly and the antiques more mellow. In the busy months, a pianist plays during the dinner hour; the inn offers outdoor dining, and wine and dessert are served on the veranda until 9:00 P.M.

Meanwhile, Eileen continues to spend some of her winter travel time in Europe looking for new recipes for the inn, so no matter what you had last time, you can count on something new to try next time.

How to get there: The inn is on Route 276 in the center of town. If you take Route 64 into town, go east on Main Street.

Fryemont Inn
Bryson City, North Carolina
28713

Innkeepers: Sue and George Brown
Address/Telephone: Fryemont Road (mailing address: P.O. Box 459); (800)
   845–4879
Rooms: 39; all with private bath.
Rates: $60 to $110, single or double, breakfast and dinner. Inquire about
   children's rates.
Open: Mid-April through October.
Facilities and activities: Breakfast and dinner open to public by reservation,
   picnic lunches available, full bar. Swimming pool, tennis courts, laundry,
   craft-and-gift shop. Located in the Great Smoky Mountains. Nearby:
   Blue Ridge Parkway, rafting, horseback riding, boating, fishing, historic
   sites, the Cherokee Indian Reservation.

   Being in this inn makes you feel rustic without sacrificing any
creature comforts. Just entering the lobby gives you a sense of being
in a different world. It's a huge expanse of space, finished in wormy
chestnut board and batten, with a stone fireplace big enough to
burn 8-foot logs. Couches and chairs are grouped for conversation
in front of the fireplace and around the rest of the lobby, along with
a couple of good-sized tables with chairs for games or cards.

   The Browns and their staff practice the kind of easy hospitality
that encourages people to talk to them and to one another.

   This is the kind of place that would *have to* have a porch with rockers for hardcore relaxing as well as for watching the view of the Smoky Mountains.

The dining room, too, is just what the location calls for, a large room with many windows and another stone fireplace.

At dinner, you could begin with vegetable soup, but I found the cheese soup a more interesting choice. You make your own salad at the salad bar. Your choice of entrees might include fresh mountain trout, turkey with pecan dressing, and Southern fried chicken. The vegetables are fresh, served family style. It's nice to be able to order good wine to go with such a meal.

Outside, the poplar shingles of the inn make it seem to be covered in bark in such a way that the building blends into the surrounding trees and landscape as though it were itself a growing thing.

Inside and outside everything is clean, polished, mowed, trimmed—the kind of perfectly kept place in the woods we fantasize about. The good thing is that it's you in the rocker or by the pool and somebody else out there on the property doing the cleaning, polishing, mowing, and trimming.

How to get there: Follow Route 74 into Bryson City. Turn right at the first paved road, ³/₁₀ mile at FRYEMONT sign.

Hemlock Inn
Bryson City, North Carolina
28713

Innkeepers: Morris and Elaine White, John and Ella Jo Shell
Address/Telephone: Bryson City; (704) 488–2885
Rooms: 25; all with private bath, some with wheelchair access. No air conditioning (elevation 1,740 feet).
Rates: $110 to $150, double; single $25 less; breakfast, dinner, and all gratuities. Inquire about long-term rates in cottages. Inquire about children's rates.
Open: Mid-April to first Sunday in November. Then open weekends only through mid-December.
Facilities and activities: Dining room open to public by reservation, no Sunday-evening meal, picnic lunches available on request. Shuffleboard courts, skittles, Ping-Pong, walking paths in the woods, wildflower tours. Located in the heart of the Great Smoky Mountains. Nearby: Rafting, fishing, hiking, birding.

I like everything about this place, especially the way guests are encouraged to slow down, unwind, and actively enjoy nature. The inn offers guests a calendar of bloom, compiled by the Tennessee Department of Conservation, listing the more familiar flowers you can find blooming in the Great Smoky Mountains National Park each month from March through September.

Each spring Arthur Stupka, the first titled naturalist of the park, spends several weeks at Hemlock Inn during the wildflower season. He shows slides and shares his knowledge of wildflowers with any guests who are interested.

The inn sits on sixty-five wooded acres with a couple of miles of hiking trails. Even sitting on the porch puts you in touch with the out-of-doors in a gentle way. The view of valleys and mountains is magnificent, and the lawn and landscaping complement that view while introducing enough order so that you don't feel you are roughing it.

The rooms blend into the scene, too. They're furnished with country antiques and furniture made by local craftspeople. It's all comfortable without being so overbearing as to take your attention away from the scenery and growing plants.

Now, dinner might distract you. The Shells don't think that studying wildflowers should mean you have to eat lamb's-quarters and sorrel. Substantial home-style Southern cooking in generous quantities becomes the high point of the day for many guests. The food is served on Lazy Susan tables, inviting you to help yourself as often as you like.

The day I was at Hemlock Inn, dinner included country-fried steak, baked chicken with dressing, green beans, frosted cauliflower, apple-carrot casserole, okra fritters, and chess pie. Let me go back to that "frosted cauliflower." It's cooked with a topping of cheese, mustard, and mayonnaise that zips up the flavor and imparts a colorful gloss to the cauliflower—hence the name "frosted." The rolls are homemade, of course, as are the pumpkin and apple chips to spread on them. These "chips" also need explanation. They're pieces of fruit in a thick syrup, like preserves, and so many guests have become addicted that the Shells now offer jars of pumpkin and apple chips for sale.

How to get there: The inn is just east of Bryson City, about a mile off Highway 19 on top of a small mountain. The turn is marked by a Hemlock Inn sign. When you make reservations, you will receive a highlighted map with full directions from all interstate highways in whatever direction you will be traveling.

Nantahala Village
Bryson City, North Carolina
28713

Innkeepers: John Burton and Jan Letendre
Address/Telephone: 4 Highway 19 West; (704) 488–2826; outside North Carolina, (800) 438–1507
Rooms: 14 in main lodge, all with private bath and television; 40 cabins, all with private bath, some with television, some with fireplace. No smoking in public rooms.
Rates: $45 to $165, single or double; $5 each extra person in room over regular number, up to maximum allowed. Rates vary seasonally. Breakfast extra. Inquire about special discounts. Children under 6 free.
Open: Year-round.
Facilities and activities: Restaurant open to guests and public three meals a day, Saturday brunch, Sunday buffet. Brown bagging permitted. Swimming pool, tennis courts, volleyball court, Ping-Pong, horseshoes, badminton, hiking trails, horseback riding. Full-time recreation director to supervise children in summer. Nearby: Great Smoky Mountains National Park, rafting, fishing.

Nantahala Village has been one of my favorite places over many years. A while ago, during some changes in ownership, things had begun to slip, but the new owners, John and Jan, have brought new energy (and lots of refurbishing) to the place; and now, if anything, it's better than ever.

The Village covers two hundred mountain acres, so the place lends itself to outdoor recreation, but the old stone lodge is a cozy place to relax inside, too. The rooms are spacious, furnished in country-style furniture. The beds are good. The showers are hot. I've stayed in some of the cabins, when I was traveling with friends, and we found each experience there just right too. John and Jan take care to book guests into cabins that fit their situations—no cliff-edge cabins for people with little kids, a romantic cabin well away from everyone else for honeymooners, and so on.

The food here has always been good in the almost-Thanksgiving-dinner style, and still is, but you now have choices of vegetarian entrees and other lighter food as well. In addition to country ham, trout, and rib eye, for instance, you could try Wild Forest Pasta, with a cheesy sauce of herbs and vegetables. Spinach lasagna and mushroom-cheese pie are other new favorites. A children's menu is offered at each meal so that you can order the kinds of things kids like in quantities appropriate to their appetites.

The view of the mountains from the dining room is so breath-taking I like to take a long time to eat. The view remains perfect, as ever. And now, with committed, enthusiastic new ownership, Nantahala Village gets better and better. That's good news for those of us who love the mountains and the Nantahala Gorge.

How to get there: The inn is 9 miles southwest of Bryson City on Highway 19.

Randolph House
Country Inn
Bryson City, North Carolina
28713

Innkeepers: Bill and Ruth Randolph Adams
Address/Telephone: Fryemont Road (mailing address: P.O. Box 816); (704) 488–3472
Rooms: 7; 3 with private bath, some with wheelchair access.
Rates: $50 to $75, per person, breakfast and dinner. AAA, senior citizen, and travel agent discounts.
Open: April through October.
Facilities and activities: Dining room and terrace open to public (reservation preferred). Wheelchair access. Wine cellar. Nearby: Great Smoky Mountains National Park, Fontana Lake, Museum of the Cherokee Indian, the Oconaluftee Indian Village, outdoor drama *Unto These Hills*, Nantahala Gorge, Smoky Mountain Railroad excursion tours, hiking, rafting, fishing, tennis, and horseback riding.

When you realize how often innkeepers of historic inns have to answer the same questions and tell the same stories, you appreciate those who can do it without losing their enthusiasm. On that score, Ruth Adams is the best I've seen. Or heard.

She's the niece of the original owner, who built the house in 1895. When I was there, she told me in considerable detail how Amos Frye had owned all the timber in sight but had been forced to sell it when the government decided that it should be national forestland. She said that he'd kept the right to lumber out of those acres for a time and consequently had set to building. It turned out to be the kind of story that gets you involved and carried on by her enthusiasm. I soaked up all the details. Later, I heard her telling parts of the story on the telephone. And that night at dinner, I heard her tell the history twice. Her last telling was as enthusiastic as her first had been.

She radiates the same enthusiasm for the inn itself. As she showed me around, she said, "All the furniture doesn't match. It's just here because it was always here." And she pointed out that one of the rooms has the same furniture with which the Fryes started housekeeping. She showed me the unconventional way that the beds were arranged in some of the rooms, just as they are in any house where you accumulate more furniture than you can accommodate. We admired an old leather chair and a rocker with a needlepoint cushion in the living room. We even got a giggle out of the old-fashioned push-button electric switches in the walls.

Ruth cooks some of the best Southern meals I've ever tasted. When you make a reservation, you have to choose from a list of entrees offered that night, and, for me, the choice was hard because they all sounded so good: Cornish game hens in orange sauce, sautéed shrimp, baked trout, and prime rib of beef. I couldn't pass up the chance for pan-fried trout. It was rolled in cornmeal and then fried in a small amount of fat in an iron skillet. Wonderful! Along with the trout, I had baked spinach Provençal, warm spiced apples, squash casserole, and a baked potato. The vegetables were fresh. They always are.

How to get there: From Asheville take I–40 west to Highway 19/74 to the second Bryson City exit. Turn right off expressway to the first street on right, Fryemont Road. Follow the RANDOLPH HOUSE signs.

S: *Lots of inns make you feel at home. Everything about this one makes you feel that it is a home.*

The Homeplace
Charlotte, North Carolina
28226

Innkeepers: Peggy and Frank Dearien
Address/Telephone: 5901 Sardis Road; (704) 365–1936
Rooms: 3; all with private bath. No smoking inn.
Rates: $68, single; $78, double; full breakfast.
Open: Year-round.
Facilities and activities: Nearby: restaurants, shopping malls, museums, antiques shops, textile and furniture outlets.

Don't even think about trying to stay here without making a reservation ahead of time. The Homeplace has become extraordinarily popular and is always busy. It has also become one of the area's most frequently photographed inns, appearing on the covers of travel guides and cookbooks, in television commercials and newspaper articles.

The inn *looks* like everybody's notion of what a country inn should be. It's a large Victorian farmhouse, painted a creamy color, trimmed in white, with rust-colored shutters. The wraparound porch with rockers looks like a set from "The Waltons."

For me, the pleasant surprise is that the interior is light and cheerful, with none of the dimness that can be part of the whole Victorian look, especially in the South, where families kept rooms dark in summer to keep them cool.

Furnished with antiques and family treasures, the inn also

serves as a sort of gallery for the primitive paintings of Peggy's father, John Gentry. Although he didn't begin painting until he was seventy-nine, his work quickly became popular. For a while, the family sold some of it, but since he died at the age of ninety-one, having painted until just six months earlier, no more of his work is for sale. It's just too much a part of the family, and it's not a renewable resource now.

The renewable resource, apparently, is the enthusiasm and energy the Deariens bring to innkeeping. They've withstood all the typical crises of innkeeping as well as some major ones, such as Hurricane Hugo, which ripped up roofs and hundred-year-old oaks in Charlotte, leaving the city without power for about two weeks. The Homeplace not only remained open but also handled two wedding receptions right after the storm hit. Somehow the Deariens managed to convince guests that having Frank cook their breakfast on an outdoor gas grill under an umbrella was fun and that candlelight was romantic.

Ordinarily, when electricity is on, The Homeplace smells like the back room of a bakery most of the time, as Peggy makes up a steady supply of homemade breads for breakfast and cake and cookies for evening tea.

The Deariens' involvement with the inn, in decorating, maintaining, hosting, and cooking, makes it a special place. (Many of the inns that no longer appear in this guide had to be dropped, basically, because the people who ran them stopped caring and their indifference showed in everything from how they handled reservations to what they served for breakfast.) A few words on the telephone, a look around the property, and a whiff of homemade cookies are all you'll need to agree with me—the Deariens aren't going to stop caring.

How to get there: From I–77, follow Tyvola Road through South Park, where it becomes Fairview Road and crosses Providence Road. Where Fairview crosses Providence, it becomes Sardis Road. Ask for a map and specific directions from other points when you make reservations.

The Inn on Providence
Charlotte, North Carolina
28226

Innkeepers: Darlene and Dan McNeill
Address/Telephone: 6700 Providence Road; (704) 366–6700
Rooms: 5; 3 with private bath, television on request. No smoking inn.
Rates: $59 to $79, single or double, extended continental breakfast.
Open: Year-round.
Facilities and activities: Swimming pool. Nearby: restaurants, easy access to downtown Charlotte.

Darlene's the kind of innkeeper who can greet you at the door in her bare feet and still look as elegant as the inn. The inn is filled with early American antiques and many pieces from New England.

Darlene collects quilts. She has taken advantage of the inn's high ceilings and large expanses of wall to display many of them.

The inn has a walnut-paneled library, a formal sitting room with a fireplace, and a lovely dining room with an oak floor. The veranda, however, steals the show. It overlooks an oval swimming pool with a brick walk, boxwoods, and flowers all around it. It has a slate floor and is screened against summer bugs. A white wicker settee and chairs invite evening conversation. When the weather is suitable, you eat breakfast here at a little white table with ladderback chairs and a pastel cloth. Pink-and-blue cushions and accessories pick up the pastel theme. Another of Darlene's quilts hangs on the brick wall. Ferns and ficus plants make it feel like a garden room.

The guest rooms are furnished in antiques, including a cannonball bed covered with a signed antique quilt in the Plantation Room. My favorite room is the suite with a queen-sized brass bed, a ceiling fan, and a nice sitting area.

Darlene's breakfasts go well beyond the croissant-and-coffee category. Her specialty is heart-shaped Norwegian waffles with berries. She doesn't serve dinner but likes to send guests to Fenwicks, a small local restaurant also on Providence Road, where the specialty is mesquite-grilled steak.

Wherever you are in the house, you can hear classical music. Together with the relaxing decor, it is a good place to unwind after a day of "city jangles" or interstate driving.

How to get there: The inn is on Highway 16 about 1 mile north of Highway 51 in south Charlotte. From I–85 or I–77 at Charlotte, take the Brookshire Freeway (Highway 16). Go south on 16 to the Third/Fourth Street exit. This will continue as 16 South, which eventually becomes Providence Road. The inn is on the corner of Providence and Rea roads.

Windsong
Clyde, North Carolina
28721

Innkeepers: Donna and Gale Livengood

Address/Telephone: 120 Ferguson Ridge; (704) 627–6111

Rooms: 5; all with private bath, separate vanity and soaking tub, deck or patio, and fireplace. No air conditioning (elevation 3,000 feet). No smoking inn. One cottage.

Rates: $90 to $95, double; single and weekly rates 10 percent less; full breakfast. Extra person in room, $20. Inquire about cottage rates.

Open: Year-round.

Facilities and activities: VCRs and extensive videocassette library, guest lounge with refrigerator and wet bar (brown bagging), piano, pool table; washer and dryer on request; swimming pool, tennis court, hiking trails, llama treks. Nearby: restaurants, Great Smoky Mountain National Park, Asheville and historic sites, Biltmore House, craft and antiques shops, horseback riding.

I like this place so much that if I use every word of praise that comes to mind you'll think it's too good to be true. Donna and Gale built the rustic log building specifically to be a small inn and their own home. It has light pine-log walls and floors of Mexican saltillo tile. The rooms are large, with high, beamed ceilings. Skylights and huge windows let in light on all sides. The building perches on the side of a mountain at 3,000 feet so that looking out the front windows in the direction the guest rooms face, you get a panoramic view of woods and rolling fields below; looking out the back from the kitchen and entry, you see more wilderness higher up and, closer to the house, the perennial gardens, terraces, and recreational facilities.

In addition to sliding glass doors to let you look down the mountain, each guest room has either a deck or a ground-level patio where you can sit to watch the llamas that the Livengoods keep in some of the lower pastures.

Donna decorated the guest rooms in witty, sophisticated styles, using mostly items her family has gathered living in distant places: hence the Alaska Room with Eskimo carvings and art and a dogsled in the corner; hence the Santa Fe Room with Mexican furniture and a steerhide rug. I like the Safari Room. Mosquito netting is draped over the head of the bed, and the room is decorated with primitive artifacts, vines, and bamboo. Dieffenbachia and other junglelike plants flank the big soaking tub in the corner. A little sculptured giraffe with extra-long legs peers out at you from the greenery.

Two new developments here may catch your fancy. The Livengoods' daughter Sara manages the beautiful herd of llamas, which not only adorn the surrounding hills but also are the focus of gourmet picnic and overnight hikes they call "llama treks." This is a delightful way to backpack without using your own back.

And higher on the hill a small cabin with kitchen, loft bedroom, and wood stove that would be nice for a family or two couples is just being opened for occupancy.

How to get there: From I–40, take exit 24. Go north on U.S. 209 for 2½ miles. Turn left on Riverside Drive and go 2 miles. Turn right on Ferguson Cove Loop and go 1 mile, keeping to the left. You'll be driving straight up some narrow, unpaved roads. The distance will seem longer than it is.

❀

S: *It seems to be the custom on these mountain roads for local drivers to pull to the side and give strangers right-of-way.*

Jarrett House
Dillsboro, North Carolina
28725

Innkeepers: Jim and Jean Hartbarger
Address/Telephone: Dillsboro (mailing address: P.O. Box 219); (704) 586–9964 or (800) 972–5623
Rooms: 18; all with private bath, some with wheelchair access.
Rates: $40, single or double; $3 each additional person; full breakfast (Saturday and Sunday only) is extra. No credit cards.
Open: Mid-April to October 31, full service. From October 31 to Christmas, rooms available only on weekends; meals available daily.
Facilities and activities: Lunch, dinner; dining room, with wheelchair access, open to public; brown bagging permitted. "Eatin' and talkin' and rockin'."—*Jim Hartbarger*

Jarrett House is famous for its food, so I'll tell you about that first. It's been a matter of pride since the inn began business back in the 1800s that the table be so generous that no one should ever have to ask for seconds. All I can say is that anybody who would dare eat more than is offered had better bring along a couple of Weight Watchers counselors.

For lunch, I had country ham (I could have had fried chicken). That was the only choice I had to make, except for a beverage. Everything else came automatically—green beans, slaw, pickled beets with onion, candied apples, browned potatoes, and a seemingly endless supply of the lightest little biscuits I've ever tasted. A squeeze bottle on the table was filled with honey for the biscuits. Jim said that after a full season he sometimes got a little tired of country ham and fried chicken, but he never got tired of those biscuits!

After all that, I wished I could have ordered a cot to take a nap. And that was just lunch. After a big dinner here, I'd need a hospital bed.

But after-meal dozing is what the rockers on the porch are for.

For serious sleeping, the guest rooms, furnished in an assortment of oak, walnut, and cherry antiques, are nice. Everything is squeaky clean, a feeling enhanced by the white chenille bedspreads. Most of the rooms have claw-footed bathtubs.

The double-wide hallway upstairs is lined with well-used antiques, old sewing machines, an unusual oak desk, and an interesting oak washstand. It all looks as if someone will be using it again in the next hour or so—no museum-sense here.

Downstairs, the Victorian parlor is almost eerie in the feeling it gives you that any second the old inhabitants will come in and sit down. In one corner, an old Bacon & Ravern piano that belonged to Jim's mother is partly covered by a lovely folded lace tablecloth. On the wall is a framed hanging of the Lord's Prayer that she crocheted when she was ninety-two years old. Something about its intricate detail and beauty makes just looking at it a prayerful act.

How to get there: Dillsboro is 47 miles west of Asheville. Routes 19A/441 and 23/19A form an intersection in town. The inn is on the corner at the intersection.

S: *Because I know how hard innkeepers work, I marveled at how rested and energetic Jim Hartbarger looked, and I commented on it. He said that it was because he enjoyed his guests and added that after years as a basketball coach, innkeeping was a piece of cake.*

The Lords Proprietors' Inn
Edenton, North Carolina
27932

Innkeeper: Sandy Hendee; Arch and Jane Edwards, proprietors
Address/Telephone: 300 North Broad Street; (919) 482–3641
Rooms: 20; all with private bath, television, VCR, and telephone.
Rates: $53 to $70, single; $80 to $120, double; full breakfast. Extra person in
room, $15. No credit cards.
Open: Year-round.
Facilities and activities: Gift shop. Nearby: restaurants, waterfront parks, guid-
ed walking tours of Edenton Historic District, Hope Plantation tours,
Somerset Place tours.

This inn has earned a reputation as one of the most elegant
and gracious inns in the state. Three separate restored buildings—
the White-Bond House, the Satterfield House, and the Pack
House—in the historic district cluster around a lawn and gardens;
these buildings house the guest rooms and three big parlors. Breakfast is served at the Whedbee House, set on a brick patio surrounded by dogwoods in the center of the complex. The Pack House was
originally a tobacco barn that was sawed in half and brought to the
grounds in two pieces. Its conversion created lodging with huge
amounts of open space, vast floors, and soaring ceilings. The guest
rooms open onto a balcony that runs around the inside of the
building and overlooks the common rooms. The feeling of openness
is accentuated by old pine floors that are covered only with area rag

rugs, and a whimsical wallpaper border that runs around the room about waist high. Old chests and chintz upholstery fit comfortably into the scene.

Edenton is on the Albermarle Sound. It differs from many waterfront communities in having kept the waterfront for parks and homes rather than commercial activities.

Edenton boasts a lot of history. Settled in 1685 and incorporated in 1722 as the first capital of the province of North Carolina, the town has kept alive the memories of its early leaders, men who signed the Declaration of Independence, supplied Washington's army in defiance of British blockades, and convinced the people of North Carolina to ratify the new United States Constitution. Nor has the town forgotten its women. A bronze teapot memorial marks the spot of the Edenton Tea Party, where in 1774 fifty-one local women resolved to eschew English tea and clothing in support of the rebelling provincial congress.

Many of the people in the community are direct descendants of those early leaders. Those descendants and others who care have turned virtually the entire community into a project of historic preservation.

Arch and Jane Edwards are deeply involved in the community and offer a special weekend package to guests for winter weekend tours of four private historic homes not usually open to the public, capped by a reception at the last home toured and a candlelight dinner in the Whedbee House on Saturday night. A call to the inn gets you full details on these uncommon weekends.

The Edwardses' hospitality extends to inviting guests to use their residential swimming pool and to tour their private home, an authentically restored house of the 1800s.

How to get there: Edenton is 90 miles east of I–95 at the junction of highways 17 and 32. Broad Street runs through the center of town.

Woodfield Inn
Flat Rock, North Carolina
28731

Innkeeper: Jean Smith

Address/Telephone: Highway 25 South (mailing address: P.O. Box 98); (704) 693–6016 or (800) 533–6016

Rooms: 18; 9 with private bath. No air conditioning (elevation 2,214 feet).

Rates: $40 to $100, depending on time of year, day of week, type of accommodations, and number in party; continental breakfast. Inquire for specifics.

Open: Year-round.

Facilities and activities: Dinner, open to public every day but Tuesday; wheelchair access to dining room. Television lounge, game area, nature trail. Nearby: Carl Sandburg House, antiques and craft shops, golf, Flat Rock Playhouse, easy access to Blue Ridge Parkway.

Woodfield Inn used to be called Farmer Hotel, which has a ring to it, but this inn deserves a classier name than Farmer. It has twenty-two working fireplaces, guest parlors filled with antiques, and three dining rooms. If you are interested in the Victorian era, the place is as informative as a museum but a lot more relaxed.

Whatever its name, the Woodfield has been an inn all the 135-plus years of its existence. History has left its marks on the building. In one room, a hole in the wood floor opens into a 3-by-10-foot room where local people hid their valuables from General Sherman's troops during the Civil War.

Much of the furniture has been in place since the inn first opened. The old brass hardware remains intact. In the entry hall, the new wallpaper is an exact reproduction of the original. An ornate and preposterously large bench and matching chair in the entry are Chinese pieces from the 1860s that the Smiths suspect were manufactured strictly for export.

The Woodfield dining room attracts people from all over the surrounding area. The main dining room is attractive without being excessive. Many hanging ferns recall the Victorian era. Dinner is served by candlelight, and the fresh flowers on the tables come from gardens on the property. The food is mountain and Continental cuisine. The selections on the menu have nearly doubled since my first visit to Woodfield Inn. These days, baked ham, mountain trout, and prime rib are the best-sellers.

Whether you go for dinner or spend a night, please allow some time for enjoying the veranda. I'm not talking just of rocking and chatting. The inn is on a little rise in the middle of a large expanse of grass that is kept mowed, but not golf-course short. The mowed-hay fragrance carried to you on the breezes of a mountain day, along with a rock garden full of dahlias and geraniums to look at, and birdsong nearly the only sound to break the silence, seem to me the epitome of what country inns are supposed to be about.

How to get there: Woodfield Inn is on Highway 25 South, 2¹/₂ miles south of Hendersonville, on the east side of Flat Rock. It is clearly marked with signs.

La Grange Plantation Inn
Henderson, North Carolina
27536

Innkeepers: Dick and Jean Cornell
Address/Telephone: State Route 1308 (mailing address: Route 3, Box 610); (919) 438–2421
Rooms: 5; all with private bath, 1 with wheelchair access. No smoking inn.
Rates: $75, single; $85, double; full gourmet breakfast in the dining room or continental breakfast in your room. Inquire about discounts for consecutive night stays.
Open: Year-round.
Facilities and activities: Swimming pool, lakeside fishing, walking trails, croquet, horseshoes. Nearby: restaurants, golf, boat ramps, swimming beaches, picnic grounds on several state recreation areas; water skiing, sailing, fishing on Kerr Lake.

I recommended this place to my friends the Jacobys and then waited nervously to hear whether they enjoyed it as much as I had. When Jay Jacoby began his report, it didn't sound good. "Everything was so empty as we drove up from Raleigh; I wondered if we were making a mistake."

I started wondering how mad at me he was.

"But then we rang the bell and Jean Cornell opened the door, and the instant we were across the threshold I knew everything was perfect."

What Jay saw as "empty" I consider "rural," which pleases me.

Being more of a city boy, Jay probably had to adjust. But there's nothing rural inside La Grange Plantation Inn. The Cornells are sophisticated innkeepers (Jean is English) with exquisite taste. The place is furnished with American and English antiques in what Jean calls "relaxed English country style."

The front parlor has a wonderful fireplace, books ranging from current fiction to history and natural studies, and no television to break the mood. The Cornells, who are great readers, count among their enthusiastic guests the owners of a bookstore in Raleigh, so it's no surprise that one outstanding feature of all the guest rooms is a good bedside reading light.

To decorate the guest rooms, Jean made the window treatments and bed coverings herself, different in each room and elegant—made of rich fabrics, full of flowers, in muted colors.

The private baths are clustered in a central location just outside the rooms; Jean provides plush terry robes for guests to move from their rooms to their bathrooms but allows that you don't have to use a robe "if you'd rather streak!"

Turning La Grange into an inn was a major project. The Historic Preservation Foundation of North Carolina described the inn in an issue of its magazine, *North Carolina Preservation,* as a "two-story double-pile Greek Revival house with Italianate brackets," the oldest part of which was built in 1770. When the Cornells bought it in 1985, it was a wreck. Windows rattled, the plaster had big cracks, and the foundation wobbled. It took a lot of time and money as well as the expertise of an architect and an architectural conservator working with a contractor to restore the house to historic preservation standards and also make it comfortable. The Cornells did the interior painting and finished the floors themselves. Today the interior and the hospitality are, as my friends the Jacobys found them, "perfect."

How to get there: From I–85 take exit 214 to N.C. Route 39 North and proceed 4²/₅ miles to Harris Crossroads. There is a state sign pointing right to Nutbush Creek Recreation Area. Turn right and proceed ⁴/₅ mile to the inn, which is on the left.

The Waverly Inn
Hendersonville, North Carolina
28739

Innkeepers: John and Diane Sheiry
Address/Telephone: 783 North Main Street; (704) 693–9193 or (800) 537–8195
Rooms: 16; all with private bath.
Rates: $75 to $89, double; single, $10 less; full breakfast.
Open: Year-round.
Facilities and activities: Nearby: restaurants, hiking, tennis, miniature golf, antiques and crafts shops; easy drive to Biltmore Estate, Carl Sandburg home, Flat Rock Playhouse.

Waverly opened its doors in 1898 and has never been closed since. Many of the guests come back year after year to cool off. Some stay for weeks at a time. Hendersonville is a mountain town where people have gone for years to escape the summer heat. Even on the hottest days you can expect to sleep under blankets at night. But don't worry about unexpected heat waves. All rooms are air-conditioned just in case.

John and Diane have between them twenty years' experience in the hotel business. They chose Hendersonville and the Waverly because they wanted to get out of the fast-track life that kept John traveling most of the time and made it hard for them to nurture family life. It's not that they work less as keepers of a small inn but that now they can work together, at home. In recent years they have contributed a high level of innkeeping professionalism to the area.

Their values line up beautifully with the family orientation that has traditionally been typical of Waverly, but I see growth here, too. These days, Waverly attracts guests in addition to those escaping the heat: overnight travelers looking for a place more interesting than a motel and vacationers looking for lodging with a personal feel. The result is a fascinating mix. You can see it on the porch—young travelers, middle-aged couples, retired people, and families with children, not just occupying rockers side by side, but talking and actually listening to one another.

It's a good setup for socializing. In addition to using the porch, guests can gather in the library or in the Victorian parlor, where a fireplace is the focal point on nippy evenings. There are sitting rooms on all three floors.

John and Diane have renovated Waverly extensively and have furnished the place with the kind of turn-of-the-century mix you'd have expected to find originally in such a home.

Waverly still emphasizes service so complete you can only think of it as personal favors. John said, "We dote on our guests. We'll take you to church, get your car fixed, answer questions, and get your travel information."

Gee, I wonder if they'd marry me?

Two additions to the inn's activities, Murder Mystery weekends and Wine Lovers' weekends, are turning out to be a lot of fun for guests and for John and Diane. On weekends when these are scheduled, the inn accepts reservations only for people planning to participate, so you don't have to worry about arriving and finding yourself in the middle of "Murder, She Wrote" if that's not what you had in mind.

For the mystery weekends, the actors check in the same as any other guests, so you really have no idea who is a player and who is not until the whole thing is over. The wine weekends include a French meal and an Italian dinner, preceded by a tasting and discussion of five French or Italian wines and served with three more. Time is set aside at the end of the meal for questions and conversation. Diane says that after either kind of weekend guests inevitably go home feeling they've made some new friends.

The Waverly Inn is listed on the National Register of Historic Places.

How to get there: Take Route 64 or 25 into Hendersonville, directly to Main Street.

Hidden Crystal Inn
Hiddenite, North Carolina
28636

Innkeepers: Richard and Jeanne Pleasants; Eileen Lackey Sharpe, owner
Address/Telephone: Sulphur Springs Road; (704) 632–0063
Rooms: 10; all with private bath and television, 1 with Jacuzzi and fireplace,
1 with wheelchair access. Cottage available. Inquire for details.
Rates: $65, single; $75, double; $85, bridal room; full breakfast.
Open: Year-round.
Facilities and activities: Dinner by reservation, brown bagging permitted, pic-
nic baskets, wheelchair access to dining room. Swimming pool, cro-
quet, badminton, paddle tennis, volleyball. Nearby: Hiddenite Center
and Lucas Mansion Museum a short walk away; Emerald Hollow
Mine, hiking, official North Carolina Bicycle Trail, folk arts.

Rock hounds know about Hiddenite. Rock hounds are those
folks who dig and sift and sluice through buckets of dirt looking for
gemstones. The town is named for the gemstone and, of course, the
inn is named for the town, with oblique reference to the Emerald
Hollow Mine just down the road. Here's how you put it all together
for a better-than-average good time.

Make reservations for dinner. Wear scrungy clothes and pack
your bathing suit and something nice to put on for dinner. Spend a
morning or an afternoon at the mine sluicing. (Take rubber gloves
if you worry about your hands.) You might want to take one of the
inn's picnic lunches, since the mine has picnic facilities. Take your

finds to Hiddenite Gems, at the mine, to arrange to have your stones cut or polished and turned into jewelry. (I now have a pendant of amethyst and one of snowflake obsidian.)

Return to the inn, being sure to take off your muddy shoes before you go in, and have a snack, lounge around the pool, look at the changing exhibits in the museum across the yard, and maybe catch a little nap. Before dinner, sip your wine in the living room and wander into the North Carolina Room to study the beautiful North Carolina gems and minerals displayed in the lighted cases. If your sluicing didn't amount to much, you may not be able to resist buying a piece of jewelry made by local silversmiths from local semiprecious stones. Do all this slowly to save energy for dinner, which is sumptuous to the point of being overwhelming. I had a creamy seafood and pasta dish with fresh vegetables and, for dessert, lemon meringue pie. You'll work out the details of your own dinner when you call for your reservations, so you may have something altogether different. The inn staff is *very* receptive to special requests.

After dinner, look around the house a little more. In the foyer, you can study a mural of the county's landscape; on the landing of the stairs, you'll notice a large smoky quartz crystal that came from the mines in Hiddenite. Then, just wander around the house, catching all the art and gem displays and antiques you missed the first time. Seldom do you find so many pretty things in one place.

By now, you should be sleepy enough to retreat to the quiet of your room. If you stay in the Garnet Room, you'll have a king-sized bed and a painting by the same artist who painted the mural in the foyer.

Morning brings a huge gourmet breakfast with as much coffee as you want, as well as anything special you may have arranged for ahead of time. If you prefer not to indulge in two heavy meals in such a short time, you can arrange for something lighter, either for breakfast or dinner, when you make your reservations.

I've just described the outing my husband and I had here; we can't wait to go back.

How to get there: Hiddenite is 65 miles from both Charlotte and Winston-Salem on Highway 90. The inn is right on the through street. You will receive a map when you make reservations.

The Lodge on Lake Lure
Lake Lure, North Carolina
28746

Innkeepers: Jack and Robin Stanier
Address/Telephone: Charlotte Drive (mailing address: Route One, Box 529A);
   (704) 625–2789
Rooms: 11; all with private bath.
Rates: $75 to $130, single or double, full gourmet breakfast. Inquire about
   discounts for week-long stays.
Open: February to January.
Facilities and activities: Lakefront, fishing, canoes, boathouse and boat rentals.
   Nearby: restaurants, 2 golf courses, hiking, tubing, tennis, horseback
   riding, antiques and crafts shops.

"The outside of the building doesn't tell the story; the view
tells the story," Robin said. The lodge is built in European hunting-
lodge style; it sort of nestles into the lakeside without calling much
attention to itself. Inside, the high, vaulted ceilings, hand-hewn
beams, and huge stone fireplaces make you think of a very *good*
hunting lodge, but Robin is right—the genius of the place is in the
long row of windows and the porch facing the lake that take full
advantage of the view that one suspects could exist only here in the
Blue Ridge Mountains.

The genius apart from the view is in the innkeepers, who've
patterned their operation on a famous inn in Mexico that they visited more than twenty-five years ago. The experience delighted them

174

so much that all this time they've wanted to go and do likewise. Now they have—in their own style. What Robin liked especially about the Mexican inn was that "it attracted great guests." So does the Lodge on Lake Lure.

It's a matter of kindred spirits. If you want Italian marble baths and gold fixtures, the lodge isn't the place to look. But if you like overstuffed chairs pulled around the fireplace, rooms with wormy-chestnut walls and four-poster beds, breakfasts ranging from banana-buckwheat pancakes to eggs Benedict, and straight-forward innkeepers with more than a tad of humor, you'll love the lodge and, by definition, become one of the great guests.

Let me illustrate that "tad of humor." The special suite at the inn, the kind that is often referred to as a honeymoon suite at inns, here is called the "Something Suite," because the Staniers don't want a special weekend to seem limited to honeymooners. The "something" is whatever special reason you want a special room. I suggested several other possible names for it because Robin said they really should get it named, but in my heart I am sure it will remain the Something Suite. I hope so.

Although an inn's history isn't as important as its beds and food, it is fun, since the beds and food are in such good shape, to know about the lodge's racy past. It was built as a getaway for the state highway patrol back in 1930, and *everybody* knows those guys didn't go up there back then to knit bonnets for their grandmothers! While you're in town, get the old-timers to tell you stories.

How to get there: From I–26, take Highway 64/74 to Lake Lure. The lodge is on Charlotte Drive, just off Highway 64/74. Turn at the Lake Lure fire station opposite the golf course. Ask for a map when you make reservations.

S: *The view from the porch dining room, across the lake to the mountains, changes beautifully minute by minute.*

Greystone Inn
Lake Toxaway, North Carolina
28747

Innkeeper: Tim Lovelace

Address/Telephone: Greystone Lane; (704) 966–4700; outside North Carolina, (800) 824–5766

Rooms: 33; all with private bath, Jacuzzi, television, and telephone, some with fireplace and private balcony.

Rates: $109 to $210, per person, breakfast and dinner, afternoon tea and cakes, and all recreational activities except golf fees. Inquire about children's rates.

Open: April 11 through New Year's weekend.

Facilities and activities: Library-lounge with facilities to store and serve alcohol brought by guests (inn is in a dry county). Lake for swimming, boating, waterskiing, and fishing; golf course, tennis courts. Nearby: hiking, scenic drives, antiques and resort shops.

I drove so high up into the mountains to find Lake Toxaway that I didn't expect to find much in the way of civilization when I got there. Then I turned off the narrow road into a drive, and the Greystone Inn seemed to rise from the lake like Camelot.

The Greystone used to be the private mansion of Lucy Moltz. When she first decided that she wanted to build a summer place in the woods beside Lake Toxaway, her husband, apparently a practical man, suggested that she camp out there for a while first to see if she really liked it. This she did—in a 14,000-square-foot tent with hardwood floors staffed with eleven servants. And that was rustic compared with the inn today.

Innkeeper Tim Lovelace has worked hard to keep the intimate feeling of visiting a private home, but make no mistake—most of us don't know any private homes as luxurious as this to visit. Every room in the inn has a magnificent view of the lake or grounds and is furnished in antiques and period reproductions similar to the furniture Mrs. Moltz had. The color television sets are hidden in armoires. The rooms are named after the wealthy and famous people who used to visit Mrs. Moltz: Vanderbilt, Rockefeller, Wanamaker.

Guests dine in the new Lakeside Dining Room, where every table has a great view of the water and the cuisine is gourmet.

But as lovely as everything is inside the inn, the outdoor activities thrilled me more. In good weather, Tim leads hikes along Horse Pasture River past three magnificent waterfalls. During the warmer months, he takes guests out on the lake on the party boat to watch the sunset. When the leaves are in color, the beauty of sailing or canoeing along the lake's 13 miles of shoreline can be an almost religious experience.

How to get there: The inn is in Western North Carolina 50 miles south of Asheville. It is off U.S. 64, 10 miles east of Cashiers and 17 miles west of Brevard. Turn into the Lake Toxaway entrance. It is clearly marked. Follow the signs 4 miles to the inn. Because you are driving steep, winding roads, it will feel longer, but keep going.

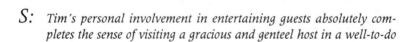

S: *Tim's personal involvement in entertaining guests absolutely completes the sense of visiting a gracious and genteel host in a well-to-do household.*

Big Lynn Lodge
Little Switzerland, North Carolina
28749

Innkeepers: Gale and Carol Armstrong
Address/Telephone: Route 226A (mailing address: P.O. Box 459); (704) 765–4257 or (800) 654–5232
Rooms: 38, plus 4 suites in adjacent building; all with private bath.
Rates: $73 to $105, double, breakfast and dinner. Inquire about single rates.
Open: April 16 to November 1.
Facilities and activities: No smoking in dining rooms. Player piano, television lounge, gift shop, shuffleboard, horseshoes, nature trails. Nearby: hiking, golf, fishing, horseback riding, gemstone mines, craft shops, potteries, weekly square dancing in town hall, easy access to Blue Ridge Parkway.

The outstanding feature about the Big Lynn Lodge is its location near the Blue Ridge Parkway and the absolutely astounding view. The cool summer days attract many people, too. From Little Switzerland, you can see the Black Mountains, Grandfather Mountain, Roan, Humpback, Iron, Beech, and Laurel mountains, and more than a half dozen others, depending on the clarity of the day. Sometimes you can sit here, practically up as high as heaven, and watch pockets of fog and haze form and dissipate so far below that they seem to have nothing to do with you. The air in the area is unpolluted and clear.

Many retired people stay here for days, even weeks, at a time.

During the peak of the season, about August, the inn has few rooms available for a single night.

The dining room does not serve fried food at dinner. The vegetables are steamed, not boiled. Each meal includes salad, meat, three vegetables, fresh homemade bread, and dessert. The food is what I think of as old-fashioned American: roast beef, trout, chicken.

Relatively few young people stay here, but the inn welcomes them, and, on occasion, the porch or lounge becomes another of those rare places where young and old meet and talk and decide that they can have a lot of fun spending time with friends outside their own age group. Down with demographics.

The rooms are comfortable and modern, in long, low buildings facing the view of mountains and valleys below. It would be hard to find any place where there isn't something spectacular to look at—wildflowers and dogwood in the spring, brilliant hardwood foliage in autumn.

Next to the main inn is a building with four condos, built in 1989. These condos are being rented as luxurious suites with king-sized beds, living and dining rooms, full kitchens, whirlpool tubs in the baths, and private balconies. And, of course, that same astonishing view.

How to get there: From the Blue Ridge Parkway, take the Little Switzerland exit. Turn left. The inn is 1 1/4 miles from the exit. From I–40, take Route 226 North at Marion. Drive about 20 miles to the top of the mountain, then turn left on 226A, which takes you directly to the inn.

The Tranquil House Inn
Manteo, North Carolina
27954

Innkeeper: James Gotsch

Address/Telephone: Queen Elizabeth Street (mailing address: P.O. Box 2045); (919) 473–1404 or (800) 458–7069

Rooms: 28; all with private bath, television, and telephone, some with wheelchair access. No-smoking rooms available.

Rates: $55 to $145, single or double, seasonal; continental breakfast each morning and wine at check-in. No charge for 1 or 2 children under 16 in the same room.

Open: Year-round.

Facilities and activities: Library with fireplace, full-service marina, touring bikes, gas grill for cookouts. Nearby: walk to restaurants and shops; Fort Raleigh National Historic Site, Elizabeth II State Historic Site, Elizabethan Gardens, North Carolina Aquarium, all kinds of fishing.

The Tranquil House Inn is strikingly attractive, inside and out. The building is a reproduction of a typical turn-of-the-century Outer Banks inn. The interior, done in cypress, furnished with light pine furniture and decorated with oriental rugs, seems as bright and sunny as the docks outside. Stained-glass windows and fresh flowers in the guest rooms whisper luxury. Perhaps because of its location right on Shallowbag Bay, a sense of quiet permeates the place, even though it is close to Manteo's tourist activities.

And, nice as it is, you probably won't spend many daylight hours in the inn, because there is so much to do in and around

Manteo. The Manteo Walking Tour takes a couple of hours and instructs you in much of the area's early history, including the mystery of the colony set up by Sir Walter Raleigh that disappeared sometime between 1587 and 1591, while its leader was away procuring supplies.

People fish and crab right from the docks here, and the inn has bikes if you want to pedal around the rest of the town.

When you need to sit down for a while, one of the most popular spots inside the inn is a little library on the first floor with rockers and a leather couch, a writing desk, books to borrow, and a gas-log fireplace for cool evenings. If you prefer to be outside when you can, you'll like the rocker-lined wraparound porches from which you can watch boats maneuvering in and out of their slips in the marina.

At dinnertime, it's fun to take the short walk to Clara's Seafood Grill, also on the waterfront, reputed to serve the best crab cakes in town. (The menu says "more crab than cake.") It's an upscale place, as is the inn, but dress is casual enough to allow for walking shoes and shorts.

How to get there: Take Highway 64 from the west or Highway 158 from the north. Follow the signs for the Elizabeth II State Historic Site. You'll see the inn on the Manteo waterfront. Sir Walter Raleigh Street leads directly to the inn.

Harmony House Inn
New Bern, North Carolina
28560

Innkeepers: Buzz and Diane Hansen
Address/Telephone: 215 Pollock Street; (919) 636–3810
Rooms: 9; all with private bath and television, telephone on request.
Rates: $55, single; $80, double; full breakfast.
Open: Year-round.
Facilities and activities: Smoking on porch only. Guest refrigerator and iron-
   ing equipment. Located in the historic district. Nearby: restaurants,
   Tryon Palace and Gardens restoration, walk to shops and marina.

If anybody ever publishes a book called *The Joy of Innkeeping,*
Buzz and Diane would have to write a chapter for it. Their professionalism and easy warmth make the name Harmony House exactly right for the inn.

The guest rooms are big and comfortable, with good beds and
lots of light. The house itself has a bizarre history, which ultimately
led to its spacious and open feel today. The circa-1850 Greek
Revival house was built by a man who had six children. To accommodate them, he made additions to the house about 1860 and
again about 1880. The kids grew up, and about 1900 two of the
sons, who both wanted to live in the house with their families,
sawed it in half and moved one half 9 feet away from the other to
add hallway, front door, staircase, and sitting room. Each family
lived in its own half for twenty years. Now it's all one house again,

but it has two stairs, halls, sitting rooms, and front doors, side-by-side. The effect is that you feel you could put in tennis courts and still have room around the edges for spectators.

Downstairs in the parlor, Diane and Buzz have assembled antiques and historic and family memorabilia. A focal point in the parlor is a pump organ from about 1875 in perfect working condition. Hearing Buzz play "Greensleeves" on the organ was a special experience.

It may be because the building is so easy to be in and the Hansens are so congenial that business travelers tend to make the inn a second home. While I was here, a lawyer stopped in unannounced with his daughter, used the phone in the inn's office, and then hurried out to the car, calling over his shoulder that the two of them would be back to spend the night on their way through tomorrow. Diane and Buzz laughed and never raised an eyebrow.

They clearly enjoy innkeeping and New Bern. New Bern is an uncommonly friendly town. The Hansens told me a story about a couple who stayed with them who were walking to a nearby restaurant where they had dinner reservations. The couple stopped to admire a well-restored old house along the way. The owners, sitting on the porch, invited the couple in to look around and have a drink. Everyone got along so well that the couple missed their reservation time completely.

How to get there: Pollock Street runs 1 block back from Tryon Place Drive, which fronts on the Trent River. Ask for a map when you make your reservation.

Pine Crest Inn
Pinehurst, North Carolina
28374

Innkeeper: Peter Barrett
Address/Telephone: Pinehurst; (919) 295–6121
Rooms: 40; all with private bath, television, and telephone, some with wheelchair access.
Rates: $45 to $65, per person, double occupancy, depending on season; single, $10 to $25 more; breakfast and dinner. Corner rooms $5 extra. Inquire about package rates including greens' fees.
Open: Year-round.
Facilities and activities: Breakfast and dinner open to the public, wheelchair access to dining room, bar. Access to Pinehurst Country Club golf course and 20 other area courses. Nearby: tennis, horseback riding, skeet shooting; fishing, sailing, and swimming on Pinehurst Lake.

You'll always find something going on at Pine Crest Inn. Most people come for the golf; Pinehurst is famous for the number and quality of its golf courses. But golf is by no means the only attraction at the inn.

The dining room is famous. Executive Chef Carl Jackson has been here more than fifty years; his assistant and nephew, Chef Peter Jackson, has been here about thirty years. Local folks as well as inn guests fill up the dining room regularly. The menu changes every day. It features everything from spaghetti to roast leg of spring lamb and homemade soups, breads, and desserts. An addition I'd like to see more often is the Happy Heart Dinner, a low-fat,

184

low-cholesterol offering available each day. As for desserts, I find the Château Margaux Sundae elegant and appropriate to our growing interest in lower-fat diets. It's made of orange sherbet, orange slices, and Château LaSalle wine.

The inn has piano-bar music for dancing in the lounge and a bartender who is also a sportswriter working in the piano bar. Sports talk is by no means limited to golf, popular as it is. The area also has good tennis and many horse farms. The local interest in horses is reflected in the recurring racing motif on draperies and upholstery fabrics throughout the inn. In one of the large corner guest rooms, most of one wall is covered with a hunt-scene mural.

For all its activity, the inn is definitely a family affair, the kind of place that includes the names and pictures of all the staff and many guests in its advertising. The easy hospitality makes you feel as though you've known everyone here forever.

How to get there: U.S. 1 and 15/501 go directly into Pinehurst. When you get into the town, follow the TO VILLAGE SHOPS signs to the market square. The inn is 1 block from the center of the village on Dogwood Street.

S: *You've heard the saying: "If God gives you lemons, make lemonade." This Sandhills area of North Carolina always makes me think that God gave the people here sand traps, so they made golf courses.*

Fearrington Inn
Pittsboro, North Carolina
27312

Innkeeper: Alan Reyburn
Address/Telephone: 2000 Fearrington Village Center; (919) 542–2121
Rooms: 14; all with private bath, television, and telephone, some with
wheelchair access.
Rates: $145 to $225, per room, full breakfast.
Open: Year-round.
Facilities and activities: Fearrington House Restaurant, with wheelchair
access, open to guests and public Tuesday through Saturday, 6:00 to
9:00 P.M., and Sunday, 6:00 to 8:00 P.M. The Fearrington Market Cafe
is open Monday through Friday for lunch and dinner, Saturday and
Sunday for brunch.

Fearrington Inn is wonderful. It's one of those cases where
there's so much to tell I'm nearly at a loss for words.

First, the inn doesn't make sense unless you know that it's part
of Fearrington Village, a growing, astonishingly tasteful planned
community near Chapel Hill. And Fearrington Village is hard to
understand unless you know that it's being created on farmland
sold by Jesse Fearrington to R. B. Fitch and his wife, Jenny. The
concept that drives the entire Fearrington Village project is to pre-
serve the farm and its buildings while creating a country village on
some of its acreage, without changing the rural feel of the place.

When you stay at the inn, you're very much a part of the village, especially if you eat (and how could you not!) at Fearrington House, the restaurant just a few steps from the inn. The restaurant, which opened several years before the inn, is in the old home place of the Fearrington farm. The inn is newly built to match the homestead.

The inn is all pale woods, wide windows, and English country decor inside and a slate courtyard with fountain defined by boxwood hedges outside. If you especially like the accessories around the inn, you can buy many of them in Jenny Fitch's shop, Dovecote: A Country Garden Shop. You can also buy a cookbook Jenny's written featuring recipes from Fearrington House Restaurant.

As Jenny explains it, the food at Fearrington House has overtones of the South, but it's not Southern cooking in the traditional sense. For instance, they might serve grits or black-eyed peas, but in new ways—black-eyed peas vinaigrette, perhaps, or grits timbale.

When I ate there, I was absolutely indifferent to whether or not the food was Southern. It was just good! I started with chilled gazpacho with dill sorbet. The dill probably came from the herb garden just outside the kitchen door. I tasted another person's smoked quail with a veal forcemeat and a red-wine sauce. Exotic. Then I dug into my entree, seared boneless loin of lamb with a bourbon-molasses-butter sauce. Certainly that's a new use of the classic Southern ingredients, bourbon and molasses.

Now there's also food for the soul here, in the form of McIntyre Book Store, an outstandingly good bookstore created in two stories of a building across from the inn. It resembles an English library. In addition to a superior collection of books, the place has comfortable chairs, a conversational grouping around a fireplace, and an active visiting-author program.

How to get there: Fearrington is 8 miles south of Chapel Hill on U.S. 15/501 toward Pittsboro.

The 1868 Stewart-Marsh House
Salisbury, North Carolina
28144

Innkeepers: Gerry and Charles Webster
Address/Telephone: 220 South Ellis Street; (704) 633–6841
Rooms: 2; both with private bath. No smoking inn.
Rates: $50 to $55, double, full breakfast. Inquire about discounts for singles and stays of more than 3 days, and about arrangements for children.
Open: Year-round.
Facilities and activities: Located in historic district. Nearby: restaurants, historic sites, golf, tennis, museums, Spencer Shops.

Chuck and Gerry, who used to live near Erie, Pennsylvania, are here for the best possible reason. They traveled throughout North Carolina and, as Gerry puts it, never saw a thing they didn't like. They agreed that when they retired to open a bed & breakfast, they'd do it somewhere in North Carolina. Ultimately, Salisbury attracted them because the town had so many homes available for historic restoration, and when their real estate agent took them to The 1868 Stewart-Marsh House, Gerry says it was as though the house opened its arms and said, "Where have you been? I've been waiting for you."

"We just loved it," Gerry says.

"It" is a nineteenth-century Federal-style home, now restored, that has a cozy pine-paneled library with a fireplace, spacious guest rooms with ceiling fans, and an elegant but simple parlor. In the dining room a 4-foot-by-7-foot pocket window has more than thirty little panes, all still the original glass. A pleasant screened porch with white wicker furniture offers a place for quiet outdoor sitting. The overall effect is light and airy. Gerry says they decided to keep the decor simple so that it would be in keeping with the house, which is not elaborate because it was built right after the Civil War, when people did not have much money to spend on houses.

Breakfast, however, is not simple by any stretch of the imagination. Gerry is always developing new specialties and uses seasonal produce. For instance, she serves fried apples with a grits and cheese and sausage casserole during the peak apple season. If you're a caffeine hound, you'll appreciate being able to arrange for early coffee—bound to bring you to breakfast in a mellow mood.

Such touches attest to Chuck and Gerry's professionalism as innkeepers. Part of their original plan included attending innkeeping workshops and working as apprentices to make sure that they were suited to the job before setting up their own inn. With innkeepers in a place they chose to be because they like it and doing work they choose to do after they had tried it, you're in for as pleasant an experience as I can imagine.

How to get there: From I–85, take the Salisbury exit, 76B. Stay on Innes Street until you come to South Ellis. Turn left. The inn is the sixth house from the corner, on the right.

Rowan Oak House
Salisbury, North Carolina
28144

Innkeepers: Bill and Ruth Ann Coffey
Address/Telephone: 208 South Fulton Street; (704) 633–2086 or (800) 786–0437
Rooms: 4; 2 with private bath, 1 with 2-person whirlpool.
Rates: $55 to $85, single; $65 to $95, double; full gourmet breakfast. Inquire about corporate rates, senior citizens' discount, and rates for stays of more than 3 days.
Open: Year-round.
Facilities and activities: Nearby: restaurants, tours of historic sites, shops, parks, golf, lake fishing.

While I was at the Rowan Oak House, a carful of women parked in the drive. They said that they were touring Salisbury and wondered if they could come in to look around.

Without hesitation, Ruth Ann let them in and took them through the house, talking cheerfully about the place the whole time.

That's the kind of person Ruth Ann is. Enthusiasm practically spills out her ears. No wonder. Bill and Ruth Ann say that finding this 1902 Queen Anne house to turn into an inn in the Salisbury historic district is a dream come true, the perfect house in the perfect town. I think they mean it.

Some of the features that so captivated the Coffeys are the

original fixtures, miraculously still in place, the stained- and lead-glass windows, and the intricately carved woodwork. At the foot of the elaborately carved staircase is a newel light unlike anything the Coffeys or any local people have ever seen. The original wallpaper is still in fine condition, too. Another uncommon feature is the fireplace in one bathroom. One room has a private porch and queen-sized bed and overlooks the garden.

The furnishings are period antiques and reproductions spiced up with such odds and ends as a dressmaker's dummy in Victorian clothes and a collection of artifacts that belonged to the home's original builder, Milton S. Brown. By artifacts, I mean his silver hair brush, a soap dish, and other personal items. It makes him seem very real.

Had Ruth Ann and Bill not found a house they liked so well, they might have opened a restaurant. Ruth Ann loves to cook. I mention it here because her breakfasts are out of the ordinary. In addition to fresh fruit and a couple of fresh homemade breads each morning, she serves such treats as egg strata, broiled grapefruit, and homemade granola. When I was there, she was experimenting with a new recipe for a poppy-seed loaf that turned out very well. The day before, she'd tried James Beard's English muffin bread. It pleased some guests; others preferred her cream-cheese coffee cake.

These goodies come to you on Wedgwood, with real silver and with linen napkins, either in the dining room or, if you prefer, in your own room.

If your morning coffee is important to you, you'll like knowing you can get it well before breakfast time.

How to get there: Salisbury is at the junction of I–85 and U.S. 52. Where Route 52 South curves toward I–85, continue straight ahead through town on Innes Street. After crossing Main, South Church, and South Jackson streets, turn left on South Fulton.

S: *Outside, Ruth Ann is perfecting the perennial gardens appropriate to the period of the house.*

The Orchard Inn
Saluda, North Carolina
28773

Innkeepers: Ann and Ken Hough
Address/Telephone: Route 176 (mailing address: P.O. Box 725); (704) 749–5471
Rooms: 9 in main house, plus 3 small cottages; all with private bath. No smoking in rooms.
Rates: $75 to $125, full breakfast. Inquire for full details. Two-night minimum stay on weekends. No credit cards.
Open: Year-round.
Facilities and activities: Dinner every night but Sunday open to public by reservation; brown bagging permitted; no smoking on dining porch. Game room, gift shop, library, horseshoes, nature trail, hiking, birdwatching. Nearby: antiques and craft shops.

This place simply overwhelmed me. It sits on eighteen wooded acres at the top of the Saluda rise, elevation 2,500 feet. All you can see in any direction are treetops and mountains. It is unbelievably quiet.

As you enter the inn from the front porch, you step into a huge living room where beautifully arranged plants, paintings, country crafts, antiques, and books all invite your attention. No matter where you turn, you see something interesting. Furniture grouped around the fireplace encourages conversation.

Guest rooms are also decorated in an upscale version of country style.

Although Ken had never cooked before opening the inn, he became the chef when the first cook they hired didn't work out. Ken turned out to be a natural talent—so good that he has attracted the attention of *Gourmet* magazine. During my visit, Ken was tickled about having found a local grower willing to sell (at a special price for the inn) all the red raspberries he grew. One of the dinner choices that night was chicken with a raspberry sauce, in addition to rack of lamb and fresh mountain trout. Ken gave me the sense that he considers the meals a serious part of the artistry that pervades the whole inn. Dining by candlelight to light classical music reinforces that sense.

Those are the features of Orchard Inn that stand out in my mind, but I have a friend who likes to stay here who sees a different set of pleasures entirely. He says, "I just like to go there and be away from the kids and enjoy the quiet and read."

Time was I couldn't imagine any waking activity more relaxing than reading, but if you're at Orchard Inn on a Saturday, you have an opportunity to make an appointment for a therapeutic massage, and *that,* my friends, leaves you so relaxed that you can't even hold a book open. The tranquil setting extends the length of time you feel that way, too.

How to get there: The Orchard Inn is in Western North Carolina, on Highway 176 between Saluda and Tryon. From I–26 north of Hendersonville, take exit 28, follow the connector road (Ozone Drive) to route 176, and turn left on 176. Drive ¹/₂ mile. The inn is on your right.

Woods House
Saluda, North Carolina
28773

Innkeeper: Dorothy Eargle

Address/Telephone: Corner of Church and Henderson streets (mailing address: Drawer E); (704) 749–9562

Rooms: 5, plus 1 suite and 1 cottage; 3 rooms, suite, and cottage with private bath. No smoking inn.

Rates: $45, shared bath; $50, private bath; $55, cottage or suite; single or double, continental breakfast. Inquire about season rates for cottage. No credit cards.

Open: May through October.

Facilities and activities: Nearby: short drive to restaurants, craft and antiques shops, golf, Blue Ridge mountain attractions.

Saluda used to be full of inns, at least a couple of dozen. Now the Woods House is almost the only one left in town. It sits at the top of a steep hill, on a large, shady piece of land, overlooking Saluda's main street. When you're here, you feel that neither the town nor the inn has changed much since it was built just before the turn of the century. Dorothy's late Victorian and turn-of-the-century antiques contribute to that feeling, as does her collection of old needlework displayed throughout the inn.

The kitchen is a real country kitchen with a wood-burning stove that's not just for show. Dorothy cooks your breakfast there. I can't think of anything that will make history come alive faster than eating breakfast surrounded by the aromas of homemade bread, coffee brewing, and the faint hint of woodsmoke that lingers around those old stoves.

Dorothy has had an antiques shop for years, even before coming to Saluda. The sure decorating touch of someone who has known and lived with antiques for a long time shows all through the inn and in the cottage that once was servants' quarters behind the house. The furniture hasn't been there forever, but it seems as though it must have been. Upstairs in the private quarters, Dorothy has a Victorian bathroom with a tin bathtub in perfect condition, and she actually uses it. It's not part of the guests' quarters, but she's so proud of it that I think she'd let you see it if you asked.

For me, the best part is the wide porch with the obligatory swings and rockers, because you can sit and enjoy the breeze while you watch the activity down on the main street and the birds in the yard. If you're an early riser, you'll find coffee set up in the dining room so that you can enjoy a cup or two on the porch before anyone even thinks about breakfast.

How to get there: I–26 takes you directly to Saluda's main street, where you will see signs directing you to the Woods House. It is on the corner of Church and Henderson streets at the top of the hill.

S: *Saluda is one of the friendliest little towns I visited anywhere in the South. The quality of crafts and antiques in the shops is outstanding. The people who run the shops are delightful, too, willing to give directions or just chat. If they're not busy, you'll probably find some of them rocking and reading or whittling in front of their stores.*

Pine Needles
Southern Pines, North Carolina
28387

Innkeepers: Peggy Kirk Bell, Peggy Ann Miller, and Kelly Miller
Address/Telephone: Route 2 (mailing address: P.O. Box 88); (919) 692–7111
Rooms: 67; all with private bath, television, and telephone.
Rates: Peak season rates from mid-March to mid-June and from September
1 to mid-November. Please call for rates. Inquire about off-season and
special-package rates. Children under 4 free.
Open: Year-round.
Facilities and activities: Breakfast, lunch, dinner, lounge for guests only.
Meeting and conference facilities, weights and workout room,
whirlpool, sauna, steam bath, heated swimming pool, lighted tennis
courts, private golf courses. Located in the sandhills of North Carolina,
known for many golf courses and horse farms.

Something new is always going on at Pine Needles, so whatever I write now, you can bet there will be more by the time you read
this.

It's not so long ago that the lobby and rooms were redecorat-
ed, so here's what you'll almost certainly find there: In the main
lobby, a dark green carpet bordered in red and white dramatically
sets off light country pine furniture and drapes and upholstery done
in tweeds and a burgundy, green, and tan plaid known as "Pine
Needles Plaid." The plaid is used throughout Pine Needles, even on
brochures.

The room has a vaulted ceiling and a raised-hearth fireplace in the brick wall along the far end. In the spring and summer, vases of flowers decorate the massive oak mantel.

The Bells built the inn mainly so that Peggy would have a place to teach golf. Certainly golf is the main attraction for most people who stay here.

Guests especially like knowing that the course will never be crowded because play is restricted to guests of the inn, if the inn is full, or will include outside players to a maximum of 140 players in off-seasons. Pine Needles has added many golf learning centers, concentrated three- and four-day schools that take as many as twenty-five people, intended for the intense golfer who wants a precise school to develop specific skills. It would be a good idea to write or call for more information, because schedules will certainly change often.

But I don't golf, and I could still stay all but forever and have a good time. The other facilities are first-class, especially the large heated swimming pool. The food is good; the wine list is above average. The area is secluded and usually quiet. (Mrs. Bell and members of the family teach an amazing number of "Golfari" sessions, basically golf workshops, for groups ranging from all women to young people. If you want a quiet escape, it is important to make sure your visit doesn't overlap with a Golfari.)

Although Pine Needles has several different kinds of guest rooms, I think I'm giving you an accurate picture of the new look by telling you that many rooms have brass headboards but are still comfortable enough that you feel free to kick off your shoes and sprawl. The Pine Needles expression for it is "casual elegance."

How to get there: Pine Needles is ¹/₄ mile off U.S. Highway 1 on N.C. Route 2 between Pinehurst and Southern Pines.

Pine Crest Inn
Tryon, North Carolina
28782

Innkeepers: Jeremy and Jennifer Wainwright
Address/Telephone: Pine Crest Lane; (704) 859–9135 or (800) 633–3001
Rooms: 4 in main lodge, 26 in 8 cottages; all with private bath, television
   with VCR, telephone, some with fireplace.
Rates: $95 to $150, double; single $10 less; continental breakfast.
Open: Year-round.
Facilities and activities: Dining room open daily for breakfast and dinner for
   guests and the public. No dinner Sunday. Full bar; library; conference
   and meeting facilities. Nearby: golf on private and open courses, swimming, tennis, crafts and antiques shops. Foothills Equestrian Nature
   center. Near Blue Ridge Parkway.

The Wainwrights are the best thing that could have happened
to Pine Crest. The energetic British couple has swept in to restore,
renovate, redecorate, and generally revive an inn that has become a
landmark in Tryon. The place has gone from looking a little sad to
stunning. If you went to Pine Crest a few years ago and were disappointed, go again! The mature, woodsy landscaping now surrounds
a revitalized inn.

The new decor, rich in hunter greens and burgundies, calls up
thoughts of an English country inn, the steeplechase and the hunt.
Everything about the place operates so smoothly and looks so professional I expected the Wainwrights to be formal and formidable.
Not their style. It's more like boundless English enthusiasm and

great good humor. These innkeepers and their staff show every sign of really *liking* each other. It creates a feeling of wonderful light-heartedness for a guest.

My favorite cottage is the 200-year-old stone bungalow that sits among trees looking like a cottage at the edge of the woods in an English village. Also, I got a kick out of the little Swayback Cottage, an old log cabin with a fireplace. The cabin has been decorated with a collection of cats. Not the live kind that run when they hear a can opener, but the cute kind that stay where you put them: paintings, porcelain pieces, metal and wood sculptures, fluffy stuffed critters draped across the backs of chairs. Regardless of the themes and exteriors, all the inn's rooms are luxurious and colorful, beautifully appointed but not screaming "decorator."

The restaurant deserves a write-up all its own. Entrees range from rack of lamb with Dijon mustard and a rosemary Madeira sauce to boneless chicken breast with herbs, shallots, and white wine. The chef emphasizes seasonal foods and complementary flavor combinations without getting silly about adding extra-exotic ingredients just for the fancy description.

Wanting to try as many good things as possible, I had small servings of both poached salmon and Maryland crab cakes, served with crisp French green beans and homemade escalloped potatoes. It was all so fresh and so perfectly prepared every bite released a little explosion of flavor. I met and complimented Chef Squires. He's skinny. How is that possible, cooking as he does?

How to get there: The main street of Tryon follows the railroad tracks. Turn onto Pine Crest Lane at the edge of town and follow it through a well-established section of homes directly to the inn. Signs mark the way.

Stone Hedge
Tryon, North Carolina
28782

Innkeepers: Anneliese and Ray Weingartner
Address/Telephone: Howard Gap Road (mailing address: P.O. Box 366); (704)
  859-9114
Rooms: 6, in inn, guesthouse, and honeymoon cottage; all with private bath,
  television, and telephone, some with fireplace, some with kitchen.
Rates: $65 to $85, double, full breakfast. Inquire about single, corporate,
  and long-stay discounts.
Open: Year-round.
Facilities and activities: Dinner for guests and the public Wednesday through
  Saturday, 6:00 to 9:00 P.M., and Sunday, noon to 2:30 P.M.; brown
  bagging permitted; wheelchair access to dining room. Swimming pool.
  Nearby: tennis, hiking, horseback riding, golf, antiques shops.

Sometimes when I've had a bad day, I imagine myself sitting
on the inn's stone patio enjoying a panoramic view of the mountains and watching squirrels skitter along the stone fence around
the patio. Soothes me every time.

The view from inside is just as lovely. The long window-wall of
the dining room looks out over the patio and an expanse of flowers,
shrubs, and a lawn that stretches down to the honeymoon cottage
by the pool. Unspoiled woodland borders everything.

Throughout the interior flower arrangements echo the outdoor flowers. As you enter the dining area, you'll see a stone fire-

place with an elegant hand-carved cherry-wood mantel. The exposed ceiling beams, doors, and all woodwork are made from cherry wood, too. And the carpet pattern resembles fallen autumn leaves. The effect is so pretty that it makes you feel like dressing up for dinner.

Because of Ray's German background, the Weingartners have added some paintings of the German countryside to remind Ray of home, and (be still, my heart!) sauerbraten, wiener schnitzel, and roladen, accompanied by homemade German noodles, now appear regularly on the menu. The regular menu also includes certified black Angus filet, veal sweetbreads, and fresh seafood.

Kathleen Pierce is the chef. Her love of cooking goes so far that she makes jam from her own berries. She prepares the inn's dinners. Everything is made from scratch.

Anneliese cooks breakfast for inn guests and reserves for herself the pleasure of making the stollen every year at Christmas. Ray serves as maître d' and the family's two sons wait on tables on weekends.

The guest rooms are furnished mostly with locally purchased antiques. The cottage by the swimming pool feels almost like a private retreat.

Indeed, all of Stone Hedge feels like a luxurious retreat, miles from any other civilization, but when you're ready to engage the world again, Tryon, with all its quaint stores and antiques shops, is only a couple of miles away.

How to get there: From I–26, take the Tryon exit (#36) to N.C. 108. Follow 108 toward Tryon for 2½ miles. Turn right on Howard Gap Road and follow the signs about 1½ miles to the inn.

Mast Farm Inn
Valle Crucis, North Carolina
28691

Innkeepers: Francis and Sibyl Pressly
Address/Telephone: Star Route 1112 (mailing address: P.O. Box 704); (704)
    963–5857
Rooms: 12; 10 with private bath, some with wheelchair access. No smoking
    inn.
Rates: $80 to $150, double; single $26 less; deluxe continental breakfast and
    dinner.
Open: January to March and May to November.
Facilities and activities: Dinner for guests and the public by reservation, din-
    ner Monday evenings for lodging guests only; Sunday lunch at 12:30
    and 2:30 P.M.; no evening meal Sunday; brown bagging permitted.
    Located in the Blue Ridge Mountains, near Blue Ridge Parkway. Near-
    by: craft shops, antiques shops, potteries, hiking, fishing, white-water
    rafting.

Sibyl Pressly considers it a good day when inn guests who
meet sitting together at the long tables during dinner adjourn to the
porch afterward to continue talking for the rest of the evening.

Francis manages to learn a little about the interests of everyone who will be eating at the inn. In the half hour or so before the
seating (6:00 P.M. or 7:45 P.M.), people begin to congregate on the
front porch, overlooking Sibyl's flower gardens, to rock and chat
and watch the mountains. The aromas that drift from the kitchen
are so inviting that when the dinner bell rings, everyone moves to

the dining room very briskly. But you can't just barge in and sit down. Francis will have worked out a seating scheme to ensure an interesting mix of people and lively conversation. Once everyone is in place at a table, he introduces everyone.

Then the food comes. During my visit we started with a fresh tossed salad with the best tomatoes I'd tasted all summer. The vegetables are from the Mast Farm gardens (in season). The entrees change daily. We had roast pork loin perfectly seasoned with garlic and black pepper. The meat was cut off the ribs, and the two were served separately. We passed platters of yam-and-apple casserole, succotash, and zucchini. The menu includes a vegetarian entree every day but Sunday. I tasted the spinach enchilada with jalapeño cheese sauce and liked it so much I had seconds. Many other guests did the same.

In the morning, I looked around the property. Mast Farm is on the National Register of Historic Places and is considered a fine example of a restored self-contained mountain homestead. The spring house, icehouse, wash house, barn, blacksmith shop, gazebo, and cabin, as well as the main inn, look much as they must have amid the daily activity when Mast Farm was originally operated as an inn in the early 1900s.

While I was looking around, Sibyl was preparing a breakfast of hot homemade blueberry muffins; fresh fruit; a delicious drink made with pineapple juice, orange juice, and bananas; and a seemingly endless flow of coffee.

How to get there: At Boone, take N.C. 105 south about 5 miles to the VALLE CRUCIS sign. Turn onto SR 1112 (the road to Valle Crucis) and go 3 miles. The inn is on the left just before you get to the village of Valle Crucis.

S: *Sibyl has published a lovely cookbook full of color photographs from the inn and the most popular recipes served in the dining room.*

Grandview Lodge
Waynesville, North Carolina
28786

Innkeepers: Stanley and Linda Arnold
Address/Telephone: 809 Valley View Circle Road; (704) 456–5212 or (800) 255–7826
Rooms: 9 in main lodge and attached porch, plus 2 2-room apartments; all with private bath, 2 beds, and television.
Rates: $85 to $100, double, breakfast and dinner. Inquire about rates for single occupancy, children, and apartments. No credit cards.
Open: Year-round.
Facilities and activities: Lunch by special arrangement, dinner open to public by reservation, brown bagging permitted. Library, game room, shuffleboard courts. Nearby: golf, tennis, outlet shopping, easy access to Blue Ridge Parkway and many historic sites.

Seems Stan came home one day from his corporate management job in Chicago and said, "I've had it. Let's do it or stop talking about it."

The other dreamer, Linda, a home economist who'd recently taken some cooking classes at the Culinary Institute of America just in case, said, "Okay, let's do it."

So they bought themselves an inn—Grandview Lodge, here in their native North Carolina. They got here in the spring of 1986; their furniture got here a few days later; their first guests checked in a few days after that.

Everyone is living happily ever after.

Stan and Linda run the inn much as it has been operated for the past fifty years. It's furnished with what Stan calls "the kind of antiques you're not afraid to sit on, but definitely not rustic. More like Grandmother's house." They've arranged two separate groupings of furniture in the living room, one for watching television and one for conversation and maybe (Stan so hopes) bridge games.

Just as Stan says the furniture's not rustic, Linda says the cooking's not Southern in the old sense. She cooks with herbs from her garden, fresh garden vegetables that a neighbor brings pot-ready, fresh local fruits, and whole grain flours. But you're not getting into health-nut meals; unless you consider barbecued beef ribs, corn pudding, and homemade ice cream hairshirt. Linda also makes her Chocoholic Tart that has in it two kinds of chocolate plus chocolate liqueur.

So many guests have asked for Linda's recipes that she wrote *The Grandview Lodge Cookbook*, which you can buy if you'd like to go home and try to cook likewise.

Grandview now offers one thing I'm relatively sure you can't find at any other inn in the South—an innkeeper who speaks Polish, Russian, German, and Hebrew. It sounds like a talent Stan might not get to use often in Waynesville, but the area is increasingly becoming known for its international folk-dance festivals, and this past season, dancers from eleven foreign countries came. Stan had a ball!

How to get there: From the U.S. 23/74 bypass, take the West Waynesville exit. Turn south to the first stop sign. Turn left onto Balsam Road and go to the first traffic light. Turn right onto Allen Creek Road. Go exactly 1 mile. Turn left at the Grandview Lodge sign and continue ²/₅ mile up a winding road to the Lodge driveway on your right. Stan and Linda will send a map when you make reservations.

Hallcrest Inn
Waynesville, North Carolina
28786

Innkeepers: Russell and Margaret Burson
Address/Telephone: 299 Halltop Circle; (704) 456–6457 or (800) 334–6457
Rooms: 8 in farmhouse, 4 on "The Side Porch"; all with private baths.
Rates: $55, single; $65 to $75, double; breakfast and dinner. Children under 6 half price.
Open: May 1 to November 30.
Facilities and activities: Breakfast and dinner open to public by reservation, brown bagging permitted on porch and in rooms. Nearby: golf, horseback riding, white-water rafting, fishing, antiques shops, outlet shops, easy access to Blue Ridge Parkway.

This is an honest-to-goodness, no-frills farmhouse. I've lived much of my life in rural places surrounded by similar white-frame, tin-roofed houses with many rooms, several fireplaces, and old-fashioned furniture. I'm thinking of the places where the furniture is antique but nobody gives it much thought because it's simply the furniture the family has always had and at one time was new furniture. These are the homes with lots of family photographs on the walls, crocheted afghans tossed over the backs of chairs, and odds and ends like silver baby cups and bronzed baby shoes on the side tables. Hallcrest Inn is just like that. The silver cup has a dent from when Russell dropped it under a rocker; the bronzed shoes were also Russell's.

Like all such farmhouses, this one has interesting quirks. For instance, the woodwork of the door facings and mantels is more elaborate upstairs than it is downstairs. Usually the fancier woodwork was downstairs where people could see it. Margaret and Russell speculate that it's reversed in their house because the original owner started with little money, but by the time he finished the upstairs rooms, he could afford more decorative touches.

Russell and Margaret are what my parents would have called "comfortable as old shoes." They clearly enjoy guests. They love the inn's view, which from 3,200 feet overlooks all of Waynesville and the surrounding mountains, with grazing sheep, tilled fields, and patches of woods. Margaret says sitting in the porch rockers is the best way she can think of to spend time at Hallcrest Inn.

Not that the Bursons spend a lot of time rocking when the inn is open. Just seeing to all the food served at the inn would be enough to keep them going. No quick mixes and instant soups here. "There will never be steam tables in *our* kitchen," Margaret said.

The food is basically Southern country, featuring Russell's homemade breads and desserts, and they pride themselves on not repeating a menu during the time a guest stays. (Once they kept up the variety for three weeks straight.)

How to get there: Two miles north of Waynesville on Highway 276, turn onto Mauney Cove Road. Drive to the end of the pavement and turn left onto a gravel road. Follow the signs on up the hill to the house. You may request a map when you make reservations.

S: *More than ever this is a family place. Russell and Margaret are joined now by their son, Martin, their daughter, Catherine, and their respective spouses and children.*

Pisgah Inn
Waynesville, North Carolina
28786

Innkeeper: Phyllis O'Connell
Address/Telephone: Waynesville (mailing address: P.O. Box 749); (704) 235–8228
Rooms: 51; all with private bath and television, some with wheelchair access.
Rates: $55 to $100, single or double, breakfast extra. Children under 8 in room with 2 adults free.
Open: April through December.
Facilities and activities: Two restaurants open to public and guests for breakfast, lunch, and dinner; brown bagging permitted. Gift shop, camp store, campground, gas station, 100 hiking trails. Located on the Blue Ridge Parkway. Nearby: fishing, scenic drives.

The new Pisgah Inn is built near the old inn. The wing of guest rooms of the new inn looks like a motel and is set up so that you park in front of your room. But the spirit of the place is that of the old inn, which you can reach by following a narrow footpath through the overgrown rhododendrons. The old building seems to teeter on the edge of the mountaintop. It's fascinating to see the old desk and lobby, read the sign giving the history of the place, and imagine what it must have been like to stay in that rather primitive building.

It's infinitely more comfortable to stay in one of the new

rooms. They are large and nicely furnished with modern furniture. Every room has huge windows and a porch facing out over the mountains. What may be lost in old-fashioned inn feeling is more than made up for by the view. The view of the mountains at 5,000 feet above sea level is awe inspiring. From Mt. Pisgah, you look down on mountaintops in every direction. Watching sunrise or sunset from this vantage point makes me almost teary-eyed.

The dining room and coffee shop have windows all around so that you can watch the day changing even as you eat. But it's not just the view that attracts diners.

Phyllis said, "Be sure to write about the trout." She was referring to the fact that if the trout served was any fresher, it would come to the table still wiggling on the plate. Although the menu includes Southern favorites like country ham, you can even have trout for breakfast. Fresh vegetables and homemade breads and desserts complement the entrees. The people at the inn say that they can accommodate tastes ranging from country boy to continental.

How to get there: The inn is on the Blue Ridge Parkway at Milepost 408.6, 25 miles south of Asheville and 20 miles north of Brevard.

Catherine's Inn on Orange
Wilmington, North Carolina
28401

Innkeeper: Catherine Ackiss
Address/Telephone: 410 Orange Street; (919) 251–0863 or (800) 476–0723
Rooms: 3; all with private bath, television, and telephone. No smoking in rooms.
Rates: $55, single; $60, double; full breakfast and evening sherry. Advance arrangement needed for children.
Open: Year-round.
Facilities and activities: Swimming pool. Nearby: walk to restaurants, museums, shopping; short drive to ocean beaches; golf, tennis, sailing.

When I first visited here, Catherine simply called her place in Wilmington's historic district "The Inn on Orange." She has changed the name to "Catherine's Inn on Orange," and that tells you something about the depth of her involvement. She decided to become an innkeeper a number of years ago because, as she told her husband, she wanted to be a hostess. And she felt that her own travel experience had taught her what people value in small lodgings.

As she sees it, when you walk through the door, you become part of her family. The feeling is not one-way. One young businesswoman who stays here regularly mentioned at breakfast that as she was driving toward Wilmington, she found herself thinking, "I can't wait to see Catherine and tell her about the new guy I went out with last weekend." I know they sat up together talking long after I'd drifted off to sleep.

Catherine says that like a good family member she tries to know when guests want to talk and when they want to be left alone.

The family sense comes also from the inn's being furnished with many antiques and family pieces that Catherine has refinished herself, including a stunning piano that once belonged to her mother and a cedar chest her mother gave her when she was twelve. The living room is cheerful but relaxing, with rose walls, a white couch, and a Persian carpet echoing the colors. Several dolls that belonged to Catherine's grandmother fit right in. The cozy upstairs library and porch have the added comfort of a well-stocked refrigerator from which you can help yourself to wine, beer, and soft drinks, just as you might at home if you could keep the refrigerator that well stocked.

Catherine's breakfasts are a delight, featuring everything from French toast to blueberry muffins and an opportunity for some casual conversation with Catherine. It's like the kind of laughing breakfast conversation we fantasize about enjoying just as soon as our own families become perfect. For some of us, an equally great delight is Catherine's leaving hot coffee in the sitting area outside the guest rooms early in the morning.

How to get there: From Highway 17 South (which becomes Market Street) into Wilmington, drive all the way to the waterfront. Turn left onto Third Street. Go 2 blocks and turn left on Orange and go 2 more blocks to the inn.

Brookstown Inn
Winston-Salem, North Carolina
27101

Innkeeper: Deborah Bumgardner
Address/Telephone: 200 Brookstown Avenue; (919) 725–1120
Rooms: 72; all with private bath and television, some with wet bar, garden
tub, whirlpool tub, and private sitting room, some with wheelchair
access. Two rooms equipped for the handicapped.
Rates: $85 to $105, single; $101 to $121, double; continental breakfast and
evening wine and cheese party. Children under 12, free; 12 and over,
$10.
Open: Year-round.
Facilities and activities: Meeting facilities. Nearby: restaurants, Old Salem,
local colleges, galleries, museums.

As an inn, this old building is in its fourth incarnation. It was
built in 1837 by the Moravians to be a cotton mill. Then it became a
flour mill and later a storage building for a moving company. The
mill was restored as an inn and a complex of specialty shops and
restaurants in 1984. It's listed on the National Register of Historic
Places.

As often happens in building within an existing large structure,
the new spaces are larger than average, with spectacularly high ceilings, surprising twists and turns, nooks and crannies, and a wealth
of visual interest in exposed beams, old brick, and historic artifacts.

More specifically: On the fourth floor, in what originally was a dormitory for girls who worked in the cotton mill, renovators found and have preserved behind glass a plaster wall full of graffiti. The old factory boiler visually dominates Darryl's Restaurant. In guest rooms, architectural features of the original building, such as brick buttresses, unusual roof slopes, and interesting spaces, have been incorporated into the design of the room.

The decor throughout the inn is early American, appropriate to the building and its Old Salem connection, without being oppressive. Quilts decorate lobby walls; country touches like hand-woven baskets, pieces of pewter, and silk flowers are scattered throughout the public areas. The huge open spaces keep it from feeling at all cluttered. In the guest rooms, furnishings are reproductions appropriate for the period set off with Wedgwood-blue stenciling around the windows.

In the breakfast room, which has brick floors and comfortable club chairs around round tables, your continental breakfast is absolutely appropriate: Moravian buns, sugar cake, and fresh fruit. If you visit Old Salem during your stay, you can pick up recipe cards for these famous Moravian delicacies.

The old Moravians were famous for their hospitality. Old Brookstown Inn is doing a remarkably good job communicating that spirit at the same time they offer the modern creature comforts you expect from a first-class hostelry.

How to get there: Coming from the west on I–40, take the Cherry Street exit. Turn right when you come to the light at the top of the ramp, onto Marshall Street. Follow the inn signs, turning left onto Brookstown Avenue. The inn is on the right. Coming from the east on I–40, take the Cherry Street exit. As you come to the light coming off the ramp, turn left onto First Street. Go 1 block, turn left on Marshall. Follow the inn signs, turning left on Brookstown.

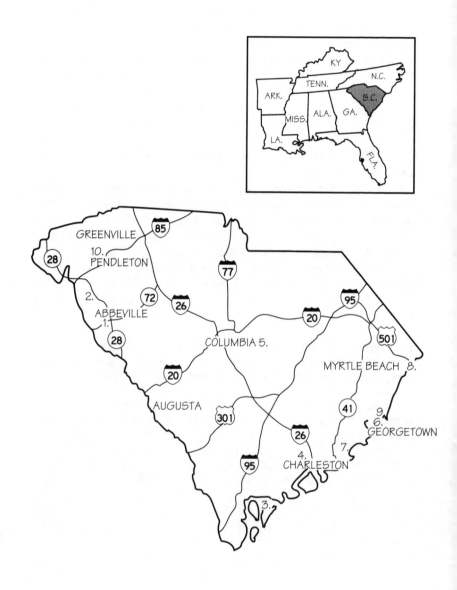

South Carolina

Numbers on map refer to towns numbered below.

The Belmont Inn
Abbeville, South Carolina
29620

Innkeeper: Janie Wiltshire

Address/Telephone: 106 East Pickens Street; (803) 459–9625

Rooms: 24; all with private bath. Pets allowed by arrangement in special circumstances.

Rates: $60 to $70, single or double, continental breakfast. Inquire about corporate rates and theater packages. Wheelchair access. Children under
12 free.

Open: Year-round.

Facilities and activities: Lunch, dinner, lounge, except Sunday. Nearby: the-
atrical productions at the restored Opera House next door; Russell
Lake for fishing, boating, swimming, and water skiing; hunting; gift
and antiques shopping in Abbeville.

Sometimes you go into an inn for the first time and everything
just feels right. The Belmont Inn is like that. What I remember most
vividly is hearing people laughing, whistling, and singing in the
kitchen before dinner. But even as I checked in, everyone was
pleasantly chatty and exceptionally helpful.

The old Spanish-style building was built as a modern hotel in
1902. For years, travelers associated with the railroad, the textile
industry, and the Opera House stayed here. But it closed in 1972
and stood empty for eleven years, until Mr. and Mrs. Joseph C.
Harden bought it. Restoration took almost a year and involved
many people in Abbeville. Almost anyone at the inn can tell you

stories about bringing The Belmont Inn back to life. Staying here, you feel like a guest not just of the inn, but of the entire community.

The relationship between the Opera House and The Belmont thrives again, too. You can make great package deals including theater tickets, dinner with wine, a drink in the Curtain Call Lounge after the show, your lodging, and continental breakfast the next morning. The package rates are always good, but they vary with the season and so does the show schedule. Activity peaks with summer theater at the Opera House.

Whether it precedes a show or not, dinner in the large dining room with its high ceilings and paddle fans is worth enjoying slowly. The menu tends toward continental cuisine without being self-conscious about it. The chef prepares veal a different way every day. After a nice meal of filleted chicken breasts Dijon with pecans, I let the waitress talk me into a slice of Irish Cream mousse cake.

With so much to do, I didn't spend much time in my room, but it was restfully simple. The old, refinished floors were bare except for a small bedside rug. A white bedspread covered the brass bed, and an antique quilt hung on one of the white walls. The room made me feel so good that I hated leaving it in the morning.

How to get there: The inn is on the corner of the town square. From Greenwood, take Highway 72 west to Abbeville, turn right onto Highway 20 (Main Street), and go to the first traffic light. Turn right onto Pickens Street. The second building on the right is The Belmont. From I–85, take Highway 28 south into Abbeville where it joins Main Street.

S: *I love Abbeville. When I walked around the town, everyone from merchants to workers in their vans waved as if they saw me every day.*

The Evergreen Inn
and 1109 South Main
Restaurant

Anderson, South Carolina
29621

Innkeepers: Myrna and Peter Ryter
Address/Telephone: 1109 South Main; (803) 225–1109
Rooms: 7; 6 with private bath, 4 with television.
Rates: $52, single; $65 to $70, double; continental breakfast and cocktail or wine.
Open: Year-round.
Facilities and activities: Dinner and bar open to guests and the public by reservation, restaurant closed Sunday and Monday. Nearby: public tennis courts, Lake Hartwell, fishing, swimming, boating.

"This is delicious. How's yours?"

"Wonderful."

"Couldn't be better."

It was early dinnertime, and I was eavesdropping shamelessly as I ate my way through an appetizer of smoked goose breast with raspberry sauce, a perfect Belgian-endive salad sprinkled with Roquefort cheese, and a really well-prepared piece of fish in a green-peppercorn sauce.

People at neighboring tables had ordered beef and veal, and I wondered if those dishes were as good as what I had. Apparently they were.

Peter is the chef. He learned his trade in Switzerland and then worked many years in good restaurants across America. No matter what I tell you about the menu now, he'll probably be serving something else when you visit The 1109 because he prides himself on changing his offerings regularly in response to what's in season and what's looking especially good at the farmer's market in Atlanta, where he goes to buy produce. But you can always count on the freshness of his vegetables and fish and the delicacy of his sauces.

Peter has been selected for membership in La Chaîne des Rôtisseurs, a worldwide French gourmet society founded in 1234. This is an honor from his peers.

Each dining room is done in different colors and patterns, giving you more the sense of a home that feeds many people graciously than of a public restaurant.

The guest rooms are in Evergreen Inn (a building next door dating from 1834), a companion to The 1109.

My favorite room in this second house is a huge, nearly octagonal room with wallpaper full of peacocks and greenery and lots of built-in walnut and mahogany shelves. There are specialty rooms, including one for honeymooners in pink and rose velvet with an exotic navy satin canopy and huge antiques.

How to get there: Going south on I-85, take exit 27 (Highway 81) toward Anderson. Turn left on Main Street and go 8 blocks. If you are traveling north on I-85, take exit 11 (Highway 24) toward Anderson. Turn left on Main Street and continue 4 blocks. The inn is on the left. Turn the corner on Hampton Street to park in the rear.

The Rhett House Inn
Beaufort, South Carolina
29902

Innkeepers: Marianne and Steve Harrison
Address/Telephone: 1009 Craven Street; (803) 524–9030
Rooms: 10; all with private bath, 2 with fireplace, 1 with Jacuzzi and television.
Rates: $100 and up, double or single (inquire for details), continental breakfast.
Open: Year-round.
Facilities and activities: Dinner by reservation on weekends. Pool table, bicycles, country club membership for golf, tennis, swimming, and restaurant. Nearby: beach, walking and carriage tours of historic sites in Beaufort, half-hour drive to Charleston or Savannah.

Beaufort does something to people. Lured by tourist literature laced with phrases like "picturesque old port town," and "nestled along the intracoastal," and "quaint historic community," people come to visit this place that time is supposed to have skipped over. And sure enough, it has.

Except for telling you that the only reason Sherman didn't burn Beaufort is because it was under Union occupation at the time, nobody gets very worked up over anything. Breezes really do "waft." The streets really are "tree-lined." Folks really do "stroll."

Next thing you know, you get to thinking that instead of visiting, you'd really like to live there.

It happened to Marianne and Steve. They left their city lives behind and the result is Rhett House, which they restored to gleaming beauty and operate in a thoroughly professional manner.

The building has wraparound verandas with classic columns and porticos, and beautifully curved entry stairs. Live oaks swathed in Spanish moss shade the house. The white exterior almost sparkles. The scene cries out to be a movie set for a Southern romance with violins playing in the background.

The rooms are furnished with assorted antiques, but everything has been chosen to keep the rooms light and bright, avoiding the slightly gloomy look we sometimes associate with antiques.

The room I stayed in was huge. It opened onto the courtyard garden, so that I could hear the fountain all night. The fireplace had a raised brick hearth. The drapes, rugs, and furniture were done in a country motif with blue-and-white gingham and ticking.

It seemed like a good idea just to stay there with the door open to the courtyard and spend the morning reading, but I didn't want to miss breakfast.

Seven of us sat around the dining room table, playing "where are you from?" and "what's your favorite inn?" and digging into bowls of huge strawberries and plates of tiny poppy-seed muffins with unromantic vigor and a most un-Southern display of energy.

Marianne gave lots of advice about nice places to see in the area and how to get there. One of her favorite places (and mine, incidentally) is Hunting Island State Park, a 5,000-acre park just 16 miles from downtown Beaufort, with several miles of perfect swimming beaches that are also uncommonly good for shelling.

At the marina, the chamber of commerce provides more information than you can possibly use about Beaufort and the area, and it offers a nice brochure for a self-guided tour of historic sites.

This inn has been enjoying a lot of publicity and the presence of some celebrity guests, including Barbara Streisand and Nick Nolte. (Not at the same time, understand.)

How to get there: From I–95 take exit 33 to Beaufort. From Savannah, follow the signs to Hilton Head Island and then to Beaufort. The inn is 1 block from the Intracoastal Waterway at the corner of Craven and Newcastle streets. Ask for a map when you make reservations.

Two Suns Inn
Beaufort, South Carolina
29902

Innkeepers: Carrol and Ron Kay
Address/Telephone: 1705 Bay Street; (803) 522–1122 or (800) 532–4244
Rooms: 5; all with private bath, television by request, telephone, 1 with wheelchair access. Smoking only on veranda and second-floor screened porch.
Rates: $83 to $91, single; $91 to $99, double; full breakfast. Inquire about special discounts.
Open: Year-round.
Facilities and activities: Gift area. Business seminar and meeting services, including computer, copier, fax, etc. Bicycles. On Intracoastal Waterway in historic district. Nearby: restaurants, downtown marina, waterfront park, shops, Hunting Island State Park beaches, Parris Island Marine Base and military museum.

When you walk into Two Suns you see a homey living room with a white-brick fireplace to your left and Carrol's weaving studio to your right. And unless the world turns upside down and goes black tonight, you'll quickly find Ron Kay, brimming with excitement and ready to tell you the story of the inn, even if he has to stop in the middle of something else to do it.

The place is worth talking about. For one thing, it is *not* an antebellum mansion. It's a restored and renovated Neoclassical Revival–style home, built in 1917 and used for some years in the 1940s as a communal home (called "the Teacherage") for local female schoolteachers. It was the first home in the community to be built with indoor plumbing. An interesting aspect of that is the brass "full body shower," brought from Philadelphia in 1916, in one of the upstairs rooms. This thing has nozzles to squirt you from both sides and several heights all at once, and it is forceful enough to have taxed Ron's ingenuity in making a shower closing that would keep water inside the shower stall.

Each guest room has its own theme and exhibits touches of Carrol's creativity in unusual window treatments, wall hangings, and such decorating touches as a stuffed parrot high up in a corner. Two of the upstairs rooms have access to the screened porch facing the bay.

The dining room, where breakfast and afternoon tea are served, could get by without much decorating from anybody, because it has windows on three walls looking out on a yard full of camellias and greenery. Like the room, breakfast is special, featuring a dish of the day along with fruits, cereals, and hot baked goods. If you have any dietary restrictions or special breakfast requests, just ask.

It wouldn't do to forget "tea and toddy hour," either. From about 5:00 to 6:00 P.M., guests mingle over tea or sherry, brandy, or wine, chatting about what they've discovered in and around Beaufort. This is definitely the kind of place where guests spend time getting to know each other. And Ron and Carrol are on hand with lots of stories about the house and community, and suggestions for good restaurants and interesting side trips.

One of the most pleasurable trips for people who enjoy the beach is a picnic on Hunting Island, a beautiful, unspoiled spot. The Kays will prepare a picnic basket for you, and if you coax just a tad, you can probably get Pebbles, the cocker spaniel, to tag along with you.

How to get there: U.S. 21 becomes Carteret, which runs directly into Bay Street in downtown Beaufort. As you drive along Bay Street, with the water on your left, the inn is on your right.

Ansonborough Inn
Charleston, South Carolina
29401

Innkeeper: Allen B. Johnson; Eric A. Crapse, assistant innkeeper
Address/Telephone: 21 Hassel Street; (803) 723–1655 or (800) 522–2073
Rooms: 37 suites; all with private bath, telephone, television, and kitchen.
No-smoking rooms available.
Rates: Spring and fall, $89 to $138, double; summer and winter, $89 to
$114, double; continental breakfast and afternoon wine and cheese.
$10 for each extra adult in suite. Children 12 and under free. Inquire
about discounts for singles, long-term stays, and corporate rates.
Open: Year-round.
Facilities and activities: Free off-street parking. In heart of waterfront historic
district. Nearby: historic sites, restaurants, shuttle transportation to vis-
itor center. Walking distance to antiques shops and downtown
Charleston.

Like so many Charleston inns, this one had a different function in its earlier time. It was a three-story stationer's warehouse
built about 1900. The building's renovation not only kept the heart
of pine beams and locally fired red brick, which are typical of the
period, but actually emphasized them. The lobby soars three stories
high, with skylights; the original huge, rough beams are fully visible, an important part of the decor.

The original plan to use the renovated building as a condo
complex didn't work out, which probably was bad news for some
investors; but it's great for inn guests now, because the rooms,

which are really suites, are huge. At least one wall in each features the exposed old brick. The ceilings are about 20 feet high. Because all the rooms were fit into an existing shell, no two rooms are exactly the same shape or size. Nothing is exactly predictable. The resulting little quirks, nooks, lofts, and alcoves add a lot of interest.

The living rooms are furnished in period reproductions with comfortable chairs and sleeper sofas to accommodate extra people. What's more, you really can cook in the kitchens. If you ask for place settings and basic kitchen utensils when you make your reservations, the kitchen will be ready when you arrive. The inn is just across the road from an excellent Harris Teeter supermarket housed in an old railroad station. I don't think it would be appropriate to whip up corned beef and cabbage or deep-fried chittlins in this environment, but the arrangement is great for preparing light meals—a good way to save your calories and your dollars for some sumptuous dinners in Charleston's excellent restaurants.

Clearly this isn't the kind of place where everyone sits around the breakfast table comparing notes about dinner the night before, but the continental breakfast (with sweet breads baked at a plantation in Walterboro) and the evening wine and cheese are set up in the lobby so that guests can sit in conversational clusters. If someone on the staff thinks that you may have something in common with another guest, he or she will take the trouble to introduce you. Indeed, the staff here is personable and helpful—attitudes you don't always encounter in Charleston hostelries. A visitor from a Scandinavian country said that if this is Southern hospitality, he likes it.

How to get there: From I–26 East, take the Meeting Street/Visitor Center exit. Go 1¹/₅ miles to Hassel Street. Turn left and go through the next traffic signal. From Route 17 South, take the East Bay Street exit, go 1³/₁₀ miles to Hassel and turn left. From Route 17 North, after crossing the Ashley River, exit to the right and go through the first traffic signal onto Calhoun Street. Drive 1²/₅ miles to Easy Bay Street, turn right, and go to the second traffic signal (Hassel Street) and turn left. The inn is on your right.

The Barksdale House Inn
Charleston, South Carolina
29401

Innkeepers: Peggy and George Sloan
Address/Telephone: 27 George Street; (803) 577–4800
Rooms: 10; all with private bath, television, and telephone, 5 with whirlpool, 6 with fireplace.
Rates: $79 to $150, single or double, continental breakfast.
Open: Year-round except December 23 through December 27.
Facilities and activities: Free parking, formal gardens. Nearby: restaurants, central to historic downtown Charleston, convenient to Spoleto activities.

Here's a success story: Start with a mess of an old house, a 1778 town house, specifically, that was bought by a landscape architect and his wife, renovated and set up with impeccable taste as an inn, and then sold as a going concern to Peggy and George Sloan. The Sloans are an energetic young couple with innkeeping in their genes. Peggy is a cousin of David Spell, whose name has become synonymous with innkeeping in Charleston (Two Meeting Street, The Belvedere), and she is the granddaughter of the woman who opened the first boardinghouse in Charleston. For his part, George says that this is something he's had in mind to do for a long time. Their verve is important because one of the sad things that often happens with long-established inns in areas like Charleston is that the people responsible for them become indifferent. Staying at such places may not be bad, but neither is it a lot of fun.

Nothing like that will happen to you at The Barksdale House Inn anytime in the imaginable future. Not only are the innkeepers involved, the inn is gorgeous. Each guest room features a different motif: traditional, French, Victorian, oriental. In them all, ceiling fans hanging from 10-foot-ceilings augment the air conditioning and make it more comfortable. The furnishings are a mixture of antiques and reproductions of the period, set off by Scalamandré borders and fabrics of the eighteenth and nineteenth centuries.

The Sloans love flowers and are growing them everywhere— in the courtyard, in hanging baskets, and around the house.

The service includes the traditional European niceties: breakfast on a silver tray, afternoon tea or sherry by the fountain, turned-down bedcovers and chocolates on the pillow, and a boniface to help arrange tours, make dinner and entertainment reservations, and work out details of the rest of your travels.

If you enjoy special events, ask about the Eastern Wildlife Expo, the Candlelight Tour, and the Festival of Homes, all of which are held yearly in Charleston. The Barksdale House is a good place from which to enjoy all these activities.

How to get there: The inn is near the corner of George and Meeting streets.

Belvedere
Charleston, South Carolina
29401

Innkeeper: David Spell; Rick Zender, manager
Address/Telephone: 40 Rutledge Avenue; (803) 722–0973
Rooms: 3; all with private bath and television. No smoking inn.
Rates: $95, single or double, continental breakfast and evening sherry. Two-night minimum on weekends. No credit cards.
Open: Year-round except December and January.
Facilities and activities: Nearby: restaurants, historic sites of Historic Charleston, carriage tours, antiques shops, museums, art galleries.

I think of David Spell as Charleston's Innkeeper. For years he kept Two Meeting Street, generally acknowledged as one of the best and most stable inns in Charleston. Recently, his niece, Karen, took over as innkeeper there and David "retired" to Belvedere, a new, smaller lodging owned by his nephew, Jim Spell.

When I say the inn is new, I'm not exactly accurate. Its use as an inn is new, but the building is old and, try to follow this, the interior woodwork is older than the exterior by about a hundred years. The building itself is a huge white mansion in the Colonial Revival style, built about 1900 and bought by a local physician in 1925. But much of its interior is woodwork of the late eighteenth century, salvaged from nearby Belvedere Plantation, which was destroyed in the 1920s to build a golf course and Navy officers' club. The physician, whose passion was woodworking, rescued the fine

Adams-style woodwork from the plantation and had it installed in his mansion. The mansion then became the inn that is called Belvedere, after the original plantation.

Enough of the history lesson. How about your creature comforts, the things we all care about? Each of the guest rooms has a high ceiling with a ceiling fan, an ornamental fireplace, antiques, queen-sized poster canopied beds, and oriental rugs.

Evening sherry and breakfast are served in an 18-foot-wide central hall upstairs that has been furnished as a living room for guests. It opens out onto a piazza that overlooks Colonial Lake and the Ashley River. Potted plants bend gently in the breeze and the white wicker furniture sparkles against the white columns and ceiling of this semicircular porch. It is the obvious place to take your breakfast on a nice morning.

Downstairs, you'll see that David has brought his fine china, brass, silver, and crystal with him to Belvedere, so in the formal rooms you can enjoy not only the transplanted woodwork, but also his museum-quality collections.

How to get there: The inn is between Queen and Beaufain streets on Rutledge. Ask for a map when you make reservations.

Elliott House Inn
Charleston, South Carolina
29401

Innkeeper: Jan Forbes
Address/Telephone: 78 Queen Street; (803) 723–1855 or (800) 729–1855
Rooms: 26; all with private bath, telephone, and television.
Rates: $100 to $130, per room, continental breakfast. Inquire about corporate rates.
Open: Year-round.
Facilities and activities: Large whirlpool in courtyard, bicycles. Nearby: walking distance to restaurants, historic sites, tourist attractions, and antiques shops.

My daughter, who spends a lot of time on business in Charleston (poor baby!), says this is one of her favorite places to stay, because the people on staff are "so sweet" and the rooms are so comfortable.

The building is a renovated three-story frame house built about 1865, expanded with a newer section. The rooms are furnished in period reproductions, with such modern amenitiies as color television hidden away in walnut armoires. Oriental rugs cover good wood floors, and oriental-patterned wallpaper carries through the theme. The rooms are all different, furnished with period reproductions.

If you stand back and inspect the entire building, you'll notice that the second- and third-floor balconies slope noticeably toward

230

the ground. Seems that the earthquake of 1886 knocked things a bit wopperjawed. Everything is structurally sound, but the result of the quake is evident in the slant of those balconies, a touch that appeals to people associatd with the place who enjoy its uniqueness.

Elliott House is ideally situated if you're planning to spend some time walking through the historic streets of Charleston. It is in the heart of downtown Charleston, a block from the antiques district in one direction, a block from famous historic sites in the other.

At the end of a day of sightseeing or business, when it's nice enough to be outside, you'll enjoy the courtyard. Designed around the whirlpool, it includes fountains and shady sitting areas and gleams with flowering plants most of the year. What a great place to enjoy a glass of wine!

It would be a mistake to relax with your wine so much that you miss dinner, however, because the inn is right next to 82 Queen, one of Charleston's better restaurants, with an exotic menu.

How to get there: Take the Meeting Street exit from I–26; go south on Meeting to Queen and right onto Queen. The inn is in the first block.

Indigo Inn
Charleston, South Carolina
29401

Innkeeper: Larry Deery
Address/Telephone: One Maiden Lane; (803) 577–5900 or (800) 845–7639
Rooms: 40; all with private bath.
Rates: $70 to $125, single or double, extra person in room $10. Includes hunt breakfast, daily newspapers, private parking. Well-behaved pets accepted. Wheelchair access.
Open: Year-round.
Facilities and activities: Small bar every day but Sunday. Nearby: historic sites, tourist attractions, and antiques shops in Charleston.

Some years ago, a road-weary James Kilpatrick wrote about the Indigo Inn in his syndicated column, noting that the people who run it "genuinely care about their guests." Usually, the first thing people mention about the inn is that it's full of blue, from the shower curtains to the exterior walls. The inn's color and name reflect the time when indigo was so important to the local economy that even the ladies of the plantation learned how to manage the crops.

It was breakfast time, and I don't think any of the guests were thinking about indigo. Dressed in shorts and walking shoes for a day of sightseeing, they came to the lobby and loaded their plates with fruit, ham biscuits, and sweet breads, all artfully arranged on a Sheraton sideboard from the 1700s under a bull's-eye mirror that seemed to magnify the food's already generous proportions.

The guest rooms are luxuriously decorated with eighteenth-century antiques and reproductions.

The three-story building encircles a brick courtyard with a fountain and a wishing pool. Large paintings of birds, deer, and other wildlife in the outside stairwells and on some of the courtyard walls fit in with plants growing there.

A few years ago, the inn began using the Jasmine House, a yellow pre–Civil War Greek Revival house around the corner, to house overflow. It has ten rooms, one with a Jacuzzi, some with fireplaces, and access to a refrigerator stocked with beer and ice. Guests are given keys to the front door so that they can come and go at will. Some prefer the Jasmine House even when the Indigo Inn is not full. The rates are higher for the Jasmine House.

Vince McPherson, who has been involved with the Indigo Inn since its opening, took me through the Jasmine House, explaining that its renovation and decoration had been a project in which the staff participated. He told me about putting together the huge antique admiral's bed, about the various renovation problems they'd solved and the decorating decisions they'd made. It left me thinking that I could go a point beyond Kilpatrick. The people here care about their guests. They also care about their inn.

How to get there: From I–26, take the Meeting Street exit. Although the address is Maiden Lane, the inn is close to the corner of Meeting and Pinckney.

The John Rutledge House Inn
Charleston, South Carolina
29401

Innkeeper: Linda Bishop; Richard T. Widman, owner
Address/Telephone: 116 Broad Street; (803) 723–7999 or (800) 476–9741
Rooms: 19 in the main house and 2 carriage houses; all with private bath, television, telephone, and refrigerator, some with Jacuzzi, some with wheelchair access. No-smoking rooms available.
Rates: $105 to $170, single; $120 to $185, double; $200 to $250, suites; continental breakfast. Extra person in room, $15. Children under 12 free.
Open: Year-round.
Facilities and activities: Full breakfast. Nearby: restaurants, walking distance to historic sites of Historic Charleston; theaters, shops, Charleston's slave market, historic tours.

A successful new inn in Charleston is good news. This one has taken connoisseurs of inns by storm, not only for its historic value and its elegance, but also for its vitality. In Charleston, some established inns seem to have reached the point of polite indifference. When you talk to people at this one, their pride in the place and their concern for guests are refreshing.

First, the history. John Rutledge, signer of the U.S. Constitution, lived here. The house was built in 1763 and is one of only fifteen homes of signers of the Constitution standing today. Also, much of the history of South Carolina was made during meetings in the ballroom and library.

As for the elegance, original plaster moldings and intricate ironwork have been restored, as have twelve marble mantels carved in Italy. At the risk of sounding disrespectful—when you look around, the phrase "really spiffed up" comes to mind. Bordered parquet floors simply take your breath away, as does the expanse of the ballroom where, in the early evening, guests are invited to mingle and share wine or sherry. If you're wearing your just-you clothes, I honestly can't tell you that you'll feel like a part of the room's history, but it is nice to go there knowing that Pinkneys and Laurens and Rutledges were once in that same space plotting the future of their state and nation. I think an honest reaction to this kind of information, though, is, "Enough already. Where do I sleep? What do I eat?"

The guest rooms are furnished in a mixture of antiques and period reproductions, with warm, cheerful colors—rose, peach, deep green, and ivory.

If you choose a continental breakfast, you'll have a tray of fresh pastries, juice, and coffee or tea delivered to your room at whatever time you specify. If you like a big breakfast to keep you going for most of the day, you can order a full breakast, for an extra charge, from a set menu. Just ask.

How to get there: The inn is near the corner of King and Broad streets. Ask for a map when you make a reservation.

Kings Courtyard Inn
Charleston, South Carolina
29401

Innkeeper: Laura Fox Howard
Address/Telephone: 198 King Street; (803) 723–7000 or (800) 845–6119
Rooms: 44; all with private bath, television, and telephone, some with fireplace, some with wheelchair access. Two are suites.
Rates: $85 to $150, single or double; $150 to $190, suites. Extra person in room, $15. Continental breakfast, complimentary wine and sherry on arrival, evening brandy and chocolates, morning newspaper, and free parking.
Open: Year-round.
Facilities and activities: Bar service in courtyards all afternoons but Sunday; Jacuzzi. Nearby: restaurants, historic sites and tours, tourist attractions, antiques shops.

The inn is a three-story 1853 building designed in the Greek Revival style.

I am endlessly fascinated by the old-city way of creating little areas of calm and quiet away from the streets with courtyards. It's done well here, with two brick courtyards filled with tropical plants and geraniums and accented with fountains: One has a Jacuzzi, and the other provides lots of shady spots for enjoying a cocktail.

The rooms are decorated individually and furnished with period reproductions. Some have canopied beds; some have fireplaces. They feel quiet, cool, and restful after you've been out pounding the Charleston sidewalks for a day.

The same tranquil feeling prevails in the lobby, where the fireplace and Audubon prints could as easily be part of a family living room as an inn. The desk of the concierge is here, too, with some very pleasant people to help with tours, transportation, and advice. I was impressed with the friendliness of the staff.

Kings Courtyard has received a nice honor. In 1989, it was one of thirty-two hotels recognized by the National Trust for Historic Preservation's new "Historic Hotels of America" program. Hotels chosen must be at least fifty years old and recognized as having historic significance.

How to get there: King Street parallels Meeting Street. From King Street, turn left on Market Street or Horlbeck Alley to park free in the city parking lot behind the inn.

S: *I consider this one of the better lodging values in Charleston.*

The Lodge Alley Inn
Charleston, South Carolina
29401

Innkeeper: Norma Armstrong
Address/Telephone: 195 East Bay Street; in South Carolina, (800) 821–2791; outside South Carolina, (800) 845–1004
Rooms: 34, plus 38 suites and 1 penthouse apartment; all with private bath, television, and telephone, some with wheelchair access, some suites with Jacuzzi.
Rates: $118 to $270, single or double; breakfast extra.
Open: Year-round.
Facilities and activities: Breakfast, lunch, dinner, and lounge, open to public and guests. No alcohol served on Sunday. Located on a restored alley in the heart of Historic Charleston, within walking distance of most historic sites. Nearby: carriage tours, Waterfront Park.

This is one of those saved-from-the-wrecking-ball stories. The whole alley of old warehouses was supposed to have been wiped out in 1973 to make way for condominiums, but the Save Charleston Foundation and some enterprising developers got into the act, saved the alley, and restored the buildings.

There's a lot of elegance in Charleston's history, which is reflected in the inn. When you arrive, you walk under a canopy, and a uniformed valet comes to park your car—or, in my case, to park my little red pickup truck. I wasn't sure how it would fit in with all that Charleston elegance, but the valet said not to worry, he'd take care of the truck as if it were his own.

A bellman, also in uniform, helped me get my bags to my room, making sure that I noticed the neatly hidden and well-stocked little refrigerator, the gas-log fireplace, and the eighteenth-century furniture reproductions. I was fascinated by one wall of the room: It still had the original brick and a huge exposed beam left from the old warehouse. The wide floor planks had the kinds of nicks and dark spots you'd expect to find in a warehouse. The floors were finished to a high gloss and partly covered with oriental rugs. From my window, I could see the steeples of some of Charleston's famous old churches.

The rooms in the carriage house are done less formally, in Country French decor, and are very spacious. Some have a second-level loft for bedroom and bath, with dining, living, and kitchen space below.

Even if you have a kitchen, though, you'll want to try the restaurant. It is known for its grand rotisserie, from which such delicacies as duck, quail, and rack of lamb come forth, to be served with new potatoes or rice. Also featured at the restaurant is a list of more than one hundred different French and American wines.

How to get there: I–26 and U.S. 17 are the major routes into Charleston. From either, turn right just before the Cooper River Bridge onto East Bay Street. Go 2 miles. The inn is on the right.

Maison Du Pré
Charleston, South Carolina
29401

Innkeepers: Lucille and Bob Mulholland; Mark Mulholland, manager
Address/Telephone: East Bay at George Street; (803) 723–8691 or (800) 844–INNS
Rooms: 15, including 2 suites; all with private bath, television, and telephone.
Rates: $98 to $200, single or double, continental breakfast and afternoon "Low Country tea." Inquire about off-season rates.
Open: Year-round.
Facilities and activities: Patios and landscaped gardens, facilities for small meetings, parties, weddings. Located in historic district of Charleston, next to the Gaillard Auditorium. Nearby: restaurants, historic sites and tours, antiques shops.

Maison Du Pré, dating back to 1804, comprises five buildings—three restored single houses and two carriage houses—surrounding a brick courtyard full of flowers, fountains, and an old well. Most innkeepers like to say that each room in their inn is different. When you consider all the nooks and crannies and assorted shapes and sizes inevitable in a collection of five old buildings, you can see that at Maison Du Pré that boast would almost inevitably have to be true.

There's a morning room, an evening room, an upstairs drawing room fitted out with a grand piano, a space for meetings and formal dining, and, of course, the fifteen guest rooms variously furnished with period furniture, antiques, and oriental rugs. The most memorable is undoubtedly the honeymoon suite, which has an old claw-footed bathtub (and a separate shower in case your love of history doesn't extend to bathing), and a fireplace. You get a chilled bottle of champagne when you rent this suite. The unusually nice courtyard and gardens unify all buildings and rooms and provide a pleasant common area in good weather.

Like so many of Charleston's old buildings, the Maison Du Pré would have been condemned had not the Mulhollands restored it. They've left their personal stamp throughout the buildings by decorating with Lucille's own oil paintings, watercolors, and pastels and her husband Bob's pen-and-ink drawings, as well as a collection of other works by Low Country artists. All of the bedrooms are named after the French Impressionist painters.

The sense of Maison Du Pré as a family project seems even stronger to me since Hurricane Hugo devastated Charleston on September 21, 1989. The Mulhollands, like many people in Charleston, fled to safety, waiting out the storm in Spartanburg, South Carolina. When they returned, they found that they couldn't get to their home on Sullivans Island but that Maison Du Pré remained relatively unharmed in the midst of all Charleston's destruction. They opened the inn for business as soon as the power was restored and moved temporarily with their two schnauzers into the little brick carriage house, trusting inn guests to forgive the presence of dogs in this situation. They're back in their own home now, but the special feeling of family shelter remains.

How to get there: The inn is between George Street and Laurens Street on East Bay.

S: *Maison Du Pré offers some excellent vacation packages and special-event arrangments worth calling about.*

Meeting Street Inn
Charleston, South Carolina
29401

Innkeeper: Simon T. Patterson
Address/Telephone: 173 Meeting Street; (803) 723–1882 or (800) 842–8022
Rooms: 55; all with private bath, television, and telephone.
Rates: $105 to $135, single or double, continental breakfast, newspaper.
　Inquire about corporate rates.
Open: Year-round.
Facilities and activities: Meeting room, Jacuzzi in courtyard. Nearby: restaurants, historic sites, Charleston tourist attractions, antiques shops.

Everything is elegant here: the miniature formal garden, the splendid fresh floral arrangements in the lobby, and the guest rooms furnished with eighteenth-century reproductions and oriental carpets. But the staff are so friendly that nobody feels intimidated.

The morning that I was sitting in the lobby, guests were hanging around in their Bermuda shorts and running shoes watching a photographer take pictures for an advertisement. A pretty girl in a maid's costume was holding a huge turkey. The photographer was snapping away. Everybody was saying silly things to make the girl with the turkey smile.

Guests came and went, business was transacted, and everybody was smiling and cheerful. This continuous, pleasant activity seems to be the norm. People who stay here really have fun. Guests congregate in the courtyard for chamber music and cocktails toward evening. During my visit, the music was provided by two flutists.

The inn is right across from the famous Charleston Market, where vendors try to sell you everything from sweet-grass baskets to specialty bean-stew mixes and fresh produce.

How to get there: Take the Meeting Street exit from I–26. Stay on Meeting Street to the 100 block.

Two Meeting Street
Charleston, South Carolina
29401

Innkeepers: The Spell Family: Pete, Jean, and Karen
Address/Telephone: 2 Meeting Street; (803) 723–7322
Rooms: 9; all with private bath, television on request.
Rates: $90 to $150, single or double, continental breakfast. Minimum two-day reservation requested on weekends. No credit cards.
Open: Year-round.
Facilities and activities: Nearby: restaurants, walk to most historic sites in Charleston.

On a scale of one to ten for elegance, Two Meeting Street is at least a twelve. Incredible. It's a renovated 1892 Queen Anne mansion filled with family antiques, oriental rugs, lamps, silver, and crystal. The Tiffany stained-glass windows and carved-oak paneling are simply breathtaking.

The guest rooms are similarly luxurious, with four-poster and canopied beds and period furniture.

The family whose antiques fill the house is the Spell family. David Spell, who was innkeeper for many years, has sold the property to his brother and sister-in-law, Pete and Jean Spell. They and their daughter, Karen, are all involved in managing the inn, while David has moved to a new, smaller inn, the Belvedere.

During a time when many family inns are being gobbled up by corporations and losing the sense of human involvement that made

244

them special, it is a joy to me to be able to tell you that all continues in the personal tradition in this inn, known for its museum-quality furnishings.

I don't want to give you the impression that the inn feels like a touch-me-not museum. It's livable. There is a small kitchen on each floor, for cooling wine and making coffee and snacks.

And staying at the inn is fun. From the piazzas, you can see everything that goes on in Battery Park. In the early evening, guests often gather on the porch for sherry or a cocktail and conversation and to watch the action in the park: kids, couples, carriages. Weddings are the best fun. As one guest said, "We sit and gawk."

A favorite story around the inn is about the time a television crew caught a guest playing the banjo as he sat on the piazza. They interviewed and filmed him as though he were a typical Charlestonian passing the time on a warm evening, and they included the piece in a documentary about Charleston life. Never mind that he was actually from Ohio, visiting Charleston for the first time in his life.

Another guest, whose hobby is collecting vintage clothing, dressed in costumes of the period all during her stay.

Dinner at Robert's of Charleston, in the Rainbow Market, is in keeping with the glamor and theatricality of Two Meeting Street. Robert sings operatic arias as he prepares the seven-course meals he serves to just fifty diners each night. As you sit in the dining room, you can hear him cooking and singing in the kitchen.

How to get there: From I–26 or U.S. 17, take the Meeting Street exit and stay on it until you come to the Battery, at the end of the street. The inn is at the corner of South Battery and Meeting.

Vendue Inn
Charleston, South Carolina
29401

Innkeepers: Evelyn and Morton Needle

Address/Telephone: 19 Vendue Range; (803) 577–7970

Rooms: 34; all with private bath, television, and telephone, some with Jacuzzi, some with fireplace, some with sitting area, some with wheelchair access.

Rates: $95 to $115, single; $105 to $145, double; $155 to $220, suites; continental breakfast and wine and cheese. Rates lowest between July 1 and September 14.

Open: Year-round.

Facilities and activities: Dinner for guests and the public by reservation Monday through Saturday, bar service with dinners in dining room, cocktails overlooking courtyard and on roof. Nearby: historic sites and tourist attractions of Charleston, antiques shops.

I walked in about 5:00 P.M. to find guests sipping wine in the sunken indoor courtyard while a piano player entertained from the main floor overlooking the courtyard. On Saturday evenings, the music includes a violin and cello. Even with the music, though, I think sometimes I'd rather enjoy a cocktail up on the roof garden, from where you can see Patriot's Point and Fort Sumter and enjoy the coolest breeze around. Off the porch is a refrigerator that you can use if you'd like to keep something not offered by the inn.

The inn is in the French merchant district, created in what was once an old warehouse. At various points throughout the inn, you can still see the old beams and old pine floors burnished to a rich glow.

The guest rooms, which vary considerably in size, have canopied and poster beds, with oriental rugs and eighteenth-century reproduction furniture. The newer suites have sitting rooms with fireplaces, Jacuzzis in the bathrooms, and wet bars.

The inn's restaurant, which used to be called Chouinard's, has a new life as The Library at Vendue. It's decorated in a warm English style reminiscent of an old library, with leather-bound books tucked into niches around the restaurant. Evelyn is proud of Chef Paul Tinsley's food, not only because it is good but also because, as she puts it, "his plates look like works of art." His seafood dishes are outstanding. Other specialties include lamb, beef, duck, and some wild game items.

For intimate dinners or private parties, you may request a separate dining room.

How to get there: From I–26, take 17 North at the Mt. Pleasant junction. Get off and take a right onto East Bay Street for 2 miles (past the old market). Take a left on Vendue Range.

Claussen's Inn
Columbia, South Carolina
29205

Innkeeper: Dan Vance
Address/Telephone: 2003 Greene Street; (803) 765–0440; outside South
  Carolina, (800) 622–3382
Rooms: 22, plus 7 suites; all with private bath, television, and telephone,
  suites with extra half-bath, some with wheelchair access. No-smoking
  rooms available.
Rates: $75, single; $100, double; continental breakfast and evening bever-
  ages. Inquire about corporate rates.
Open: Year-round.
Facilities and activities: Small conference room, outdoor Jacuzzi. Nearby:
  restaurants, University of South Carolina campus, state capitol buildings.

On the outside, Claussen's Inn still looks like an old bakery in
the middle of a busy business area where people come for all kinds
of food, wine and beer, movies, antiques, and fine clothing. The
bakery is listed on the National Historic Register.

When you first walk in, you're struck by the open, skylit lobby
with comfortable overstuffed couches and chairs and lots of blooming plants. The second-floor loft overlooking the lobby has more of
the same furniture. A water fountain on the main floor trickles the
whole place calm.

The rooms are decorated with antique reproductions, queen-
and king-sized beds, and large baths that blend comfortably with

the restored brick and roof supports and the Mexican terra-cotta. Most of the rooms have 20-foot ceilings, and several have loft bedrooms.

The loft suite I saw has hardwood floors, full-length windows, an airy sitting area on the lower level, and a staircase that winds to the four-poster bed in the loft. The overall effect is bright and open.

Claussen's offers the amenities you'd expect: turn-down service with chocolate and brandy in the evening and, in the morning, a complimentary continental breakfast and a newspaper to read under the skylight.

As for food, Claussen's is within walking distance of restaurants offering Greek, American, Italian, continental, and fast food. If you're in the mood to frolic, there are pubs, dance clubs, a comedy club, a movie theater, live-band clubs, a pool and hotdog joint, and even a couple of dives.

Claussen's caters to corporate travelers, but I can't imagine anyone not enjoying a stay here—no matter how uncorporate he or she may be.

How to get there: From I–277, exit left onto Harden. Turn right at Greene Street; from I–26, take the Cayce/West Columbia exit and follow Route 321 to Harden. Turn left on Harden. Go to Greene Street. Turn left onto Greene Street.

S: *This is probably the only way I can go into a bakery without doing myself bodily harm!*

The Shaw House
Georgetown, South Carolina
29440

Innkeeper: Mary Shaw
Address/Telephone: 8 Cypress Court; (803) 546–9663
Rooms: 3; all with private bath, 2 with dressing room; television and tele-
    phone by arrangement.
Rates: $50, single or double, full breakfast. No credit cards.
Open: Year-round.
Facilities and activities: Bicycles, bird-watching. Nearby: restaurants, golf, ten-
    nis, marinas, antiques and gift shops, museums.

When a reader is disappointed by an inn I have recommended,
I hear about it; I seldom hear when guests enjoy an inn. The Shaw
House is a notable exception. Because it has only three rooms, I
debated whether or not to include it in this book. Now I am glad I
did. I've heard repeated praise for Mary Shaw and her little inn. It
has two outstanding features: a spectacular location overlooking
Willowbank Marsh, and Mary Shaw.

First, the marsh. It's a bird-watcher's dream. The bird-watchers
I know would be pleased to slog around out here, identifying one
hard-to-find bird after another. But from The Shaw House, on a little bluff overlooking the marsh, they can sit at the breakfast table by
the great picture windows in the corner and see more birds than
they would right out in the grasses. Guests who are serious about
bird-watching bring their binoculars and books and note pads right
to the table.

Now, Mary, a tiny, perky woman who favors bright-colored clothes, is a natural-born Southern storyteller who also has the knack of hospitality. The house is full of antiques. She can lead you on a tour of the rooms, telling stories about when and how she and her husband, Joe, acquired or inherited each piece. In the telling, the rice bed, the Eastlake chair, the English dressing table from the early 1800s, the rare petticoat mirror—all take on reality as furniture that living people used over generations.

Mary enjoys her guests. In the evening, she offers wine and cookies and snacks. In the morning, she prepares a mammoth breakfast and gives you your own pot of coffee. Her casserole of grits, cheese, and sausage is so popular that she has had copies of the recipe printed for all who ask. If you stay several days, you'll see that Mary sets the table with different dishes and linens each morning.

The Shaw House is an easy place to be. You can come and go without ceremony and rely on Mary for whatever advice you need about local historic sites and restaurants.

On her recommendation, I tried the River Room Restaurant, an easy walk from the inn. It's a small place, with a tiny bar and a nice variety of wines. Iced tea is served in wide-mouthed Ball jars. People dress casually. I had a fine crab salad and some of the best fried onion rings I've tasted in a long time. The onions were cut into thick slices and the breading was not the typical heavy cornmeal bomb, but a crispy, tempuralike batter. If you go there, try to be early. Because the dining room is so small, no reservations are accepted.

How to get there: Route 17 goes through town. Turn away from the business district onto Orange Street. Make a quick jog left. You will see the street signs for Cypress.

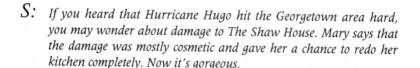

S: *If you heard that Hurricane Hugo hit the Georgetown area hard, you may wonder about damage to The Shaw House. Mary says that the damage was mostly cosmetic and gave her a chance to redo her kitchen completely. Now it's gorgeous.*

Village B & B
McClellanville, South Carolina
29458

Innkeeper: Cheri George
Address/Telephone: 333 Mercantile Road: (803) 887–3266
Rooms: 1 with private bath, telephone, television, and kitchenette. No
    smoking inn.
Rates: $55, single or double, continental breakfast. No unmarried couples.
    No credit cards.
Open: Year-round.
Facilities and activities: McClellanville is a fishing village. Nearby: boating,
    national forest hiking trails, hunting; midway between Charleston and
    Georgetown.

My finding this place proves that I lead a serendipitous life.
The fact that it survived Hurricane Hugo proves that Cheri is doing
something right.

My part of the story is that when I was driving south from
Georgetown to Charleston on Route 17, I saw a small sign and followed it along some back roads to the inn. Cheri's story is more
dramatic. Both her family home and the inn floated off their foun-
dations in waves of the Atlantic that devastated most of McClellanville. Somehow the Georges managed to get the buildings back
where they belong, and, with elbow grease and paint and determi-
nation, they got everything back the way it was.

Village B & B, only about a mile from Route 17 on an unpaved road, lies in the middle of a large lawn with woods behind and with fields edged with live oaks and their requisite Spanish moss across the road.

It's the smallest inn I've ever visited, but it definitely *is* an inn. The room is 20 feet by 20 feet in a wing completely separate from the owners' house. The pale floor, sanded and finished old southern pine, is so striking that it practically stands up and says hello. The teal wallpaper complements the floor without being too dark because of all the big white-curtained windows that let light in and let you look out at the rural countryside. A large bath and dressing area extend to the rear. The set-up is ideal if you are traveling with children because it is so spacious.

The antique iron beds, dressed in fluffy white and peach covers, had been in Cheri's family for three generations. When she decided to open the inn, she hauled them from the barn and had them blasted and painted white.

At a round table near the door, Cheri serves your breakfast: blueberry or honey bran muffins, fresh ambrosia, and coffee or tea. The overall effect is amazingly relaxing.

While Cheri chatted at the table, I studied the large watercolor seascapes on the walls and wondered where she'd found such nice art, intending to ask her about it before I left. Before I got around to it, she made an off-hand mention of "Matthew's paintings" and indicated a bin of some for sale I'd somehow overlooked in the corner. In his spare time, her husband, Matthew, paints local outdoor scenes, birds, flowers, and shells.

I don't claim to be an art critic, but I have to tell you, I was so taken with Matthew's work that it took me an hour to narrow the choices down to five favorites and then another half-hour to decide on the two I just had to have. When I got them home, my framer admired them lavishly. Now Matthew's print from an oil, of a boy fishing off the end of a dock at twilight, hangs in my office; a watercolor of a lighthouse seen from under a dilapidated, barnacle-encrusted pier delights me in the bedroom.

And that's what I mean by leading a serendipitous life.

How to get there: From U.S. 17, turn at McClellanville at the caution light. Follow the signs to the inn.

Chesterfield Inn
Myrtle Beach, South Carolina
29578

Innkeeper: Bob Chapman
Address/Telephone: 700 North Ocean Boulevard (mailing address: P.O. Box 218); (803) 448–3177
Rooms: 31 in inn, 26 motel units adjacent; all with private bath, television, and telephone. Wheelchair access to some motel rooms.
Rates: $60 to $128, double; single $27 less; breakfast and dinner. Children welcome; inquire about special rates.
Open: Year-round except December and January.
Facilities and activities: Dinner open to the public by reservation. Heated pool, beachfront. Nearby: tennis clubs, golf, outlet shopping malls.

When I first found this inn, quite by accident, I couldn't believe it—a little island of old-time stability smack in the middle of the beachfront glitz of a major ocean resort area.

It's not just that the building is brick and wood instead of plastic and chrome. The inn's key people have been here a while, too. For instance, the current innkeeper is a cousin to the previous innkeeper, and their relatives were here back in the 1930s and '40s, which creates a wonderful sense of continuity.

This is not a fancy place. It's a place you can take the kids to and not have to worry about their sitting too hard in a chair or scuffing up expensive rugs. And you don't have to yell at them not to play on the elevators because there aren't any. The building is only three stories high.

The lobby looks like a huge family room, with wood walls painted white and an assortment of tough, comfortably worn country-style furniture.

The dining room, which has an unbroken view of the ocean, is wood paneled with a terra-cotta floor. Outside the dining-room windows, lots of wood rockers line the porch, and a lawn connects the porch to the beach. During the summer months, when the beach is guarded, the hotel provides beach chairs and umbrellas for guests.

Myrtle Beach is part of the Grand Strand, 55 miles of wide, white bathing beaches. Somewhere around Myrtle Beach you can find every tourist amusement in the book, including many outlet stores, and then retreat to the inn for dinner when it all gets too much for you.

The food is what you might call "Southern-style country." The menu always offers a choice among three or four entrees and includes three vegetables, mostly fresh, and fresh seafood.

Although the inn does not have full facilities for the handicapped, some of the motel rooms are accessible, and the staff often and willingly help guests in wheelchairs get to the restaurant through a rear door with only a small step. They welcome your questions if you have any doubt about whether the place could work for you.

How to get there: Take U.S. 501 into Myrtle Beach. Turn left onto Broadway and go to the first light. Turn right onto Oak and drive a short block to Seventh Avenue North. Turn left and drive 3 blocks to Ocean Boulevard, which is the oceanfront street. The inn is at the corner of Seventh Avenue North and Ocean Boulevard.

Serendipity
Myrtle Beach, South Carolina
29577

Innkeepers: Cos and Ellen Ficarra
Address/Telephone: 401 71st Street North; (803) 449–5268
Rooms: 12; all with private bath, refrigerator, and television.
Rates: $62 to $87, double, continental breakfast. Inquire about fall, winter, and children's rates.
Open: March 1 to November 30.
Facilities and activities: Heated pool, Jacuzzi, shuffleboard, Ping-Pong, gas grill. Nearby: 1½ blocks to beachfront; restaurants, tennis, golf, fishing, outlet shopping.

Cos and Ellen like people. People like them. When you stay at Serendipity, if you spend any time in the common room, where breakfast is served and where people just wander in to sit and sip something cold, you'll talk to a lot of friendly and interesting people—the Ficarras, guests, and local friends of the Ficarras.

The inn itself is *very* pretty, *very* clean, *very* comfortable. That's not always true of lodgings in vacation centers.

The furnishings and decor are several notches above beach standards for artistic interest and aesthetic appeal but still sturdy enough to accommodate children. The Ficarras are knowledgeable collectors of fine antiques and art, and even though they don't spread a lot of that really good stuff around the inn, I think the level of their taste still affects the look of the grounds and guest rooms.

In the Oak Room, for instance, two antique lion's head oak chairs from Pawleys Island dominate; in one smaller room, Holly Hobbie wallpaper is lifted beyond cliché by a quilted bedspread and a signed Norman Rockwell print.

All the rooms have good reading lights and chairs and, just in case you didn't bring a book, you may choose one from what Ellen and I laughingly called the "trashy novel" selection of paperbacks in the common room. Guests leave books they've finished and take others, and Ellen adds those she's read, so the collection is ever-changing. To me, places that are set up for readers rank high.

Likewise, Ellen's breakfasts are a cut above the usual B & B continental because, instead of going for the near-ubiquitous croissant, she serves breads baked by a local German friend, along with hard-boiled eggs, cereal, bagels and cream cheese, and her own specialties, differing from day to day. When I was there, she had prunes stewed with apples and spices that were so good I tried to duplicate them when I got home. Other guests raved about her warm brown Betty.

As for dinner, Cos and Ellen recommend two Italian places that are as special in their own ways as Serendipity itself. The Villa Mare is a neighborhood Italian restaurant/pizzeria with low prices and high quality, good for getting a meal without a fuss. The Villa Roma, for more important meals, offers fresh hand-cut veal, fresh pasta, and breads made on the premises. The proprietors came from Rome and they know how to do it right! The Ficarras eat at these places themselves whenever they can. They also recommend Cerro Grande, a new authentic Mexican restaurant with good food and music on Saturday nights, all at reasonable prices.

How to get there: Take Highway 17 (King's Highway) to 71st Avenue North. Turn east toward the ocean. The inn is just off the highway, behind hedges.

Sea View Inn
Pawleys Island, South Carolina
29585

Innkeeper: Page Oberlin
Address/Telephone: Pawleys Island; (803) 237–4253
Rooms: 20; all with private half-bath, showers at ends of halls, some with air conditioning.
Rates: $90, single; $65 to $75, per person, double occupancy; 3 meals a day. Weekly: single, $610; $430 to $500, per person, double occupancy; 3 meals a day. Minimum two-night stay. Priority given to stays of a week or longer. Inquire about spring watercolor and fitness weeks. No credit cards.
Open: Last week of April through October.
Facilities and activities: Beachfront and umbrellas, crab dock in salt marsh. Nearby: boating, fishing, naturalist's studies in the salt marsh and surrounding area.

Pawleys Island is a small sea island, 4 miles long and one house wide, where the people are proud to say that nothing changes and nobody hurries. You won't find any commercial activity here, just what Page likes to call "barefoot freedom at its best."

Guest rooms are plain but comfortable. The living room has a brick fireplace, grass mats on the floor, and couches and chairs upholstered in pastel rainbow colors. There are good books everywhere.

Many watercolors, mostly beach and water scenes, hang on the walls. They are the work of artists who take the week-long watercolor workshop held at the inn early each spring. Some of the pictures are for sale.

You can hear and see the ocean from practically every point in the inn, including the dining room. Meals served here emphasize Low Country foods such as gumbos and black-eyed peas with corn bread, and seafood in some form each day. The desserts range from a creamy chocolate pie to a light and fluffy peanut butter pie.

If you're here for the early spring "shape-up week," when people come to shake off winter lethargy and exercise back to fitness, the meals feature vegetarian entrees, seafood, and whole grains.

During the rest of the season, sunning, swimming, and shelling take up guests' time. Toward the end of the day, they sometimes gather on the porch facing the marsh, where they keep their spirits on the shelves and in the refrigerator for an afternoon cocktail. Even if no other people show up, you're not exactly alone on the porch. You can talk to the green parrot in the big white cage. I don't know his name. He wouldn't tell me.

How to get there: From Route 17, turn at the PAWLEYS ISLAND sign onto the connector road. In less than a mile you must turn left or right. Turn left. The inn will be about 4 telephone poles south of the chapel.

Liberty Hall Inn
Pendleton, South Carolina
29670

Innkeepers: Tom and Susan Jonas
Address/Telephone: Liberty Hall; (803) 646–7500 or (800) 643–7944
Rooms: 10; all with private bath and television. No smoking in guest rooms.
Rates: $52 to $62, single; $57 to $67, double; extended continental breakfast. Cot or additional person in room, $15.
Open: Year-round except for major holidays.
Facilities and activities: Dining room open for dinner for guests and the public Monday through Saturday; reservations appreciated; full liquor service. Located in Historic Pendleton, which is on the National Register of Historic Places. Nearby: golf, Lake Hartwell, Clemson University, many historic sites.

They didn't know I was coming. Knowing Liberty Hall had changed hands, I decided on impulse one day to stop in. The housekeeper said the new innkeepers, Tom and Susan, were in the kitchen getting ready for a big luncheon and told me to go on back. The two were so cool you'd think they had crazy ladies claiming to be the authors of travel guides wander into the kitchen every day of the week.

The kitchen was a spotless expanse of stainless steel. A crowd was due in thirty minutes, and all Tom and Sue had left to do was wash some lettuce leaves. So that I could sample their luncheon offering, they fixed me a plate of really good chicken salad with rice and mandarin orange sections and garnished with fresh spinach, black-seeded Simpson lettuce, and fresh tomatoes ("we didn't want to serve just any old chicken salad," Tom said) and poured me a glass of white wine. Then, never once looking ruffled, Sue showed me the changes they've made at Liberty Hall.

The inn is still comfortably furnished with many of the same period antiques and lots of Williamsburg blue, rose, and burgundy in the draperies, bed covers, and linens; the beds are still firm and comfortable. Sue has added to those basics lots of little personal items: books, family pictures, knickknacks, her mother's needlework, and quilts from her own collection. And, being a reader, Sue saw to it that every room has a good lamp on each side of the bed. The overall effect is that you can settle into a room as comfortably as if your own mother had fixed it up for your visit.

Outside, thriving herb and vegetable gardens provide seasonings and salad greens, and the Jonases's son, Alex, who has become a competitive gardener, is trying to grow the biggest pumpkin in South Carolina.

I haven't heard anything about pumpkin pie! But the dinner possibilities just get better and better here, with crab cakes, a spectacular 8-ounce beef tenderloin filet marinated in a special sauce, plus local pasture-raised veal, chicken, and seafood entrees always among the choices. Dinners are single price, fixed menu, with a choice of entrees. There is no set menu in the restaurant. Tom and Sue say that fresh ingredients and inspiration determine what they offer.

Tom continues to refine and expand his wine list, always trying to take wine seriously while keeping the offerings in a price range that doesn't require you to take out a second mortgage to buy a bottle of wine.

How to get there: From I–85, take exit 19B toward Clemson and follow U.S. 76/28 almost to Pendleton where Business 28 turns to the right. The inn is on the right, shortly after you turn. From U.S. 123, take 76/28 to Pendleton and turn left onto Business 28. Go past the town square. The inn will be on your left.

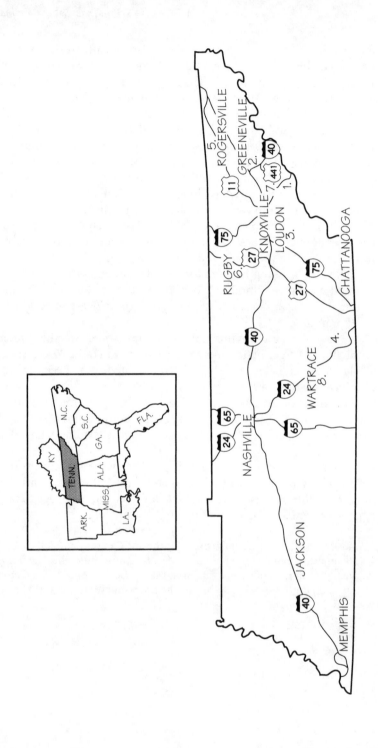

Tennessee

Numbers on map refer to towns numbered below.

Buckhorn Inn
Gatlinburg, Tennessee
37738

Innkeepers: John and Connie Burns
Address/Telephone: 2140 Tudor Mountain Road; (615) 436–4468
Rooms: 6, plus 4 cottages, 1 guest house; all with private bath, cottages and guest house with television, refrigerator or kitchenette, and fireplace.
Rates: $95 to $250, double, full breakfast. Only traveler's checks, personal checks, and cash accepted.
Open: Year-round, except Christmas.
Facilities and activities: Fixed-price, set-menu dinner for guests by reservation, $18 per person. Ice available. Small conference facilities. Spring-fed lake stocked with bream and bass. Located on 35 acres. Nearby: hiking, swimming, tennis, racquetball, basketball, skiing, golf, shopping, and tourist activities. Close to Gatlinburg.

I found some changes during a return visit to Buckhorn Inn. John and Connie Burns had taken over as innkeepers. The inn was designed by John's grandfather and was owned and operated by John's uncle for many years. Robert, Rachel, and Lindsay Young now own it, and John and Connie run it for them.

Everything looks better than ever. And the short drive up the hill from the glitz of Gatlinburg bringing you to the simple white building well settled into mature landscaping and woods still soothes your jangled nerves, as does the view of the highest peaks of the Smokies.

Inside, the living room and dining room are divided from each other in one big, long room by a large stone fireplace in the middle of the front wall. The chairs and love seats are cool and summery looking in new upholstery.

From here, doors open out onto a narrow porch separated from a well-manicured lawn by a low hedge. From the lawn, stone steps lead to a footpath that wanders into the woods.

Once when I stopped here, I met an elderly woman who had first visited the inn when someone gave a trip here to her and her husband as an anniversary present. She has come back every year since, even though her husband has passed on. And I met a young couple entranced with the grand piano, the rockers, and the generous supply of books. I think they had come intending to follow a full-steam-ahead schedule of hiking, fishing, and fitness but had been lulled into rocking and reading instead.

The inn has always been known for its good food and that, too, is better than ever. Everything is home cooked daily, from breads to desserts. A professional chef on staff has been creating sophisticated menus. At breakfast, for instance, your choices, in addition to standards such as country ham and eggs, might include a strawberry or walnut waffle with bacon or Buckhorn's own version of müesli cereal. At dinner, they serve up meals such as pesto chicken with basil cream sauce, preceded by chablis cheddar soup, accompanied by rice pilaf, salad, and a fresh vegetable, and finished off with a dessert of fresh strawberries, honey, and cream.

How to get there: Take U.S. 441 to Gatlinburg and turn onto U.S. 321 north at Gatlinburg Chamber of Commerce corner. Follow U.S. 321 north about 5 miles. Turn left at Buckhorn Road and go ³/₄ mile. Turn right at BUCKHORN INN sign. The inn is ¹/₄ mile on the right.

Big Spring Inn
Greeneville, Tennessee
37743

Innkeepers: Jeanne Driese and Cheryl Van Dyck
Address/Telephone: 315 North Main Street; (615) 638–2917
Rooms: 6; 5 with private bath, 2 with fireplace, telephone and television on request. Smoking in designated areas only.
Rates: $60 to $75, single; $65 to $80, double; full gourmet breakfast. Advance arrangement for children under 12.
Open: Year-round.
Facilities and activities: Picnic lunches and dinner by special arrangement, brown bagging permitted. Library, swimming pool. Nearby: walk to Greeneville historic sites; Great Smoky Mountains, champagne balloon rides; local dinner and outdoor concerts.

Jeanne has the good innkeeper's knack of making you feel as though you've known her forever. She and Cheryl are a mother–daughter team, and their sense of family somehow includes their guests as well.

The inn is full of special little touches that make you feel that Jeanne and Cheryl took pains to prepare for your visit: fresh flowers, fruit, and cookies in your room, along with a basket containing shampoo, deodorant, and the other little things you tend to forget when you're traveling.

The inn is housed in an old three-story brick Victorian building in remarkably good shape, and in furnishing it, Jeanne and Cheryl have used both antiques and reproductions, concentrating on comfort. My room seemed especially restful, with the blue of the walls and carpet echoed in the shades of a woven coverlet and in the bouquet of blue miniature irises on the nice oak library table.

Just outside the room, a library for guests invites browsing. At bedside, I found leather-bound editions of *Jane Eyre* and *Stories of Edgar Allan Poe.*

Truth to tell, however, I didn't spend a lot of time reading because by the time I had finished Jeanne's dinner, I was too sleepy. She served flounder in a light wine sauce with white grapes; steamed, herbed carrots; and a fresh salad made with a tomato that actually tasted like a tomato. We had muffins that were just faintly sweet, a perfect accompaniment to the fish. And for dessert, strawberries cardinal—fresh strawberries in a raspberry-kirsch sauce with almonds. Good, good.

One of the nicest new offerings at Big Spring Inn is the gourmet picnic basket for two, a lavish spread including a woven basket that you get to keep.

It's also worth noting that the herb garden, started in 1986, has matured and gotten bigger each year; its bounty shows up in all seasons in herb butters, herbed eggs, pestos, and salads with edible flowers.

Finally, Big Spring Inn offers a number of special vacation and honeymoon packages, ranging from a Christmas weekend to several different cooking-class weekends and a fall foliage celebration. Do ask about these.

How to get there: The inn is 75 miles northeast of Knoxville. From the south, leave I–81 at exit 23 (Greeneville–Bulls Gap). Follow Business 11E to Main Street. Turn left. The inn is the seventh house on the left after the third stoplight. From the north, take exit 36 (Baileyton Road) off I–81 and go 14 miles to the stoplight. Turn right onto North Main and continue to the corner of Nelson. Turn right onto Nelson and then left into the drive.

River Road Inn
Loudon, Tennessee
37774

Innkeepers: Pam and Kent Foster
Address/Telephone: River Road (mailing address: P.O. Box 372); (615) 458–4861
Rooms: 6, including 2 suites; all with private bath, 1 with large Jacuzzi and kitchenette, 1 with separate nursery with crib. Some pets accepted with advance notice.
Rates: $65 to $85, double, full breakfast. $10 each additional person.
Open: Year-round.
Facilities and activities: Swimming pool, fishing, nature trails, boating, farm animals. Nearby: short drive to restaurants, Great Smoky Mountains National Park, Knoxville and Oak Ridge, Watts Bar, Tellico recreational lakes.

The Foster family has created that rare gem, an inn that *welcomes* children and accepts some pets happily. The Fosters have young children themselves and had the inspiration to turn that into an asset, making the place into an inn/farm alive with a pony and new colt, baby chicks, ducks, and geese. They mow the grass from the house all the way back to the barn, so it is a pleasant walk. About halfway between the house and barn is a swing set for children. And the nursery room has a wicker crib decorated with a Peter Rabbit motif. (The nursery is in the restored slave quarters, assuring that the sound of a crying babe doesn't fill the house.)

That's important, because this inn is still a treat for adults who enjoy good historic preservation and imaginative decorating in rural settings. The inn is a Federalist home built circa 1857. The foyer is furnished with an antique grandfather's clock from Ireland, a French needlepoint chair, and a blue-velvet Victorian parlor set that echoes the color of the morning glories in the original cabbage-rose wallpaper.

The double parlor is furnished with some excellent Victorian and Empire pieces, but the attractions are the baby grand piano and the large fireplace, both of which invite guests to gather and make friends.

Pam loves celebrating the seasons and uses seasonal decorations and fresh flowers from the property all through the house.

Pam also loves being an innkeeper, loves this inn, and loves the good feelings that come with a successful project as the family continues improving the property. She designed new drapes to frame the windows without obstructing the view and says with pride, "They turned out great!"

And probably because Pam's enthusiasm is contagious, everybody loves her. Other innkeepers in Tennessee speak highly of her; guests leave rave notes: "Pam, your personality is a real asset!" and "This house is fantastic and it's so lucky to have you to breathe life into it."

I should mention also that Pam breathes life into sightseeing by keeping information about the area in her computer to plan and print out day trips and restaurant recommendations for you.

How to get there: From I–75, take exit 72 toward Loudon. Go ¹/₂ mile to Queener Road. Turn left and follow Queener to River Road. Turn right. The inn is on the left.

Adams Edgeworth Inn
Monteagle, Tennessee
37356

Innkeepers: Wendy and David Adams
Address/Telephone: Monteagle Assembly; (615) 924–2669
Rooms: 10, plus 1 suite with kitchenette and fireplace; all with private bath, some rooms with fireplace or wheelchair access. Smoking on verandas only.
Rates: $55 to $125, single and double, continental breakfast. Two-night minimum on special weekends.
Open: Year-round.
Facilities and activities: Dinner by reservation. Gift shop. On grounds of Monteagle Assembly. Nearby: golf, tennis, Tennessee State Park, wilderness and developed hiking trails, Sewanee University of the South, Monteagle Wine Cellars.

Occasionally someone opens an inn that seems destined from the beginning to become a classic. I believe Edgeworth is such an inn. David and Wendy put uncountable hours of study, thought, and travel into defining the kind of inn they wanted. Then they put at least that much into finding the right building in the right location. They wanted a good-sized inn, in a rural setting, elegant but not formal. They wanted a full-service inn, serving dinner as well as breakfast.

The three-story Victorian house, nearly one hundred years old, on the grounds of the Monteagle Assembly (sometimes called "the

Chautauqua of the South"), is perfect because it was built as an inn. Outside, David and Wendy expanded established perennial gardens to enhance the sense of rural seclusion. It looks like everything has been growing here forever.

Inside, they refurbished and brightened the interior without hiding the wood floors or changing the inn's warm character. They brought a large, eclectic collection of museum-quality art, as well as antiques and interesting mementos they and their grown children have picked up in world travel. Also, they have some wonderful items from the years Wendy's father spent as a United States ambassador, including the gold-edged ambassadorial china upon which Wendy serves dinner.

Some of the guest rooms have been designed around quilts made by her mother and grandmother that Wendy uses as bed covers. The library and guest rooms overflow with books. Classical music deepens the feeling of serenity in the sitting areas and floats out onto the shady porches.

If you prefer an active retreat to a sedentary one, the state park and wilderness areas offer more possibilities than you could explore in a lifetime. Because David has family with homes on the Assembly grounds, he knows the area intimately and takes pleasure in sharing. You can, he asserts, even find places to go skinny-dipping. The facilities of the Assembly offer more sedate versions of swimming and walking.

Dinner deserves a write-up of its own. When Wendy dims the lights in the formal dining room, most of the illumination comes from candles, except for small lamps shining over each of the paintings in the room. Often a piano player or guitarist provides music.

We had an appetizer of smoked salmon with Russian black bread and Vidalia onions. Of the several choices of entrees, I especially enjoyed the chicken breast filled with fresh herbs. We had a variety of lightly cooked and sauced fresh vegetables, and a colorful salad of arugula and greens with Camembert. For dessert Wendy served fresh strawberries and kiwi in a custard sauce with a hint of either caramel or maple. Maybe both. The flavors were subtle enough to keep me wondering.

It doesn't get any better than this.

How to get there: From I–24 take exit 134. Turn right. In the center of the village you will see a steel archway with a MONTEAGLE ASSEMBLY sign. Turn through the arch. Once on the grounds, turn right at the mall sign and right immediately at Chestnut Hill.

Hale Springs Inn
Rogersville, Tennessee
37857

Innkeepers: Ed Pace and Sue Livesay
Address/Telephone: 110 West Main Street; (615) 272–5171 or (800) 272–5171
Rooms: 10; all with private bath and television, 9 with working fireplace.
Rates: $45 to $65, double; inquire about rates for single; continental breakfast.
Open: Year-round.
Facilities and activities: Dinner for guests and public Monday through Saturday, brown bagging wine permitted. Restored formal gardens and gazebo. Nearby: walking tour of Historic Rogersville, many historic sites in upper East Tennessee; Smoky Mountains, Cherokee Lake, swimming, tennis, golf.

Hale Springs Inn is just one-half block away from the courthouse. It was Election Day when I was there, and from the dining-room windows I could watch voters come and go while supporters of one candidate or another wandered around waving signs. It seemed right to be observing contemporary political activity from the inn where presidents Andrew Jackson, James K. Polk, and Andrew Johnson all stayed (not together, mind you).

The inn was built in 1824. Skilled restoration has kept its historic interest alive without sacrificing comfort. The rooms are all big and bright, with high ceilings, good plumbing, and cheerful decor. All the rooms but one have a working fireplace.

I like the fact that when the rooms are not occupied, their doors are kept open so that you can see how each one is furnished. You can pick up a self-guided–tour brochure and go through the inn one floor at a time, noting such things as an authentic East Tennessee bed, wardrobe, and chest of drawers in the John McKinney Room, and a mantel in the Andrew Johnson Room that was brought from Philadelphia by wagon in 1824.

The restaurant in the inn balances history and contemporary tastes equally well. The costumes of the service people, the decor, and the music all reflect the Colonial period, as do the menu and recipes. A typical Colonial dish is Rosemont chicken, containing breast of chicken and Virginia ham with a light grape sauce. The specialty of the house is prime rib of beef, fashionable in any century.

How to get there: Rogersville is on Highway 11W about 65 miles east of Knoxville and 30 miles west of Kingsport. Follow the main street into the center of town to the town square and the inn.

Newbury House
at Historic Rugby
Rugby, Tennessee
37733

Innkeepers: Historic Rugby
Address/Telephone: Route 52 (mailing address: P.O. Box 8); (615) 628–2430
Rooms: 5, plus 2 cottages; 3 rooms with private bath, both cottages with private bath and one with wheelchair access.
Rates: $58 to $68, double; single $10 less; full breakfast at New Harrow Road Cafe and continuously available coffee or tea.
Open: Year-round; February 1 to December 31 for tours.
Facilities and activities: Cafe open for breakfast and lunch daily; for dinner Friday and Saturday; brown bagging wine permitted. Tour of historic buildings, craft commissary, bookshop, "gentlemen's" swimming hole (now for ladies, too). Nearby: Village is at Boundary A of the Big South Fork National River and Recreational Area; hiking, rafting, fishing.

For this place to make any sense to you, you need to know that once upon a time in England all the good jobs and positions of power went to the first sons in English families. Second sons didn't get much of anything. Thomas Hughes was a reformer who tried to change that by starting the Rugby colony in the wilderness of Tennessee as a place where second sons could create their own world and still enjoy British ways. Like most utopian attempts, it never quite worked, partly because no one prepared those younger sons for what they were getting into.

Staying here may not have been a lot of fun for those unprepared English sons, but it's great for a tourist today. In addition to getting a glimpse into the life of another time, you get the pleasures of a nicely kept inn with good beds, some exposure to the local mountain culture, and access to wonderful crafts.

Although the inn is carefully attended, this is not the kind of place where you lounge about chatting with the innkeeper. You'll find a letter on your bed telling you about the possibilities of the whole village. Your interaction is with the entire village and its staff, all of whom are educated to answer questions not only about Historic Rugby, but also about the surrounding area. Even breakfast is an interaction with the village, because it is served in the village cafe, where you have a choice of continental or full Southern breakfasts. It's all spelled out for you on a Victorian menu card.

This Victorian theme is echoed in a new, successful Victorian book shop.

The craft commissary has improved steadily in recent years and is considered by some visitors to be better than any other in the state. Much of the work is done by local people and by people who take the workshops Historic Rugby sponsors in weaving, quilting, making white-oak baskets, cornhusk crafts, and the like. Write for a full schedule. You may choose to plan your visit here to correspond with one of the workshops.

How to get there: Rugby is on Route 52, between Elgin and Jamestown, Tennessee. From I–75, take State Highway 63 east, then go south on Highway 27 to Highway 52. Go west on 52 about 6 miles. From I–40, go north on Highway 27 or 127 to 52.

Blue Mountain Mist Country Inn
Sevierville, Tennessee
37862

Innkeepers: Norman and Sarah Ball

Address/Telephone: 1811 Pullen Road; (615) 428–2335

Rooms: 11, plus 1 suite; all with private bath, 2 with Jacuzzi, 4 with wheelchair access. Five 2-person cottages with Jacuzzi and fireplace. No smoking inn.

Rates: $69, single; $79 to $125, double; full breakfast, continental breakfast for late risers. Extra person in room, $15.

Open: Year-round.

Facilities and activities: Television room, conference room, outdoor Jacuzzi, permanent horseshoe court, volleyball and badminton, walking trail. Nearby: restaurants; short drive to Pigeon Forge, Gatlinburg, and Great Smoky Mountains National Park; crafts community.

Blue Mountain Mist is a *new* Victorian-style farmhouse built in 1987 specifically to be used as an inn. Consequently, the interior is bright, cheerful, and spacious, escaping the sense of gloom and spaces being forced into unnatural uses that sometimes afflicts old mansions converted to inns.

The inn is in the foothills, where you find lots of rolling farmland and can see in all directions. The Balls have built the inn on a portion of the farm belonging to Sarah's parents, and the family feeling pervades the operation. Quilts and furniture from Sarah's family are part of the inn's decor, and a picture of the inn drawn by Sarah's son, Jason, in 1987 when he was in kindergarten, hangs framed in a position of honor at the foot of the stairs near the front door. Sarah's mother stops in regularly with fresh flowers for the inn, and folks do a lot of visiting.

Visiting is encouraged by cozy upstairs and downstairs sitting areas, each with a fireplace, and by the rocking chairs on the big wraparound porch from which you have a great view of the surrounding countryside as well as the inn's nicely kept grounds.

The guest rooms, furnished with country antiques, are as airy and pleasing as the common areas of the inn. The Rainbow Falls Room, however, stands in a class by itself. It has a huge hot tub set up on a platform behind a stained-glass window in a rainbow falls design crated by a local stained-glass artisan. The carpet, drapes, and bedding pick up deep greens and blue-greens from the stained glass, producing an effect so stunning that people who've heard about it sometimes stop at the inn and ask to see it.

The Sugarlands Room, usually used as the bridal suite, catches your imagination too. The hot tub in this room is on a platform in a windowed turret, with a view of the mountains. The room is decorated in white, mauve, and mint green.

The five cottages in the wooded area behind the inn are a new feature. Designed for two people, each cottage has a queen bed, fireplace, kitchenette, two-person Jacuzzi, porch with swing, and a grill and picnic table in the yard.

How to get there: From I–40, take exit 407 onto Highway 66 south, proceeding through Sevierville to Pigeon Forge. In Pigeon Forge, turn onto Lower Middle Creek Road at The Old Mill and continue 2³/₁₀ miles to Jay Elle Road. Turn right. The inn is 1¹/₂ miles on the left.

Von-Bryan Inn
Sevierville, Tennessee
37862

Innkeepers: D. J. and Jo Ann Vaughn

Address/Telephone: 2402 Hatcher Mountain Road; (615) 453–9832 or (800) 633–1459

Rooms: 5 in main house; all with private bath, some with whirlpool. Separate chalet with whirlpool, 3 bedrooms, kitchen, living room, fireplace, decks, hot tub.

Rates: In main house, $80 to $125, double; $12 each additional person. In chalet, $160 for up to 4 people; $12 each additional person. All rates reduced by 10 percent for stays of 2 or more nights Sunday through Thursday. Two-night minimum stay in chalet.

Open: Year-round.

Facilities and activities: Garden room with hot tub, upstairs television lounge in main house, swimming pool. Nearby: restaurants; short drive to Pigeon Forge, Gatlinburg, and Great Smoky Mountains National Park; crafts community.

Von-Bryan Inn is on top of a mountain near the Great Smoky Mountains. Not near the top, *on* it. The view includes the Smokies and Wears Valley and treetops in the clouds. The inn is set up to make the most of the view, especially the garden room, a nice protected spot inside from which you can sit in a corner hot tub big enough to hold eleven people and watch the sunset from the windows. The outdoor pool seems to float above clouds and mountains, and from there the view is panoramic. While I was here, I saw men stand in the yard looking across the valleys and deciding, without even going inside, that this was a place to which they must bring their wives.

I could've told them that it's nice inside, too. The living room has a stacked-stone fireplace and attractive, unobtrusive furniture grouped for conversation.

Each of the guest rooms has a special delight, a special view or an unusual bed, for example, but the Red Bud Room is unlike anything I've ever seen. It has a king-sized bed against a natural paneled wall, windows along another wall, a sitting area with a love seat, and a big cherry-red hot tub in the corner. Red simply dominates the room. Jo Ann says that it's one of the most requested rooms and theorizes that folks who would find a red hot tub just too racy at home get a kick out of it on vacation.

Speaking of Jo Ann, if personable innkeepers are important to you, you'll enjoy Von-Bryan. Jo Ann is thoroughly competent and produces a gourmet breakfast without a flick of the eyelid, but she's easy, chatty, and comfortable, all at the same time. D. J. has a green thumb and also is a good conversationalist. When I visited, I lingered much too long over breakfast because we got to talking about everything from food and plants to our earlier careers, and I couldn't make myself leave.

Among the nice little treats you can arrange for yourself if you stay here are helicopter pickup and delivery to the inn, dinner by reservation, and picnic baskets. I didn't experience the helicopter trip, but given the view and the height of the mountain, I think it would be a sensational experience. And, given the proximity of all the hiking trails and picnic facilities in the Smokies, I think a picnic basket would be a special pleasure, too.

How to get there: From Highway 321, turn onto Hatcher Mountain Road (the inn's sign marks the turn) and follow inn signs all the way to the top of the mountain. Ask for a map and more detailed instructions when you make reservations.

Walking Horse Hotel
Wartrace, Tennessee
37857

Innkeeper: George Wright
Address/Telephone: 110 West Main Street; (615) 389–6407
Rooms: 25; 12 with private bath, 13 share baths. Wheelchair access.
Rates: $48, private bath; $38, shared bath; $62, suite; single or double, breakfast extra.
Open: Year-round.
Facilities and activities: Lunch open to public 7 days a week; dinner open to public Monday through Saturday; no bar service; brown bagging permitted. Wheelchair access to restaurant. Wartrace is a center for walking-horse activities. Nearby: ten minutes to Shelbyville, the walking-horse capital; Bell Buckle, known for outstanding crafts.

I met the folks at the Walking Horse Hotel and fell in love. They are genuinely nice people, helpful primarily because it's second nature to them and only incidentally because it's good for business.

George is passionate in his involvement with the Tennessee walking horse. He is passionate in his restoration of the old hotel. The two belong together because the first Tennessee walking horse, Strolling Jim, was developed by Floyd Carothers, the owner of the hotel in 1939.

Today the hotel houses the world's largest collection of Tennessee-walking-horse pictures. Some of the pictures, which date as far back as 1930, were already there when George took over the hotel, but he has added many more.

Out back in the stables where Strolling Jim lived, near a headstone marking his grave, George has created the Walking Horse Center, complete with real horses, memorabilia, and films. If you're interested, George will tell you about the pictures, show the films, explain the memorabilia, and let you watch some actual walking-horse training as he works with his walker, Perfect Ten.

He has concentrated on getting the guest rooms scrubbed clean and painted; he has spent money on basics like good, specially made mattresses rather than on decorating. And in the restaurant, under the direction of his mother, Pauline Wright, he offers what he calls Southern Gourmet cooking.

All the breads and desserts are made on the premises. Entrees include steaks, Tennessee country ham, and Southern fried chicken as well as a gourmet hotel special, such as shrimp creole or chicken rosemary, each day. The recipes are from Pauline's own collection. She and George like to emphasize that the food they serve at the inn is the same as what they've eaten at home over the years. (Not long ago, I asked George how he could eat so well and never get fat. He said, "None of our desserts have calories. All our waitresses will tell you that.)

As for what to do after dinner, George suggests sitting on the corner balcony and watching the trains go by.

How to get there: George says, "If you can find Wartrace, you've found the hotel." From I–24, take exit 97 to State Route 64. Follow 64 into Wartrace. The inn is next to the railroad tracks.

❁

S: *The names people give their properties give you an idea of the special humor of the area. I saw "Chigger Hill" and a little farm with the sign "Oleo Acres, the Cheaper Spread."*

Indexes

Alphabetical Index to Inns

Inns with Restaurants or That Serve Dinner by Special Arrangement

Inns with Wheelchair Access
(L Denotes Limited. Ask for Details)

Inns with Swimming Pools

Inns on or near Ocean Beaches
(* Denotes on Beach)

Inns on or near Lakes
(* Denotes on Lake)

Inns Recommended for Business Travelers

Inns with Very Social Innkeepers

Inns Especially Suited for Children

Secluded and Peaceful Inns

Inns in Splendidly Restored Houses

Inns That Forbid or Restrict Indoor Smoking
(* Denotes Restriction)

About the Author

Sara Pitzer is a North Carolina–based freelance writer. Before she began writing books, she worked as a feature editor and writer for a Pennsylvania newspaper and wrote for magazines. She considers herself, above all, a reporter, and she prides herself on describing what she sees objectively and accurately.

In addition to *Recommended Country Inns: The South,* Sara has written *Pennsylvania: Off the Beaten Path; North Carolina: Off the Beaten Path; How to Write a Cookbook and Get It Published; Buying and Selling Antiques;* and *Enjoying the Art of Southern Hospitality.*

She lives in the country with two dogs, half a dozen cats, and a patient husband.